MW01265362

THE CULTURAL IMPACTS OF CLIMATE CHANGE: SENSE OF PLACE
AND SENSE OF COMMUNITY IN TUVALU, A COUNTRY THREATENED
BY SEA LEVEL RISE

A DISSERTATION SUBMITTED TO THE GRADUATE DIVISION OF THE
UNIVERSITY OF HAWAI'I AT MĀNOA IN PARTIAL FULFILLMENT OF
THE REQUIREMENTS OF THE DEGREE OF
DOCTOR OF PHILOSOPHY
IN
PSYCHOLOGY
MAY 2012

By
Laura K. Corlew

Dissertation Committee:
Clifford O'Donnell, Chairperson
Charlene Baker
Ashley Maynard
Yiyuan Xu
Bruce Houghton

Keywords: Tuvalu, climate change, culture, sense of place, sense of
community, Activity Settings theory

1

For Uncle Ed

and

Father Tom

Rest in Peace.

ACKNOWLEDGEMENTS:

This research was funded in part by the University of Hawai'i Arts and Sciences Student Research Award, the Society for Community Research and Action (SCRA) Community Mini-Grant, and the University of Hawai'i Psychology Department Gartley Research Award. This research was conducted with the support of the Tuvalu Office of Community Affairs, especially with the aid and guidance of the director, Lanieta Faleasiu, whom I thank dearly. I also extend my thanks and my love to Sir Tomu M. Sione and his family for welcoming me into their home. I would like to thank each of the interview participants, as well as every person I met in Tuvalu. In these past few years I have received a great deal of support from members of government agencies and NGOs, religious leaders, and private individuals. Thank you all for speaking with me and sharing with me your time, your knowledge, and your care. I would also like to thank my dissertation committee and especially my adviser, Dr. Clifford O'Donnell, for guiding me through this process. Finally, I would like to thank my husband and research assistant, Michael R. Corlew. Thank you for coming with me on this journey.

3

ABSTRACT:

The Psychology of Climate Change is an emerging field that focuses on human causes and impacts. The APA (2009) report noted a developed-nations bias in the current body of research. I add that there is also a continental bias. The current study explores the cultural impacts of climate change in Tuvalu, a developing island nation in the South Pacific projected to become uninhabitable in the next 50 to 100 years due to sea level rise. This study explores the Psychological Sense of Community and Sense of Place in Tuvalu's cultures, and applies Activity Settings theory to Tuvaluan cultural contexts and change. This study utilizes semi-structured qualitative interviews, ethnography, photographic images, and archival research. This research was conducted in collaboration with the Tuvalu Office of Community Affairs. Thematic analysis revealed that climate change is considered within the context of other cultural changes that Tuvaluans are facing. Tuvalu has a strong guest and gift culture, including a responsibility of community members to share resources and give of themselves by participating in community-supporting events. Tuvaluan identity is strongly related to home island identity. Funafuti is the urban center of Tuvalu and is undergoing a heightened period of development and cultural change. The outer islands are spaces in which traditional cultural activities, language, and values are most strongly practiced, although the outer islands are also experiencing modernization, development, and subsequent cultural changes. Tuvaluans are "renowned as being adaptable" and have a long history of successful adaptation to outside influences and changes in culture. Adaptability and other cultural strengths allow Tuvaluans to maintain their traditional lifestyle while simultaneously embracing cultural changes. Climate change is currently affecting the land, weather, and sea in Tuvalu, and consequently the lives of people who live there. Individual and community adaptations are being actively engaged. The 2011 drought and other events showcase cultural strengths that Tuvaluans naturally activate in response to disasters and slow-stressor changes. Tuvaluans also rely on their faith in God. Tuvaluans are adamant that they must implement every possible measure to protect their country from climate change, and will not consider migration at this time.

4

Table of Contents

List of Images

6

8

Chapter 1

1.1 Introduction

Overview of global climate change. The United Nations Framework Convention on Climate Change (UNFCCC) in 1992 named its ultimate objective as the "stabilization of greenhouse gas concentrations in the atmosphere at a level that would prevent dangerous anthropogenic interference with the climate system" (UNFCCC, 1992). The "dangerous anthropogenic interference with the climate system" (hereafter referred to as "climate change" or "global climate change") has been a concern for some time. For example, the U.S. National Academy of Sciences published a brochure in 1957-1958 warning that because "our industrial civilization has been pouring carbon dioxide into the atmosphere at a great rate" there may occur "a marked warming effect on Earth's climate" which may "cause significant melting of the great ice cap and raise sea levels in time" (as quoted in NOAA, 2010). Since the Industrial Revolution, carbon dioxide, along with other greenhouse gasses, has been released increasingly into the atmosphere largely through the burning of fossil fuels (IPCC, 2007). As levels of greenhouse gasses increase, higher levels of heat from the sun are prevented from escaping the atmosphere, thereby causing a rise in temperature. This rise in temperatures has induced changes in global climates (above and beyond changes in weather), and is projected to cause increasingly significant and perhaps devastating effects in the next 50 to 100 years (Karl, Melillo, & Peterson, 2009).

Worldwide, some anticipated (and current) changes include ocean acidification, glacial melting, desertification, crop loss, forest loss, increases in pests (including weeds, bugs/insects, and viruses), reduced overall rainfall but more frequent damaging storms, and sea level rise (CCSP, 2008; IPCC, 2007; USAID, 2009). Recent studies point to the likelihood of an average global sea level rise of 1 meter by 2100, and several more meters of subsequent centuries given current trends in carbon pollution (Fletcher & Richmond, 2010; Marra, Merrifield, & Sweet, 2012; Weiss, Overpeck, & Strauss, 2011). Global climate change poses a number of problems to developing coastal and island nations around the world who are uniquely vulnerable to structural degradation and resource loss in addition to being singularly unequipped financially to implement the high levels of adaptation and mitigations efforts necessary for the long-term disaster of climate change (Barnett & Campbell, 2010; Parks & Roberts, 2006). As an indicator of the high level of climate change risk, global financing entities such as the World Bank and the African Development Bank have begun requiring development proposals to address long-term project feasibility within the changing climate so as to protect future investments (USAID, 2009).

The Secretariat of the Pacific Regional Environment Programme (2011) named climate change as one of its four strategic priorities due to its high level of threat to the livelihoods of those in the Pacific. Pacific Island Developing Countries (PIDCs) are currently struggling with sea level rise, greater and more frequent storms, saltwater inundation to fertile soils, freshwater

9

salination, drought, land erosion, coral bleaching and a decrease in natural resources such as taro and fish (Bhattarai, 2011; Burns, 2003; CCSP, 2008; Normille, 2010; Sharma & Gosain, 2009; Spenneman, 2006; USAID, 2009). In the Pacific, seasonal and decadal weather trends like the El-Nino Southern Oscillation (ENSO) and the Pacific Decadal Oscillation (PDO) will intermittently exacerbate or even reverse climate change trends over the next century since these trends are often associated with severe wind, weather, and sea changes (Chowdhury et al., 2010; Coelho & Goddard, 2009; Marra, Keener, Finucane, Spooner, & Smith, 2012; Shea, 2004; Timmerman & McGregor, 2010). At times the combination of short- and long-term changes will manifest in disaster scenarios (Spennemann, 2006). On the long term, many low-lying island nations (e.g., Tuvalu) are projected to become uninhabitable, or for their land to disappear entirely beneath the rising sea (Ede, 2003; Funk, 2009; Hunter, 2002; Mimura, et al., 2007; Patel, 2006; UNFCCC, 2005). Such countries are faced with unprecedented legal and moral questions regarding the future of their people, such as whether they can maintain sovereignty, government, citizenship, and control of their waters if their country's land no longer exists (Friedman, 2010). Indigenous Pacific populations must also contend with a threat to cultures whose traditions are intricately connected to their ancestral lands (Farbotko & McGregor, 2010).

Overview of the psychology of climate change. The Psychology of Climate Change is a growing field. In 2010, the American Psychological Association's (APA) Task Force on the Interface Between Psychology and Global Climate Change released a report compiling previous research and suggesting future directions in psychological research on global climate change (Swim, et al., 2010). The task force identified six key areas in which psychological research can positively contribute to humanity's understanding of and response to climate change, including 1) human understanding of climate change risk; 2) contextual and psychological mechanisms that promote environmentally destructive behaviors; 3) psychosocial effects of a changing climate; 4) adaptation and coping; 5) psychological barriers which may impede proactive behaviors; and 6) the role of psychologists in limiting climate change.

Psychology has much to offer climate change studies. Sound scientific understanding of climate change issues is at once essential and insufficient to the success of climate adaptation plans (Finucane, 2009). In addition to climate models, decisions-makers must understand the local relevance of proposed actions, ways of understanding risk, sense of place, community power structures or hierarchies, and other drivers for behavior or inaction which will affect responses to scientific recommendations (see, e.g., Budescu, Broomel, & Por, 2009; Fritze, Blashki, Burke, & Wiseman, 2008; Kempton, 1991; Kidner, 2007; Leiserowitz, 2005; Rogan, O'Connor, & Horwitz, 2005). Planning and response to climate change include a number of unknowns. In the physical sciences, there exists a significant amount of uncertainty within models and projections. Of course, "In scientific terms, 'uncertainty' is not the same thing as 'doubt'; nor is uncertainty, by itself a cause for disagreement" (Niepold, Herring, &

10

McConville, 2007, p. 4). The social sciences contain similar uncertainties that must be explored, as is discussed in the APA report on climate change.

In addition to the necessity of psychology's involvement in climate change studies, the APA task force also noted that the current body of research suffers from a developed-nations bias, in that a majority of the research has been conducted in wealthy, developed nations. I will add that current research further suffers from a continental bias. Consequently, previous research and current knowledge may not be relevant to developing island nations. Citizens of countries such as Tuvalu, with a landmass of less than 26 km² that may become entirely submerged with sea level rise, are likely to experience the threat of climate change differently than citizens of the United States. Furthermore, indigenous peoples and other populations that have lived in one place and developed cultures attached to that place over many generations experience a threat to their land uniquely due to a heightened sense of place (Fried, 2000; Oneha, 2001). Therefore, these developed-nations and continental biases reflect serious gaps regarding the psychology of climate change. My dissertation research in Tuvalu would seek to address these gaps by exploring Sense of Place, Sense of Community, and Activity Settings theory in a developing country with an indigenous population under critical threat from climate change.

Psychological studies in Tuvalu are scarce and have not previously focused on climate change. For example, Taylor (2000) studied individual and community coping in the aftermath of a tragic dormitory fire, focusing on Post-Traumatic Stress Disorder (PTSD). Studies of cultural and other human impacts of climate change in Tuvalu have only been conducted in fields other than psychology. In Development Studies, Allice (2009) found the Church of Tuvalu plays an intricate role in Tuvaluan understanding of and response to climate change, and Dix (2011) discussed the need for government and donor agencies to balance sustainable development with climate change adaptation. In Theology, Lusama (2004) discussed biblical interpretations of climate change used with the population in Tuvalu.

In Geography, Connell (2003) explored the interconnections between development and climate change. Bhattarai (2011) assessed mangrove forests in Tuvalu and the Pacific region, including consideration of the increased climate change threat to human populations as mangroves disappear. Paton (2008) and Paton & Fairbairn-Dunlop (2010) explored Tuvaluan perspectives and agency in creating a better future for themselves and their communities. Locke (2009) discussed the intricately connected influences of development, population changes, and climate change as drivers for domestic (between-island) and international migration. Farbotko (2005; 2008; 2010a; 2010b) has critically explored international narratives about Tuvalu that dismiss or undermine the agency of Tuvaluans as actors on the national and global scale who develop their own fate in a dynamic culture and changing climate.

Anthropology is another field that has been increasingly prolific in exploring the human impacts of climate change (Rudiak-Gould, 2011), including in Tuvalu. Chambers and Chambers (2007) critically reviewed video documentaries about climate change in Tuvalu as part of their longitudinal

11

research on the culture in Nanumea (see, e.g., Chambers & Chambers, 2007; Chambers, 1984; Chambers & Chambers, 2001). Goldsmith also followed up longitudinal research on the role of the Church of Tuvalu (1989) by exploring the imperfect fit of popular theories of governance to the unique issues faced by Tuvalu as a developing microstate, including climate change (2005). Lazrus (2009a, 2009b) deeply explored Tuvaluan citizenry perspectives on climate change and the government's desire to maintain their homeland while navigating complicated national, regional, and global political spheres.

Many of these studies directly address social and cultural impacts of climate change in Tuvalu and as such can positively contribute to the knowledge base of the psychology of climate change. However, none of these studies are based within the field of psychology, and therefore do not directly address psychological concepts or theories. The current research adds to this knowledge base by specifically exploring the psychological theories and definitions with Sense of Place and Sense of Community, as well as the concepts of Activity Settings theory, with an aim to address the gaps in the psychological study of climate change.

Overview of Tuvalu and climate change. Tuvalu is a low-lying island nation in the South Pacific that is projected to become uninhabitable in the next 50-100 years due to sea-level rise associated with global climate change (Hunter, 2002; Mimura, et al., 2007; Patel, 2006). This developing country consists of nine small islands and atolls, and has a total landmass of 25.63 km². Tuvalu has been experiencing sea level rise and associated problems for decades (Ede, 2003; Funk, 2009; Hunter, 2002; Pacific Country Report, 2006). The Tuvalu Meteorological Office has kept track of the sea level since 1990 and has documented this rise. Saltwater inundation is a problem on the islands because salination kills *pulaka* (giant swamp taro that is the traditional staple crop) and other plants, leaving the saline land barren and even more susceptible to increasing erosion (Bhattarai, 2011; Burns, 2003; Corlew, 2010 field notes). Funafuti, the capitol atoll, has already lost one of its islets to erosion and another is soon to follow (Bayer & Salzman, 2007; H. Vavae, personal communication, August 12, 2010). Erosion in Tuvalu and other atoll nations are often associated with land displacement, in which parts of an island are washed away while another area of the island increases, which may result in a net loss of no land mass but has major implications for infrastructure regardless (Webb & Kench, 2010).

Climate change is a very salient issue in the country. The government has been vocal in the United Nations, through the Alliance of Small Island States (AOSIS), and in other international forums on the topic of climate change (Sheehan, 2002). Tuvaluan representatives have made powerful and sometimes emotional appeals in political and scientific forums to maintain pressure on foreign governments to attend to the human impacts of climate change on small states (Farbotko & McGregor, 2010; Nine, 2010). The official position of Tuvalu is not to negotiate for migration at this time. Tuvalu instead negotiates for global mitigation efforts to stem the causes of these devastating climate changes, and for local adaptation efforts to protect the Tuvalu people in their

12

homeland (General Environment Briefing, 2010). The threat of sea level rise as part of global climate change is a social and environmental justice issue faced by the people of Tuvalu, who are not responsible for global climate change (Parks & Roberts 2006), but who are facing massive consequences.

A brief introduction to Tuvalu culture and history. Previous estimates for Tuvalu's cultural history date back about two thousand years. Most of the genealogical records only reach back three or four hundred years. However, a new archeological discovery has uncovered evidence of human inhabitation in an underwater cave dating back 8,000 years. Geological record shows a massive rise in sea level starting 14,000 years ago, and new speculation is that this gradual change to the Pacific islands has wiped out much of the early evidence of Pacific Islander activity. Linguists hold that Tuvalu's unique language structure is about two millennia old.[1]

During the 1500s, Tuvalu was spotted several times from exploratory vessels, though was rarely sighted during the next two hundred years. In 1819, Tuvalu was renamed the Ellice Islands after Edward Ellice, a Member of Parliament and the owner of the Rebecca, the ship which is credited with Tuvalu's rediscovery. Christian missionaries from the London Missionary Society arrived in Tuvalu in 1861. Tuvaluans embraced Christianity, which is now considered to be part of the traditional culture and lifestyle, and is interwoven in major facets of Tuvaluan life (Goldsmith, 1989; Dix, 2011). In 1877, Tuvalu was taken under British jurisdiction, and in 1915 became part of the Gilbert and Ellice Islands Colony. Kiribati and Tuvalu were grouped despite having little language or cultural connection to one another. Tuvaluans participated as workers on Banaba (Ocean Island) and in Nauru during the phosphate mining boom, but Tuvalu as a country has limited commercially exploitable resources (Hughes & Gosarevski, 2004). Tuvalu gained independence on October 1st, 1978, after voting also to separate from Kiribati.[2] The nine newly independent islands reverted to their traditional name of Tuvalu, which translates to "group of eight" (T. Sione, personal communication, July 31, 2010). The ninth island, Niualakita, is populated by a small group of families from the overcrowded island of Niutao.

During colonization, Tuvalu developed a parliamentary system of governance patterned after the British system (Goldsmith, 2005). Tuvalu maintained traditional systems of elder rule or guidance that became legalized in the Falekaupule Act of 1997 (Paton & Fairbairn-Dunlop, 2010). Each island has its own *Kaupule* or town council that is overseen by a national *Falekaupule*.[3] The largest employer in Tuvalu is the government on Funafuti. Tuvalu's population has increased dramatically since it began trading with foreigners. In 1866, the population was 2,812; increased to 3,994 by 1931 and to 8,229 by

---

[1] http://www.tuvaluislands.com/history.htm

[2] http://www.tuvaluislands.com/history2.htm

[3] *Falekaupule* is also the name of the Niutao *maneapa*. Some of the islands refer to their *Kaupule* as the *Falekaupule*.

13

1979, just after Independence (Tuvalu Millennium Development Goals Report 2010/2011). The population was estimated at 11,636 in 2005[4] and has shown a recent annual population growth rate of 1.8% (Tuvalu MDG Report, 2010/2011). Of those, just under half live on urban Funafuti, with the remainder spread out among the more rural outer islands with populations ranging from 35 to 1,591 people.[5] Additionally, in 2006, there were 2,625 Tuvaluans living in New Zealand, 37% of whom were born in New Zealand.[6] Other Tuvaluans have migrated for school or work to other countries or are employed as mariners on international vessels. Tuvalu's population is increasing its global movement (Lazrus, 2009).

Tuvaluans lived a traditionally subsistence lifestyle. Their main food sources were *pulaka*, coconut, fish, crab, and other foods naturally available in the land and sea. Tuvaluans cultivated these foods and used island resources for clothing, housing, tools, and other materials. Each island traditionally had its own cultural practices, including gods, *aliki* (chiefs), and clan structures. On a smaller scale, each family had a unique set of expert skills that defined their role within the community. Each family member also had a set of roles and responsibilities to the family, divided along gender and generational lines. Marriage was decided upon by the family (as opposed to the individual), guided by parents and other elders who also negotiated with the families of prospective spouses. Since its connection to the British nearly two hundred years ago, Tuvaluan cultures and ways of life have shifted dramatically and adapted significantly to outside influences and ever-changing contexts. As will be discussed in Chapter 4, many of these adapted cultural norms continue to play a powerful role in Tuvaluan daily life.

Tuvalu was the third poorest country in the world until 1999 when they were assigned the country domain name .tv (Baram, 2005a,b). Tuvalu now leases out the domain name to various television stations and programs around the world (Commonwealth update, 1999; Homer, 2000). With the income from .tv, Tuvalu has increased its infrastructure and funded the securing of a seat in the United Nations. Tuvalu is in a period of rapid development, especially on Funafuti. Tuvalu's tallest structure, the three-story Government Building, has been erected. Roads are paved and new houses build at an astonishing rate (Corlew field notes, 2010). Since 1980, there has been an increasing migration to Funafuti (Encyclopedia of the Nations, 2003). With 2.79 km² of total land area in the atoll, the population of Funafuti is 4,492 (Central Statistics Division, 2010a), roughly 45% of Tuvalu's entire population.

Since colonization by the British, the Tuvalu people have adapted to much of Western culture (Munro, 1982). Many people leave the country for school or work, and a large number have immigrated to New Zealand, Fiji, and

---

[4] http://tuvaluislands.com/about.htm
[5] http://tuvaluislands.com/islands/islands.html
[6] http://www.stats.govt.nz/Census/about-2006-census/pacific-profiles-2006/tuvaluan-people-in-new-zealand.aspx

14

Australia. However, in Funafuti I was told by community members, leaders, and cultural experts that it is difficult if not impossible to fully maintain Tuvaluan culture when not in Tuvalu because 'the Tuvalu way' is inextricably connected to the Tuvalu islands themselves (Corlew, 2010). The culture and land are joined through this close personal attachment to one's home island (Munro, 1982). For example, each island maintains close-knit community organizations in which individual members are jointly responsible for the organizational functioning and wellbeing of all members. A person's home island is at once their identity, their family, their community, their pride, and their responsibility. These community ties are maintained even after migration to the highly populous Funafuti, where neighbor islands each have their own *maneapa* (see Image 1).

Tuvalu's collectivist traditions struggle outside of a Tuvalu context when people immigrate or travel outside of the country for school or work. One woman, when describing her years outside of the country said, "We had many more opportunities, but we suffered there" because of the disconnect from family, neighbors, and the close-knit community (Corlew field notes, 2010). Another woman reported that many Tuvaluans, especially from the rural neighbor islands, do not want to leave, even knowing what lies in store with sea level rise. "They don't want to move. They don't want to move because they say that if they move, they don't have a home. This is their home. That's how they live" (Corlew field notes, 2010). One Tuvalu woman who works with climate change efforts told me that when she gives presentations to people from other countries, they always ask if she will migrate when the time comes. She always

Image 1. Vaitupu island community *maneapa* on Funafuti (Corlew, 2010).

15

tells them, "No, I don't want to go. I was born here and I will die here" (Corlew field notes, 2010). Such statements are in line with previous literature regarding sense of place and psychological sense of community among indigenous peoples (Bishop, Colquhoun, & Johnson, 2006; Foster-Fishman, Nowell, Deacon, Nievar, & McCann, 2005; Fried, 2000; Oneha, 2001).

Sense of place. Sense of place is an overarching concept regarding people's relationship to a physical and/or natural environment (Jorgensen & Stedman, 2001; Rogan, O'Connor, & Horwitz, 2005). In the psychological sense, "place" is not only a physical location, but also the human interaction with that location. The human interaction, or 'sense of place' may include emotional connections to places (Manzo, 2003), place attachment, and place identity (Altman & Low, 1992, Knez, 2005; Proshansky, Fabian, & Kaminoff, 1983; Twigger-Ross & Uzzell, 1996). Place attachment and place identity are often considered to be strongly interconnected, in that while place attachment develops so too does one's identity in connection to that place.

> "Through extensive interaction with a place, people may begin to define themselves in terms of ... that place, to the extent that they cannot really express who they are without inevitably taking into account the setting that surrounds them as well" (Ryden, 1993, as quoted in Stedman, 2002, p. 563).

A person's sense of place is not bound by any specific spatial range, but in fact can include interacting attachments to multiple ranges (Hidalgo & Hernandez, 2001). For example, a Tuvaluan may experience a place attachment and resultant place identity with their family home, village, island, and country. Indeed, I often heard invoked the identity "we Pacific Islanders." These identities are not mutually exclusive (a family home is within a village within an island within the country within the Pacific Ocean). The place identity most strongly invoked at any given time may be contextually dependent (e.g., on another Tuvaluan island, home island identity may be particularly strong, whereas in Great Britain, the Pacific Islander identity may be invoked).

Sense of place has been studied through multiple models (i.e., Breakwell, 1992; Knez, 2005; Stedman, 2002), all of which connect positive sense of place with positive psychological wellbeing. Breakwell (1992) developed a four-process model for sense of place, which included place identification, place continuity, place-related self-esteem, and place-related self-efficacy. In Breakwell's model, place attachment and identity served as a function of people's desires to identify themselves distinctively by location, to maintain residency in a familiar or otherwise psychologically compatible location, to feel good about or proud of their location, and/or to care for their needs within their location. Knez (2005) added to this model a fifth element, climate, which also contributed strongly to place identity when connected to urban- versus country-person attitude. An incongruity between person attitude and climate may be harmful to place identity. Indigenous peoples' health and wellbeing are often intricately connected with their land due to a heightened sense of place (Oneha, 2001). Furthermore, Fried (2000) found that community displacement from places of high attachment and identity can lead to widespread grief and negative community outcomes.

Sense of community. Sense of community is the level of connection a person feels to a community (Brodsky, 2009; Sarason, 1974). Sense of community is composed of four major components: (a) a feeling of belongingness, or the extent to which people perceive themselves to be members of the community, (b) influence of the community on the individual and vice versa, or a mutual degree of impact of a person on the community and of the community on a person, (c) a sense of needs fulfillment though community involvement, or the satisfaction one gains from active community membership, and (d) an emotional connection to the community and community functions (McMillan & Chavis, 1986). Sense of community is commonly considered to have a necessarily positive influence on a person's psychological welfare, however Brodsky (2009) proposes that across contexts, sense of community may be positive, neutral, or negative. Brodsky offers members of the Revolutionary Association of the Women of Afghanistan (RAWA) as an example of people who have a strong sense of community, but who are oppressed within that community. Similarly, while I was in Tuvalu most people I spoke with praised the strength of the collectivist traditions and importance of community for the wellbeing of the Tuvalu people, but several people also included the caveat that the financial contributions to community organizations and the obligation to care for others who are struggling means that most people find it difficult or impossible to lift themselves out of poverty in this developing nation. However, none disputed the importance of community connection to wellbeing.

Sonn and Fisher (1998) argued that the sense of community propagated through community networks and organizations is a major strength for community resilience against adversity and change. Even when people are prohibited in some way from participating in the larger community, they may find ways to develop a sense of community through church groups or extended family networks. In Tuvalu, people who migrate from neighbor islands to Funafuti maintain their sense of community despite lack of access to their home island resources and structures by developing organizations that are home-island specific. Similarly, I spoke with Tuvaluans who had migrated to New Zealand. They told me they maintained ties with other Tuvaluans in New Zealand though Tuvalu community events and activities, though it was not the same as in Tuvalu where their community is constantly surrounding them.

Sense of community may manifest differently in indigenous groups than in Western groups. For example, Bishop, et al. (2006) found five components of community conception among Australian Aboriginals including kinship structure, language groups, skin groups, education, and knowledge. Therefore measures created among dominant groups in Western societies may not be universally valid. For this reason, qualitative measures are recommended to explore and legitimize indigenous conceptualizations of community (Bishop, et al., 2006; Foster-Fishman, et al., 2005).

17

Activity Settings theory. Activity Settings theory offers a useful means of exploring cultural norms and changes. In Activity Settings theory, the setting itself becomes the unit of analysis, including all of the tangible and intangible elements that comprise the setting: people, schedules, power hierarchies, values, expectations, time spent, actions and behaviors, etc. The activities may be recurrent or single events. The actors may be regular or in constant flux. Such elements contribute to the makeup of the activity setting. In analysis, the activity setting therefore includes the space and the actors as well as the actions and all relevant goals and motivations. When a group of people participate in shared activity settings, they begin to develop intersubjectivity, or shared interpretive meanings of events in their lives (Gallimore, et al., 1993; O'Donnell, Tharp, & Wilson, 1993; Vygotsky, 1981). These shared meanings and shared interpretations of events by a group create a 'culture' of thought and experience. In fact, heightened intersubjectivity stemming from extensive interconnectivity in shared activity settings will increase the cohesion of a group (O'Donnell & Tharp, 2012). Over the long term, deep and lasting cultures are created and sustained by extensive sharing of activity settings.

Using activity settings as the units of analysis allows cultural and community psychologists to examine the components that contribute to a shared culture. By exploring intersubjectivity through a wide range of activity settings, researchers can begin to understand patterns of knowledge, value, interpretation, or behavior in a community (O'Donnell, 2006). Conversely, by exploring the individual components of activity settings, researchers can begin to deconstruct highly valued or particularly important elements that make up the culture's identity. The study of culture is much larger than any individual or event. Activity Settings theory offers a means to navigate complex systems of values, communication styles and patterns, behavioral rules, goals and intentions that contribute to a shared culture.

Photography. Photography has been used extensively in cultural and community psychological studies as a qualitative methodology that empowers research participants to engage actively as experts of their communities within a study (Foster-Fishman, et al., 2005; Wang & Burris, 1994). It has previously been used for a wide variety of research purposes, including the social influences on health and wellbeing (Cooper & Yarbrough, 2010; Ornelas, et al., 2009; Rhodes, Hergenrather, Wilkin, & Jolly, 2008), social activism and reconciliation toward liberation (Lykes, Blanche, & Hamber, 2003), community service experiences among adolescents volunteers (Cardazone, 2010), youth perceptions of the Costa Rican tourism industry (Anglin, 2012), identity and narrative memory (Harrison, 2002), the social dynamics of place (Nowell, Berkowitz, Deacon, & Foster-Fishman, 2006), studies with vulnerable populations (Jurkowski & Paul-Ward, 2007), and for community and youth empowerment interventions (Carlson, Engebretson, & Chamberlain, 2006; Wilson, Minkler, Dasho, Wallerstein, & Martin, 2008). These studies used a research method called Photovoice in which participants direct the research through the images they chose to share. Blending photographic images with interviews and other research methods is a particularly valuable tool for research with indigenous communities whose experiences may not otherwise be adequately captured by many Western methodologies (Cooper & Yarbrough, 2010; Harrison, 2002; Lykes, Blanche, & Hamber, 2003). Images of realities in which normative structures are highly divergent from psychology's mostly Western audience allows for a more precise description of indigenous experiences and interpretations. This enhanced ability to communicate about participants' lives increases the verisimilitude commonly induced by the detailed narrative, or "thick," description of qualitative research (Creswell, 2007).

1.2 Methods

Preliminary studies. In the summer of 2010, I traveled for two weeks to Funafuti, Tuvalu for gathering of preliminary data to develop my research proposal in collaboration with key community stakeholders (Corlew, 2011). By working on site in Tuvalu, I was able to collaborate effectively with multiple community members who are stakeholders in the topic of my research in both professional and personal capacities. Their face-to-face involvement in the choices about specific research questions, sources for data, methods of inquiry, and analysis paradigm ensure that the research will be both truly representative of the experiences of Tuvalu within this topic and will be meaningful to the people of Tuvalu. This trip further deepened my own understanding of the culture and community climate of this country. Although the focal data for this dissertation were collected in the second visit (see below), the extensive ethnographic data gathered in this preliminary research trip were used in analysis to offer support to resultant themes, to thicken the interview data of the second study, and to offer a context to cultural norms and values. This preliminary research trip used exploratory methods, which I will describe below. I will also describe the themes that resulted from this study as they relate to the development of the second study.

Prior to traveling to Tuvalu, I contacted representatives of multiple organizations by phone and email. I found these organizations online. They included government agencies and NGOs who work with the environment, climate change, community wellbeing, or Tuvalu culture. The general script for these contacts was to explain who I was, that I had read about their agency online, and to ask if I may meet them when I came to Tuvalu. I received positive responses from about half of my contacts, and received no response from the rest. Emails to two organizations were bounced back to my inbox. A representative from one organization, the Luaseuta Foundation that works for community wellbeing in a variety of capacities including through climate change issues, contacted me multiple times offering advice for my travels and also offering a place to stay with his uncle, Sir Tomu Sione[7].

---

[7] See Appendix A: Reflexivity for a discussion of my entrance into the community.

Agency/organization interviews. While in Tuvalu, I met with representatives from agencies I had contacted. Many of these organizations were based in Tuvalu and Tuvaluan-led, however, other organizations were run jointly with or entirely by Japanese researchers. Japanese organizations included the Foram Sand project (which is a research project seeking to combat sea level rise and erosion by literally *growing* new sand) and Tuvalu Overview. Tuvalu Overview[8] is known for two main projects in Tuvalu: their efforts to photograph every Tuvaluan and collect their stories and genealogies for historical record, and their project to prevent erosion by planting mangroves. I had the opportunity to join Tuvalu Overview in a trip to plant mangroves in Funafuti's southernmost islet, a flat strip of land whose beach extends far into the lagoon at low tide, but is completely covered at high tide (see Image 2). I was invited (separately, by nearly every agency in attendance) to a climate change progress report meeting that was attended by government environmental agencies, the Funafuti *Kaupule* (town council), the Taiwanese Ambassador, the Japan International Cooperation Agency (JICA), Foram Sand, Tuvalu Overview, and another Japanese organization that proposed during the meeting to carry out a "beach nourishment" project in Funafuti to protect the most populous islet against sea

Image 2. Mangroves planted on Funafala islet in Funafuti by Tuvalu Overview (Corlew, 2010).

---

[8] http://www.tuvalu-overview.tv/eng/

20

level rise and erosion. The research, aid, and other funding that come from Japan and Taiwan were noted as critical to ongoing efforts to protect Tuvalu from the changing climate.

I visited a number of Tuvaluan agencies as well, including the Ministry of Natural Resources, Energy, and Environment; and the Tuvalu Meteorological Society; the Office of Community Affairs; the Ministry of Health; the Office of Cultural Affairs; the Office of Women's Affairs; the Tuvalu National Archives; and the Tuvalu Association of NGOs (TANGO). Though several of these agencies were expecting me to stop by at some point during my trip, I entered all of these interviews without an appointment. I went to the offices, explained who I was and the purpose of my visit, and asked if I may schedule a time to meet. In all cases, the people I met with opted to speak with me at that time, and in multiple cases invited me back to meet with other individuals or invited me to other relevant meetings or events. I interviewed these individuals predominantly on their topic of expertise. The general framework for each interview was to discuss (a) the function, research, activities, or findings of that office; (b) climate change, culture, and/or community issues in general in Tuvalu; and (c) ideas or advice they could offer to me about learning more while I was in Tuvalu or for my research directions.

Lay interviews/conversations. I also had the opportunity to interview or converse with lay Tuvaluans on the topics of climate change, community, and culture.[9] These conversations took place with visitors to the Sione family home; during visits to others' homes; during parties or community events; in public locations such as the street, library, or airstrip (see Image 3); or in public businesses or offices. If the interviewee was introduced or referred to me for a specific purpose, our conversation typically focused on those specific topics. Other conversations typically wandered about topics concerning Tuvaluan community, cultural, traditions, and history—things that any tourist may discuss with a local. People took a great deal of interest in my background, family, studies, and reasons for visiting Tuvalu. Approximately 1,000 people come to Tuvalu each year (Central Statistics Division, 2010b). In this small and tight-knit community many people felt quite comfortable asking me as many questions as I asked them. I realized early on that in Funafuti it was quite common for people to have migrated from other islands. A favorite line of questions for me quickly became to ask about a person's home island. People were almost always very willing and excited to tell me about their home island.

---

[9] During lay conversations, I typically steered clear of climate change issues for the most part to minimize psychological discomfort. However, climate change would become a topic of conversation when (a) the interviewee asked why I was in Tuvalu and continued the discussion on the topic of climate change after I told them, or (b) the interviewee was referred to me as someone I should speak with about climate change because of their level of knowledge or involvement with the topic.

Participation/observation. Largely because of my good fortune in being invited to stay with a family, I had the opportunity to observe and participate in a large number of family and community activities. These included everyday cultural activities such as family meals, prayer, games, and morning and bedtime rituals. I was also invited to special events such as a National Children's Day festival at Nauti Elementary School, an inter-island volleyball game at Funafuti's court,[10] a night out at a nightclub, an evening dance rehearsal for a three-day long festival which occurred the weekend after I left, a celebratory lunch to honor ten new inductees into the police force, a going-away party for a close friend at another friend's home, dinner and karaoke at the Taiwanese Ambassador's home, and a Ministers' dinner at the Prime Minister's home (see Image 4). Most touching of all, the Sione family threw a traditional family going-away party in my honor the night before I left in which dozens of family members came to see me off.

Image 3. The Funafuti airstrip is a recreational gathering place (Corlew, 2010).

Field notes. During agency interviews, lay conversations, and participation/observation, I took copious field notes to record all of this ethnographic data. Though I brought a digital voice recorder with me, it was rarely appropriate to use it. In most cases, I was able to take notes during the conversations; this includes all agency interviews and many lay conversations. During some lay conversations and many participation/observation instances, I was not able to take notes during the event, but was able to write down my recollections in great detail soon thereafter. I also kept a day-to-day journal of

---

[10] Even on Funafuti, different islands may own their own sports courts, *maneapa* (traditional gathering place), or other social spaces that are used for that island only unless they host an inter-island activity.

events to record my progress, the order of events, my thoughts about what I was learning, and ideas for my research. I reviewed my field notes daily, and as my ideas began to take form, I regularly conducted "check-ins" with interviewees. During these "check-ins," I would bounce my thoughts and ideas off of interviewees to see if they held "a ring of truth" and most importantly, made sense in a Tuvaluan context. In my experience, the people I spoke with were more than happy to compare their Tuvaluan conceptions against my American ones. In this way I was able to refine explicitly my ideas as I progressed through this preliminary study.

Image 4. Ministers dinner in Prime Minister Apisai Ielemia's *fale lau* (Corlew, 2010).

Throughout this trip, I explored ideas for the exact research focus and methods that would best address the broad topic of "climate change and Tuvalu" so as to reflect both private and professional understanding of the threat of climate change while being culturally responsive to the values, norms, and priorities of Tuvalu. I gathered information and research advice from the above sources, and established a collaboration with Lanieta Faleasiu, the Director of the Office of Community Affairs. By the time I met with Ms. Faleasiu, I had had the chance to speak to everyone mentioned above. I also had the opportunity to "check-in" with many of them and refine my ideas about what may work in Tuvalu. Ms. Faleasiu had been referred to me by multiple interviewees, and though we did not have a scheduled appointment or a specific referral, I greatly anticipated meeting with her. I wrote up a basic research justification and proposal including a brief operationalization of terms and potential research questions. For research methods, I offered multiple suggestions though no specific plan. I also had no specific plan for participants. When Ms. Faleasiu and I met, we discussed each of these items in great detail.

Resulting themes. The interviews, conversations, observations, and collaboration with Ms. Faleasiu yielded the following themes:

(a) The importance of cultural communities from Tuvalu's individual islands to individual, family, and community identity. Tuvalu has nine islands and atolls (Nanumea, Nanumaga, Niutao, Nui, Vaitupu, Nukufetau, Funafuti, Nukulaelae, and Niulakita). People from different islands may have different accents and dialects, but the language spoken on each island is mutually intelligible among all of the islands, save Nui. Each island has its own Kaupule (town council), its own customs and culture, and traditionally, its own gods. Family and community connections are of the utmost importance to the Tuvalu people. People are typically highly involved with women's groups or youth groups (distinct to each island), island community groups, and church organizations. Even on Funafuti, people maintain close connections with other people from their home islands through these organizations. Tuvaluan identity is intricately connected to island community (Munro, 1982).

(b) The importance of both land and community to the wellbeing of the Tuvalu people. Because Tuvalu is a collectivist society, Tuvalu custom holds a strong value for caring for the needs of others. To paraphrase what one woman told me, "Nobody ever starves in Tuvalu." It may be a developing nation, and Tuvaluans may be very poor, but they take care of each other. No one will ever go hungry because they can depend upon their family and their island community to care for them. On one's home island, there is also the ability to gather food from the land. Every inch of Tuvalu is owned by Tuvaluans. Even government property and the airstrip are leased from Funafuti families who own the land. For this reason, when people migrate from other islands to Funafuti, they do not have the same access to land resources as do families from Funafuti. This makes food more expensive, because it cannot be supplemented by growing. Island community groups may also have to adapt because of a lack of access to land. For example, the Vaitupu women's group on Funafuti does not gather pandanus leaves for their traditional weaving crafts. Instead, they sew pillowcases or make other crafts from purchased cloths. Home island, physical land, and island community are highly interconnected in the lifestyle and wellbeing of the Tuvalu people.

(c) The collectivist nature of community activities and projects. Most Tuvaluans are involved with their community. One woman told me she "would wonder about" a person who stayed off by themselves and was not involved in community groups, indicating it would be very strange behavior. I was also told that losing access to this close community network is very hard on the psychological wellbeing of Tuvaluans who have moved to other countries. When I visited the Tuvalu Association of NGOs (TANGO), I asked them what sorts of projects they have found to be successful or unsuccessful. The answer

was the projects that involve the community tend to last, whereas independent projects that are not based within the community tend to fail in a year or less.

(d) The need for community research to be based within the Tuvalu community with data and results beneficial to and accessible by Tuvalu people. Community research has a greater chance of being supported and successful if it involves community members actively. There is also a strong need in Tuvalu for research dissemination within the community. While visiting the Tuvalu National Archives, I spoke with the National Archivist about the dearth of books and materials written in Tuvaluan, and a similar shortfall of materials from foreign researchers about Tuvalu. She named a number of research projects from multiple countries, whose researchers had come through the archives to gather information, but had left nothing behind. These included graduate theses and dissertations. She asked me specifically to send her a copy of my dissertation for the Archives. Ms. Faleasiu later confirmed that this was a common issue Tuvalu faced, and that responsible researchers should share the knowledge they gained with Tuvalu.

(e) The official Tuvalu position with respect to global climate change at this time is to negotiate only measures that will allow the Tuvalu people to maintain their homeland. Sir Tomu Sione, my host family's patriarch and the Tuvalu Minister of Health, shared with me a government document on Tuvalu's official positions regarding climate change (General Environment Briefing, 2010). This document called for strong actions by specific foreign governments (including the United States) to reduce emissions immediately. "We need a commitment to targets for the **year 2015**. Setting targets for 2050 is too far away" (bold in original). The document calls for adaptation funding by wealthy nations for developing nations who are falling victim to climate change and indicates that the Tuvaluan government will not negotiate for migration at this time.

Sir Sione explained that if Tuvalu negotiates for migration at this time, the nations that ought to reduce their emissions may further stall the process. They may decide that the lands of certain countries are acceptable losses because the people will be safe. However, the loss of the Tuvalu homeland is not acceptable. If there comes a time when the people must move to survive, they will move to survive. But until that time, "we will fight to keep our country, our culture and our way of living" (General Environment Briefing, Annex 1.3).

Ms. Faleasiu and I discussed each of these points with specific attention to developing a research framework for the second, more directed study that would successfully operate within the thematic guidelines. In this way, the research methods of the second study and its outcomes will be useful and beneficial in Tuvalu. The research plan utilized the resulting themes in the following ways: (1) the second study must address the multiple cultural communities from Tuvalu's islands rather than seeking to identify a single "Tuvalu" culture; (2) the research must address the importance of both the communities and islands to the Tuvalu people, as well as the intersection of island and community to the identity and wellbeing of the Tuvalu people; (3) the research will include a cross-section of community members; (4) the research will be conducted in collaboration with the Office of Community Affairs to ensure a Tuvaluan stake in the research methods and outcomes, as well as to ensure the benefit, usefulness, and accessible dissemination of research data and outcomes to the people of Tuvalu; (5) photography will be used; (6) the research will be framed within the social and environmental justice imperative that the Tuvalu people maintain their homeland.

Collaboration. Ms. Faleasiu agreed to serve as collaborator and Tuvalu adviser throughout the entire research development, implementation, and analysis process. She has offered advice on ways to help the study function well in Tuvalu. She has answered questions I have posed about the study design. She has had the opportunity to review project materials and proposals. Dissemination materials will be prepared and disseminated under her advisement. It is my hope that the data gathered from this study will also be a useful addition to other ongoing research in the Office of Community Affairs.

Second Study. The current research delves into the sociocultural concepts of sense of place and sense of community of the Tuvalu people within the larger framework of the Psychology of Climate Change. This study explores the distinctive cultural identity, values and customs that are unique among Tuvalu's islands. The current research is aligned with Tuvalu's official position that land and culture are precious and must both be protected for the survival and wellbeing of the Tuvalu people. Therefore, the threat of climate change is not only to the physical islands, but also to the cultural communities of Tuvalu.

Research questions. This study explores four specific, but interrelated themes: sense of place; sense of community; interconnection between sense of place and sense of community within the culture; and future projections regarding climate change. The specific research questions are as follows:

1) What is the relationship between land and the wellbeing of the Tuvalu people (sense of place)?

2) What is the relationship between community connections and the wellbeing of the Tuvalu people (sense of community)?

3) What is the relationship between land and community connections (sense of place and sense of community) in Tuvalu culture(s)? and,

4) How might global climate change affect the Tuvalu community as well as the land?

Research site. The research site is the Funafuti atoll in Tuvalu. Funafuti is the capitol of Tuvalu and the most populous of Tuvalu's nine islands with 4,492 inhabitants (Central Statistic Division, 2010a). As the political and economic capitol, Funafuti has experienced a population influx in recent years from the neighboring islands (CRISP, 2007). Funafuti is also home to the University of the South Pacific, Tuvalu campus, bringing a further influx of young adults seeking higher education from Tuvalu's other islands. Funafuti has resident communities from neighboring islands who typically maintain their home island identity through active involvement with island-specific organizations, women's organizations, church functions, and other community gatherings. On Funafuti, neighbor islands may have their own *maneapa*, volleyball or tennis courts, or other physical structure owned and actively utilized by that island community. Funafuti is therefore a prime location to engage with community members from multiple islands regarding their cultural community values, norms, and wellbeing. Furthermore, neighbor island community members currently residing in Funafuti are uniquely able to speak to the importance of community connection to their home island, since their communities must actively devise ways to maintain organizational and cultural traditions away from their home island.

Procedure. I traveled to Funafuti for three weeks during December 2011 to January 2012. During this trip, my husband Michael R. Corlew, also traveled with me and served as my research assistant. As a history student, he was also conducting his own research on the recent history of the market economy shifts in Tuvalu through oral histories. In his study, I served as research assistant. Ethnographic and other data collection included a combination of recorded interviews, non-recorded interviews, informal conversations, participatory observation, photography, and copious field notes. Several participants have also added to or clarified data via email and the social networking website Facebook. Those who have email addresses received a copy of their transcripts to review and make corrections, additions, subtractions, or clarifications. Several participants were contacted for advice, feedback, and additional information during the data analysis and writing process.

Interviews. Interviews were conducted in person in Funafuti in participants' offices, homes, or the homes of family members by myself and/or my research assistant.[11] The interviews began with the informed consent process, introducing the participant to the research topics and giving a brief overview of the types of questions they would be asked. The interview continued with a semi-structured conversation covering the following themes:

1) "About your home island," i.e., The land and physical structures on your home island; The community on your home island; The culture on your home island; The ways in which people interact with the land during daily activities and special events; Community networks and organizations on your home island (who they are, what they do, etc.);

2) "About your life/community on Funafuti," i.e., Differences in way of life between your home island and Funafuti[12]; Your island community's functions and activities on Funafuti; Maintaining your island's culture on Funafuti; The ways in which people interact (or cannot interact) with the land on Funafuti during daily activities and special events; Home island community networks and organizations maintained (or not maintained) on Funafuti;

3) "Ways in which your land/physical structures and community life are connected to each other on your home island and/or Funafuti", i.e., They ways in which individuals or groups interact with the land; The ways in which community activities need or utilize land; The ways in which community identity is strengthened by land; and

---

[11] As noted in the Participants section, below.
[12] Not applicable to participants from Funafuti.

27

4) "Future projections with climate change," i.e., How climate change might affect your community's land and structures; How climate change might affect your community's culture and way of life.

Non-recorded interviews. Two participants with whom I conducted an "official interview" declined to be recorded, and one of these participants requested anonymity. I was allowed to take notes during both of these conversations. The topics of these interviews included those mentioned above, and in one case, explored extensively the role of religion in Tuvalu daily life and culture. Notes from these interviews were included in the coding process, as described below.

Informal conversation. During my travels I was often in the company of people who were very interested to discuss study themes, especially related to the Tuvalu culture and changes over time, including climate change. These conversations did not include an informed consent process, and in most cases I did not take notes during the conversation but recorded them into my field notes as soon as possible afterwards. Information from these conversations is used to thicken the data gathered from the formal interviews.

Participatory observation. I was very fortunate once again to be included in the family celebrations, activities, and daily life with Sir Tomu Sione's family. My travels were during the holiday season, and as such, I was able to participate in Christmas, Boxing Day, and New Year's celebrations with the Niutao island community as well as with my host family. I was also present for a birthday celebration and a funeral. Special events and everyday activities were recorded with field notes, photographs, and/or video. These experiences were weighted in the analysis and bring thickness and depth to the other data.

Photography. I had originally intended to conduct a series of focus groups or interviews, incorporating the Photovoice methodology. Participants would be interviewed, would then go out and take photographs of important objects, places, or events, and would then return for a second interview about the photographs. However, logistical issues prevented this series of events from being completed with most participants. Participants were asked to take or share previously taken photographs to serve as examples of important values, places, events, or cultural norms that are important in portraying Tuvalu. One participant, "Jopeto Major," drove around the island and took 79 photographs to portray the important aspects of Tuvaluan life on Funafuti. We later sat down to discuss each of these photographs. Another participant, Ken T. Sione, sat with me at his family's computer and searched through old videos of Tuvalu culture. These videos included home movies and also clips from Gerd Koch's research. Ken used these videos as a focal point for explanations about Tuvaluan daily activities, cultural materials, and events in Niutao, describing items and behaviors to me in detail as they occurred and recounting stories of his participation in events like bird hunting, fishing, and basket weaving.

Several interviewees mentioned items or places that were available for me to take pictures of after the interview. I also took many photographs and several short videos of cultural activities in daily living and special events that can serve as examples of Tuvaluan culture. In addition, photographs were collected via Facebook from Stephen Boland, an Australian working with the Ministry of Finance in Tuvalu. These photographs were taken during the 2011 drought and show the community and land impacts of this extreme weather event. I contacted Mr. Boland for permission to use these pictures in the study to thicken the participants' descriptions of the 2011 drought.

Field notes. As in the preliminary research trip, I took copious field notes. When it was appropriate to take notes during a conversation or activity, I did so. If note-taking was inappropriate at the moment, I would record information as soon as possible after the fact. As in the preliminary study, I was able to "check in" with several participants, and especially with Tomu Sione as my host family's patriarch and with Lanieta Faleasiu as the study's collaborator.

Participants. Nineteen interviews were audio-recorded from sixteen participants, representing all nine islands. Niutao was the island most strongly represented, as I gathered interviews from a wide cross-section of Tomu Sione's extended family. Two additional interviews were conducted that were not recorded. Seven of the participants were women and eleven were men. Four elders (over 65) are included in this sample, all of whom were men. Eight young adults (under 35) were interviewed, of whom six were women and two were men. All participants spoke English with at least a very strong conversational fluency. Three participants chose to use an altered version of their names, and one participant whose interview was not audio-recorded requested complete anonymity. All audio-recorded participants consented to have their interviews and transcripts donated to the National Archives and the Office of Community Affairs. One recording will not be donated because the interview inadvertently captured a conversation with the family doctor. The participants are briefly introduced below.

Table 1. Participants by Demographics

Participant	Home Island	Other Island(s)	Sex	Age Bracket	Occupation
Sir Tomu M. Sione	Niutao	Funafuti	M	Elder (65+)	Politician; old man of southern Niutao clan
Ken T. Sione	Niutao	Funafuti	M	Youth (Below 35)	Police officer
"Kou"	Niutao	Funafuti	F	Youth (Below 35)	Homemaker
"Sueina Hindu"	Niutao	Funafuti	F	Youth (Below 35)	Homemaker
Vete Savaio	Niutao	Funafuti	M	Middle Age (35-65)	Civic engineer; sports
Nalu Nia	Niutao	Funafuti	M	Elder (65+)	Educator; historian
Feue Tipu	Nanumea	Niutao, Funafuti	M	Middle Age (35-65)	Professor

Alamai Manuella Sioni	Nanumea	Funafuti, all outer islands	F	Middle Age (35-65)	Director, Office of Cultural Affairs
Kokea Malua	Nanumea	Funafuti	M	Elder (65+)	Politician
Rev. Alefaio Honolulu	Nanumea	Nukulaelae, Niulakita	M	Middle Age (35-65)	Reverend, EKT
Rev. Tafue Lusama	Nukulaelae	Vaitupu, Funafuti	M	Middle Age (35-65)	General Secretary, Ekalesia Kelisiano Tuvalu
Beteteba Aselu	Nukulaelae	Funafuti, all outer islands	F	Youth (Below 35)	Social Analyst
S. Metia Tealofi	Nukufetau	Funafuti	M	Elder (65+)	Politician; hotel industry
"Jopeto Major"	Nukufetau	Funafuti	F	Youth (Below 35)	Student
Matakina Simii	Nui	Funafuti	F	Youth (Below 35)	Director, Fusi Alofa
Lanieta Faleasiu	Nanumaga	Funafuti	F	Youth (Below 35)	Director, Office of Community Affairs
Anonymous			M		
Noa Petueli	Funafuti		M	Youth (Below 35)	Assistant Archivist, Tuvalu National Archives

Sir Tomu M. Sione is the "old man" or head of the southern Niutao clan and the patriarch of his family. He is a former Governor General and Member of Parliament who has served in government for over 40 years before retiring in 2010[13]. He is also my Tuvalu family's patriarch. His interview was conducted by my research assistant and myself.

---

[13] 1970-1974 Member of Parliament; 1975-1978 Minister for Commerce and Natural Resources; 1982-1988 Member of Parliament; 1989-1995 Minister for Home Affairs and Natural Resources; 1996 Governor General; 1997-1998 Member of Parliament; 1998 Speaker of Parliament; 1999-2008 Member of Parliament; 2009-2010 Minister of Health

Ken T. Sione is Tomu's youngest son, and my brother in Tuvalu. He is from Niutao, but grew up predominantly in Funafuti. He is a police officer who works with the prison on Funafuti. Ken was interviewed twice. In the second interview, he showed me a number of videos about Tuvalu culture and Niutao life to explain activities and the uses of various cultural items and resources. His interviews were conducted by myself only.

"Kou" is Ken's wife, and my sister in Tuvalu. She is also from Niutao. She has attended the University of the South Pacific, Tuvalu campus, but discontinued her studies when she got married. Her interview was conducted by myself only. She chose a name variation that connected her to her husband.

"Sueina Hindu" is Tomu's daughter-in-law, by marriage to his son Hindu. She also chose a name variation that connected her to her husband. Hindu is a seaman, currently away on the standard eleven-month contract. Sueina lives in Funafuti with the family while he is away. Sueina is also my sister. Her interview was conducted by myself only.

Vete Savaio is Tomu's cousin. He was among the first generation of Tuvaluans sent away for education in other countries, and was Tuvalu's first civic engineer. His interview was conducted by my research assistant and myself.

Feue Tipu is Tomu's nephew. He is from a Niutao family, but was adopted into a Nanumea family and so can speak prolifically about both islands. Although they are of different generations, Feue and Vete are close in age and have many shared experiences with foreign education and Tuvalu's recent economic development. Feue is a professor at the University of the South Pacific in Fiji. His interview was conducted by my research assistant and myself.

Kokea Malua is an elder from Nanumea and a former Minister of Parliament. He was a child during World War II when the Americans were in Tuvalu. The people of his island were evacuated during that time to live on Lakena, a small island that is used for *pulaka* pits and other farming. I was referred to Kokea by the Tuvalu National Archives. His interview was conducted by myself only.

Nalu Nia is an elder from Niutao. He is highly knowledgeable of Niutao's culture and history, and authored the Niutao chapter in *Tuvalu, a History* (Faaniu & Laracy, 1983). Nalu served in Tuvalu's education system for much of his career. I was referred to Nalu by the Sione family. His interview was conducted by my research assistant and myself.

S. Metia Tealofi is an elder from Nukufetau and a former Minister of Parliament beginning before Tuvalu's separation from Kiribati and subsequent independence from the British Empire. Metia was a young adult during WWII and was employed by the Americans on Funafuti at that time. I was referred to Metia by his granddaughter Jopeto Major. His interviews were conducted by my research assistant only.

"Jopeto Major" is a student at the University of the South Pacific who is from Nukufetau. She would like to be a politician, but realizing there are few opportunities for women in Tuvalu politics, her next goal is to be a lawyer.

31

Jopeto's name is a nickname derived from her parents' and grandfather's name. Jopeto is an amalgam of their names, and Major is the English translation of "Metia." Jopeto was interviewed twice. In the second interview she explained the importance of the 79 photographs that she took around the island of Funafuti to describe life in Tuvalu and the issues faced by the community. Jopeto was not referred to me; I met her in the community. Her interviews were conducted by myself only.

Matakina Simii is the head and founder of Fusi Alofa, Tuvalu's disabilities center in Funafuti. Kina is from Nui, although she spent much of her education years away from her home island. She founded Fusi Alofa after recognizing a need in the community and tenaciously pursuing its fulfillment for several years. I was referred to Kina by Lanieta Faleasiu. Her interview was conducted by myself only.

Noa Petueli is from Funafuti. He is the Assistant Archivist at the Tuvalu National Archives and takes care of their digital archives and information technology. He is also a student at USP, Tuvalu campus, studying Information Sciences. I met Noa at the Tuvalu National Archives. His interview was conducted by my research assistant only.

Alamai Manuella Sioni is the Director of the Office of Cultural Affairs in Tuvalu. She is from the island of Nanumea, but grew up in Kiribati. As a Cultural Affairs Officer, she has intimate knowledge of the cultures and activities of each island in Tuvalu and is keenly aware of current cultural shifts occurring on Funafuti and the outer islands. I was referred to Alamai by a number of people. Her interview was conducted by myself only.

Beteteba Aselu is the Social Analyst at the Department of Community Affairs, conducting community surveys on the outer islands. She is from Nukulaelae by blood, though she grew up in Fiji and only first came to Tuvalu as an adult. Her grandfather's boat was lost at sea as a young man, and wound up settling abroad. Her father achieved his lifelong dream of seeing his father's homeland just before his retirement, reuniting with their Nukulaelae family who had never known what had happened or that this side of the family continued on. Teba came to Tuvalu to "learn what it means to be a Tuvaluan," and took the job conducting island surveys as a means to connect with the culture. Like Alamai, she is highly knowledgeable about Tuvaluan ways of life on each of the islands. I was referred to Teba by the Sione family. Her interview was conducted by myself only.

Reverend Tafue Lusama is the General Secretary of the Ekalesia Kelisiano Tuvalu (EKT, Tuvalu Christian Congregation). Tafue is the leader of the climate change initiatives with EKT, and an outspoken leader of climate change education nationally and internationally. I was referred to Tafue by a number of people, including Alefaio Honolulu. His interview was conducted by my research assistant and myself.

Lanieta Faleasiu is the Director of the Office of Community Affairs and the Tuvalu adviser for this study. She chose also to participate in the interviews as a woman from Nanumaga and as a person who is greatly interested in Tuvalu cultures and her future regarding climate change. I was referred to Lanieta during the preliminary study by a number of people. Her interview was conducted by my research assistant and myself.

The two unrecorded participants included a young man from an outer island living in Funafuti who chose to remain anonymous in the study because he did not want to be thought of as being critical of the government. The other unrecorded interviewee was Reverend Alefaio Honolulu, who is a minister of EKT. He has served as a pastor on Niulakita (the island with the smallest population in Tuvalu) and Nukulaelae. His grandfather was Hawaiian (George Holomoana), hence Rev. Honolulu's name. I was referred to Alefaio by a number of people. His interview was conducted by my research assistant and myself.

In reporting, these participants will be referred to by their first name. This is not meant as a sign of disrespect to the participants, many of whom are highly respected community leaders. Rather, my experience in Tuvalu is that people are rarely called by their last name or by a title. The first name is most commonly used when addressing or referring to another person whether or not that person is present. I will follow this convention here. All other participants who were interviewed during the preliminary studies or with whom I conversed in informal settings during either field research trip to Tuvalu will remain anonymous in the reporting of this study due to the lack of an informed consent process. The exceptions to this rule will be reporting about conversations or activities with members of my host family that are stories one would reasonably assume would be shared by family members, even to a wide audience, and follow-up conversations that clarify information from the interviews. These exceptions are used sparingly.

Dissemination. Because of the expressed need for data that is gathered by foreign researchers to be left in Tuvalu upon completion, this project will also have a dissemination phase centered on dissemination in Tuvalu. All recorded and transcribed interviews, save one, will be donated to the Office of Community Affairs for future use by Tuvaluan researchers. As possible and appropriate, reported materials such as this dissertation and a results book will be shared with the Office of Community Affairs, the Tuvalu National Archives, and with participants. This dissemination phase is funded in part by the SCRA Community Mini-Grant.

Operationalization of key concepts. In accordance with the research questions, data gathering and analysis focused heavily on the following terms: (a) sense of place, and wellbeing; (b) sense of community and wellbeing; (c) sense of place—sense of community interaction and wellbeing; and (d) future projections regarding climate change.

Terms are operationalized as follows:
a) "Sense of place" is defined as the social identity that is connected to place and the psychological or emotional attachment to place. Wellbeing in connection to place will be defined as the positive interaction between one's sense of place and one's physical, emotional, social, and/or psychological health.

b) "Sense of community" is defined to include the four major components as outlined by McMillan & Chavis (1986), i.e., a feeling of belongingness, mutual influence between the community and the individual, a sense of needs fulfillment though community involvement, and an emotional connection to the community. Wellbeing in connection to sense of community will be defined as the positive interaction between one's sense of community and one's physical, emotional, social, and/or psychological health.

c) "Sense of place—sense of community interaction" is defined to include ways in which sense of place and sense of community are inherently related to each other, such that the sense of place is meaningless without the community or the sense of community is impossible without the place.

d) "Future projections regarding climate change" will include near-term projections such as current actions or short-term plans, to long-term projections such as how Tuvaluans in three generations may live and maintain their culture.

Exploration of themes. In addition to serving as a framework for process, the five themes that resulted from the preliminary study were beneficial to the collection of rich data in the second study. Each theme served as a foundation for exploring community activities, networks, values, and customs during the interviews. Sense of place and sense of community were overarching concepts guiding the interviews and photography, as well as data analysis. However, detailed descriptions through narrative and imagery were prompted during data collection based upon the cultural themes as follows:

(a) The importance of cultural communities from Tuvalu's individual islands to individual, family, and community identity. Participants were prompted to discuss specific ways in which they maintain island identity, both on their home island and on Funafuti. They were asked to share stories from group activities, explain how or why groups were formed, or evaluate how island groups strengthen island identity. Participants were prompted to discuss words, phrases, or concepts that have important cultural meaning (i.e., in-group terms or concepts that, when mentioned, others in their cultural community understand without the need for further explanation).

(b) The importance of both land and community to the wellbeing of the Tuvalu people. Participants were asked to share examples for how land interconnects with community activities, or how the lack of land impedes them. They were prompted to consider specific ways in which community members care for each other or act together for the group's benefit. They were asked to share stories regarding how access to land and community has benefited individuals or groups, or how lack of access has been detrimental.

(c) The collectivist nature of community activities and projects. Participants were encouraged to think about their daily lives and the ways in which they work with others. These activities and projects may be everyday occurrences such as meal sharing or evening song groups; or may be special occasion events such as community celebrations.

(d) The need for community research to be based within the Tuvalu community with data and results beneficial to and accessible by Tuvalu people. Data collection took place in participants' homes or a comfortable community setting. Participants were prompted to consider their daily settings, what these places mean to them, and how people interact with these settings.

(e) The official Tuvalu position with respect to global climate change at this time to negotiate only measures which will allow the Tuvalu people to maintain their homeland. Participants were asked to think about the preceding discussions and consider ways in which climate change may affect these many aspects of culture. Participants were not asked about migration, but about their projections for the future of Tuvalu's culture and community. The cultural activities discussed served as examples for discussion on how climate change may affect culture, and ways in which the community can strive to preserve culture.

Data analysis. The interviews were audio-recorded and transcribed in full. The transcriptions and selected photographs by participants or by myself (relating to participant interviews or themes) were analyzed with the assistance of NVivo9 Qualitative Analysis Software. Coding began with a line-by-line microanalysis (Strauss & Corbin, 1998) in which each data point was coded for both the literal statement and figurative meaning. Coding relied heavily on the operationalized terms listed above, as well as the resultant themes from the preliminary study. Coding was also open to emergent themes that fall outside of the research questions and focus. This openness to emergent data is particularly important because I am a foreigner to the site and participants. Even with collaborative efforts meant to minimize researcher bias, it is vitally important to maintain awareness of potential discrepancies between researcher conceptualization of the research questions and topics and the participants' conceptualizations of the research questions and topic.

Following the initial line-by-line coding process was a quasi-deductive axial coding process. Coding patterns and themes were interpreted and continuously referred back to the individual data points and to other related themes and patterns (Creswell, 2007). Once again, axial coding focused heavily on the operationalized terms and preliminary themes, but was also open to emergent themes. Coding themes were discussed with Ms. Faleasiu and several Tuvaluan participants prior to the coding process, and open communication continued via email during analysis and reporting.

Writing style of this dissertation report. This dissertation report is an academic endeavor in partial fulfillment of my PhD. However, this report is also the result of a years-long process that included the time and efforts of myself, my husband/research assistant, and many Tuvaluans. The openness, care, and generosity of the Tuvalu people made this possible. They have shared a great deal of knowledge with me so that I might learn about 'the cultural impacts of climate change.' This knowledge is theirs, and will be left behind in their care.

Accordingly, this report will be written predominantly in lay language to increase accessibility to non-academic readers, including as appropriate, a narrative reporting format (Creswell, 2007). This narrative style will not

35

fictionalize the data, but will contextualize it within experiences or themes. These narratives will include my own experiences in Tuvalu as well as stories told by participants to relate information during the interview. Throughout Results Sections I and II, I will utilize participants' voices through quotations and photographs as much as possible to maximize the appropriateness of this paper's representation of Tuvalu and Tuvaluans.

Citations will be included throughout, but to the best of my ability jargon will be reserved for the technical sections of this report that include explanations and explorations of psychological methods, theory, models, and analyses. Lay readers who are uninterested in these things can feel free to skip these sections without losing access to the knowledge I have learned in this journey. Technical sections will include theory and nuance, and are intended for academic audiences as well as lay audiences with specialized interests. All data, stories, photos, and information that came from Tuvaluans will be reported in the non-technical sections.

A note on cultural change. Culture is dynamic in nature, and perhaps more so in our increasingly globalized world. Tuvalu culture has been in a process of recorded change for hundreds of years, since the first sporadic contacts with Westerners from the 1500s to the 1800s.[14] Oral histories, songs, and Tuvaluan legends of the first Tuvaluans show that the island power hierarchies, interisland affiliations, modes of worship, and other cultural traditions have been in flux for as long as there have been people in Tuvalu (Goldsmith, 1989). I mention this so as to be clear that when I discuss culture changes in the Results sections, I am not talking about Tuvaluan culture being *lost*. Culture is not lost. Culture is tenacious. It adapts and survives. Two examples of cultural survival and change that are familiar to Western audiences include the Native Americans/American Indians, and the Native Hawaiians.

From before the first American invasion and the beginnings of colonialism in the New World, colonizers have purposefully and systematically sought to destroy native peoples and cultures (Hall, 1997; Mann, 2005; Zinn, 1980). Through violence, legal maneuvering, schooling, adoption, relocation, and countless other efforts over a period of 500 years extending to the present day, foreigners and then Americans have sought to remove Native Americans from "our" shores. From the beginning of this process, we have been telling each other that Native American culture has been lost, or is nearly lost, or will soon be lost (Gunn Allen, 2003; Kilpatrick, 1999). Documents from hundreds of years ago written by colonizers have stated uncomprehendingly that the Native American cultures are gone. We still hear this refrain today. And yet after 500 years of extended, determined, focused, and often violent efforts by colonizers to end Native American people and cultures, they are still here with us. Culture is persistent. Culture survives.

---

[14] http://tuvaluislands.com/history.htm

The second example is that of Native Hawaiian culture. The Kingdom of Hawai'i was illegally overthrown by the U.S. government just over a hundred years ago. Native Hawaiians are now a very small minority in Hawai'i. Some people argue about whether "Part Hawaiians" should count as Native Hawaiians. Some people argue that even the Kingdom of Hawai'i did not represent "real" Hawaiian culture anyway, because there was no unified Kingdom pre-contact. Dr. Noenoe Silva states that these arguments are ridiculous. She explains that there is this idea in Western minds that the very instant Captain Cook first set his foot on Hawaiian soil that somehow Hawaiian culture was corrupted irrevocably and anything that has happened since then is no longer "real" Hawaiian culture. This idea is absurd. "We are Hawaiians," she says. "What we do is Hawaiian culture" (N. Silva, personal communication, February 2, 2011). Culture adapts and it changes over time. Outsiders do not have the authority to declare what is and is not "real" in a culture, nor to declare it "lost" as it changes.

There is no moment in Tuvaluan history in which what happened was "real" and from which any deviation meant that the culture was "lost" or "fake." I want to be clear that when I discuss the changes to Tuvaluan culture that are happening over time, I am not extolling the loss of something that once was, as Westerners are notoriously prone to do.[15] I am explaining the shifts that Tuvaluans are experiencing and talking about. These cultural changes are important in the lives of Tuvaluans now, just as past changes were important to the lives of Tuvaluans before, and subsequent changes will define the lives of Tuvaluans in the future.

Chapter Summary

This chapter introduced the major topics that will be explored in this dissertation. The chapter includes a description of methods and theories driving two qualitative exploratory studies. There is an introduction to the psychological theories and concepts related to sense of place and sense of community, as well as the concepts and terminology of Activity Settings theory. The chapter provides a brief overview of the psychology of climate change, and of the human impacts of climate change in Tuvalu. These topics will be explored in great depth in the following chapters.

Results Section I contains four chapters that discuss the dynamic cultural context of Tuvalu in which climate change is being introduced. Chapter 2 explores various ways in which the guest and gift cultures of Tuvalu manifest in daily life and in cultural expectations. Chapter 3 discusses life on the "outer islands" as a group, compared to life on the urban Funafuti. Chapter 4 directly addresses the dynamic nature of cultural life in Tuvalu with examples of changes that participants noted in their daily lives as well as with examples of systemic changes. Chapter 5 explores the historical drivers of change, including Christianity in Tuvalu as well as political and economic changes.

---

[15] See Chapter 8 for more exploration of this topic.

37

Results Section II contains two chapters that explore the human impacts of climate change within this dynamic cultural context. Chapter 6 will explores ways in which climate change indirectly and directly affect Tuvaluans. Chapter 7 discusses the ways in which Tuvaluans have agency in their current actions and future plans with climate change. There is also discussion of the complex understanding and response of Tuvaluans to climate change. Finally, Chapter 8 includes the theoretical discussion and conclusion of this dissertation by answering the research questions, applying psychological theory to the results, critically exploring examples of international discourse on climate change in Tuvalu, and addressing the limitations and implications of this research.

Results Section I

Manuia te laukele	Fortunate is the land
Manuia te ulufenua	Fortunate are the palm trees
Manuia te moana	Fortunate is the sea
Ke ola lakau	May the trees live
Ke to mai te sau mai te lagi	May dew fall from heaven
Ke manuia te nofoaiga a te aliki	May the aliki's territory prosper
Ko tagata katoa o te fenua	All the people of the island
Ke fiafia ki te aliki	Should rejoice at the election of the aliki
Ke manuia tena nofoaiga	May his territory prosper

—Excerpt, Niutaoan Blessing (Koch, 1961, p. 100)[16]

Creating the Context: Tuvaluan Cultures and Ways of Life

In the process of discussing cultural norms and the impacts of climate change, it quickly became apparent that many Tuvaluans do not consider climate change as an isolated event. Rather, the potential impacts of climate change are considered within the context of the many ongoing shifts in the recent history of Tuvalu. In fact, the issues of climate change are so highly integrated with other cultural issues that it is impossible to discuss climate change without a thorough discussion of culture.

In this section, I will discuss Tuvalu's guest culture and gift culture. I will give a brief introduction to the overarching values and ways of life that are commonly considered universal to the "outer islands" as a group. I will then explore life on Funafuti. Next, I will discuss modernity and the cultural changes occurring with food, school, work, and generational shifts. I will explore recent changes in Tuvaluan culture according to major events in Tuvaluan history. I will discuss the coming of Christianity in great detail, because although it constitutes a major cultural shift in Tuvaluan way of life (in the 1800s), Christianity is so completely integrated with Tuvaluan culture as to be considered a traditional value. Other major events include colonization by the

---

[16] When German ethnologist Gerd Koch (1961), also known in Tuvalu as Keti, traveled to Tuvalu, he spent a significant amount of time on Niutao, my family's home island. It was in Niutao that he recorded this blessing during the inauguration of a new *aliki* (chief). The results sections will begin with excerpts from this blessing. Although the blessing was published some fifty years ago, I sought permission from Sir Tomu M. Sione, as the head of his clan in Niutao, to quote these words here. By framing the discussion of the impacts of climate change in Tuvalu in this culturally enriched blessing, I hope to set the context of this report to that of Tuvalu's experiences with climate change, according to Tuvalu's needs and Tuvalu's way of life. This blessing calls for all good things to be granted to the new *aliki* and his island and people. In the face of a changing climate and uncertain future, its significance remains as strong as ever.

39

British, World War II, phosphate mining in Banaba/Ocean Island, separation from Kiribati, independence from Britain, and the domain name assignation of .tv and the subsequent influx of development funds and modernity. This section explores the context in which climate change is happening in Tuvalu.

Chapter 2

Guest Culture/Gift Culture

When I first arrived in Tuvalu, I had a list of people and organizations with whom I hoped to speak. About half of them I had contacted before by email, but even those who had invited me to stop by and talk had not scheduled a time or made any firm plans. Upon my arrival, I set about what I was sure would be a slow process of walking around the island, introducing myself and justifying why someone should bother to talk to me, scheduling a (hopefully not too distant) future time to come back for an actual meeting, and then walking on to the next place to repeat the process. I expected this because I am American. I come from a place where "time is money" and where important people who know things want plenty of advanced scheduling time to make sure eager students don't clog up their day pestering them with questions. Ever-respectful of people's time, I would never have presumed to force my presence into the offices of my list of people. At most, I really, really hoped I'd get the opportunity to speak with them before my trip was up.

What happened instead was that I would walk into an office and get about as far as "Hi, my name is Laura" before I would be invited to come in, sit down, and talk. In almost all cases, the person I sought out dropped what they were doing and spoke with me like we were old friends. An exception was when someone was out of the office and another person offered to speak with me instead, and then also told me when I could return to speak to the woman I originally sought, *and* referred me to several other people who might be of interest. There were many occasions of this. Tuvalu is a small country. Certainly if I was speaking to one person about culture or climate change, they could think of five other people I should speak to. Several times I was referred to people specifically because they were used to speaking with foreigners; they would know what types of questions I would ask, and would have the information ready. These referrals were meant to make my life easier, and to make my short trip more productive. On the Thursday before I left, a woman asked me if I could come back on Monday. "Wait," she said after I agreed to this, "When are you leaving?" "Tuesday," I told her. "Oh, well maybe we had better speak now." Apparently one day was cutting it too close. What if something came up on Monday? There would be no more chances.

I never quite got over my surprise at how willing people were to sit down and talk with me, a stranger, with no notice and little context for my presence. I had never realized how much time I spend explaining myself and justifying myself to the people I want to talk to, until I didn't have to do it. Again and again in Tuvalu, people were perfectly willing to welcome me into their offices, even into their homes. During my second trip, several elders were suggested as potential participants. "Just go by and talk to him," we would be told, "He lives up the road, four houses down from the speed bump." My husband and I would wander up to knock on doors or call into open houses, "Hello? We're looking for so-and-so. Is this the right house?" "Come in, come in!"

People were very conscious of me as a foreigner, in a very welcoming way. "Hawai'i? Oh, my cousin's wife has family there!" or "Ah, yes, the Americans came here during World War II!" I'm familiar with this exchange. In Hawai'i, when you meet someone new you often run through your degrees of connection. "Where do you live? My aunty lives in that neighborhood. Do you know ___?" I appreciated this familiar ritual in Tuvalu. Even though I was from another country, the people I met sought ways to connect, to make us familiar to each other. I was fortunate to have connections in the community through my host family. In addition to explaining who I had spoken with before, who had referred me to speak with them, I was able say "I'm staying with Tomu Sione and his family," to which the response from the younger generations was often, "Ahh, Grandpa Tomu." From elders, I often heard, "Oh, Tomu! I served with him in government."

What I was learning was that Tuvalu has a very strong "guest culture," in the sense that there is a very powerfully held value that one ought to be welcoming to others. Tightly connected to this is a "gift culture," which includes the sense that one must be willing to give of themselves, of their resources, of their time and heart to family, community members, and strangers alike. These interconnected concepts of giving and welcoming are manifested in a vast number of ways in Tuvalu.

Welcoming with food. Food is one such way. We met Matakina Simii at Fusi Alofa for her interview, but this was after we had missed meeting each other on Boxing Day in her home. After the recorded interview, Kina told us about the food she had prepared on Boxing Day so we could have a real Tuvaluan breakfast. We thanked her and apologized for missing it. In truth, I felt quite honored by her welcoming efforts. When we visited Nalu Nia in his home, he interrupted the interview to call for some chilled coconuts to be brought for us to drink, and asked us repeatedly throughout the interview how we liked them. Even in Hawai'i this is an extremely rare treat; we raved about the kindness and he smiled. "Before you came, I was sitting here and I read and I asked one of my grandsons to climb up the tree and give us some coconuts with my friends." During my first trip when I stayed at Tomu's house, I was told in no uncertain terms that I was family now and that I was invited to eat every meal with the family. During the second trip, Michael and I stayed at the Filamona Guesthouse, but spent most of our days at Tomu's home when we were not out collecting other interviews. During Sueina Hindu's interview, she called out to the women at the outdoor kitchen:

SUEINA:	[Speaks in Tuvaluan] They're asking, are you two eating?
LAURA:	Oh.
MICHAEL:	I don't think so.
LAURA:	Yeah, not now. We already ate, just now.
MICHAEL:	Yeah.
SUEINA:	[Speaks in Tuvaluan]. They worry you're not eating [Laughs].

During mealtimes, guests and male elders eat first. I was often instructed "to open the table" at a gathering, another sign of the emphasis placed on welcoming guests.

Welcoming feasts. When honored guests come to an island community, it is very common to welcome them with a feast and *fatele* (dance). These guests and these events are well-remembered on into the future. Anne and Keith Chambers are anthropologists who began traveling to Tuvalu in the early 70s. They spent years on the island of Nanumea, and are very fondly remembered by the people we met on Funafuti who are from Nanumea. Feue Tipu nodded to us once and told us they were "like you. They were respectful and asked a lot of questions" (Corlew field notes, 2011). The Chambers also reported a great deal on Tuvaluan guest and gift cultures (see, e.g., Chambers & Chambers, 2001). Says Feue, "I think the Chambers have recorded how many kinds of people exchange goods." Kokea Malua, an elder from Nanumea spoke of them happily, and recounted with great pride hearing that they had enjoyed the welcome they received on his home island:

> When [a friend of Kokea's] first came here [to Funafuti] he received a letter from the Chambers, Keith and Anne, and the letter was regarding his Members of Parliament on Nanumea. And they said they can't forget about their time in here. America is a great country [Laughter] you know, big things in there. And he was touched, you know, this was the old man here on Nanumea, he was touched when he said that 'things are very good here, you know, as Americans.' They had a function, you know, or something like a ball. It was a lot of people, really good food, but he said they can't forget when they were in Nanumea.

The fact that Nanumea's function rivaled even an American ball was definitely a point of pride. Decades later, Kokea could still tell me many stories about how his island had welcomed the Chambers.

If someone is regarded as a "guest" by a family or the *Kaupule* (Town Council), it is very common for their visit to be marked with a function. But in modern times, the line between a guest and someone who merely comes to work can become unclear. For example, Teba Aselu told us about "one story in Niutao. There was this *palagi*[17] that came to fix the Telcom. He traveled to all the islands." But there seemed to be confusion on the islands. Was he a guest or not? "You know, because he is just doing his job," Teba explained. He traveled from south to north to service the telephones for all of the islands, but he was not greeted as a guest in any of the islands. He was not offered a feast or function, or even invited into people's homes for food and drink. But one island welcomed him, not as a worker, but as a guest. Teba said:

> In Niutao they – every house that he goes to, the people call to him. And then when he finished his work, the community actually provided

---

[17] White person, foreigner

43

him with a feast. So that's what he said. Out of all the islands, it is the first time they ever acknowledged what he is doing.

He was so gratified to be recognized as a guest rather that as someone just passing through doing his job that he secretly gave them free Telcom in thanks. Teba said:

> They could make a call anywhere in the world, speak for as long as they want for one whole year. Anyone on the island could do that... They call and speak to their families in New Zealand for so long. People are talking so long. "It must be so expensive," and they're like "No, it's free." [Laughter] "How come it's free?" You know, it's really expensive to call from here. "No, it's free." So they found out later, the Telcom, so they sent someone to try and fix that thing [laughter] and that was when it ended.

Welcoming family. Islands have guest houses that are especially built and maintained by the community for the welcoming of guests. Alamai Manuella Sioni explained that this work is done for free. When the Vaitupu guest house was built, she said, "The whole island community helped. The women go and cook the food and serve it to the men. The men will be working. No charge. Takes months. It was months. So we still have that kind of spirit." It has been explained to me by multiple people that if someone is going to visit one of the outer islands and they have no family on that island, a family might 'adopt' that person so that they have someone to care for them during their stay. When this happens, that family is yours for life. Teba and I discussed this seamless blending of welcoming guests and welcoming new family members:

LAURA:	When you travelled to the islands, where do you live?
TEBA:	With families. In some places, if I don't have families, there is always a couple of guest houses where we could stay. But I try my best, if I am travelling by myself, I try to live with my family. Or if I am travelling with my team, and we would prefer to stay together, then we would stay at the *Kaupule* guest house. On my time off I go and visit my families.
LAURA:	Do you have family on all of the islands?
TEBA:	I have families in – I have some families that I just made on my trips [Laughter] I'm not even related to. [Laughter]
LAURA:	We have family too, in Niutao [Laughter]
TEBA:	Yeah, Tomu! [Laughter]
LAURA:	Yeah. [Laughter]
TEBA:	Very nice. And yeah, I made families that I am not even related to. I got to know them through my work. And so I stay with them. It's very good.

This practice of adopting guests as family has a very long history in Tuvalu. Sir Tomu Sione told me the story of Christianity first coming to Niutao back in 1861 (Sogivalu, 1992). Tomu said:

44

So when the two missionaries came to Niutao, they are not allowed to come out from the shore. So the high chief from Niutao said "You stay on the beach, lie on the beach, sleep on the beach. You are not allowed to come out. If you disobey then it's not my problem. You'll be punished by the people or you'll be slaughtered or killed by the people." So they stayed there for 2 or 3 days. Then the island decided … 'please take my two missionaries up.' So he changed his mind. They accepted the mission… My grand grandfather took the Niuean pastor, because he is single and more younger than the Samoan pastor. His name is Sione. This one my father calls him. So he took his guidance… to look after the welfare of the missionary. So my grandfather took that Niuean. He looked after him, fed him, until two years later and then this pastor completed his contract. So the Niuean pastor asked my grandfather "Can you come with me to my home island?" And my great grandfather said "Yes." So they went. That's why I have a connection with the Niuean people.

Three generations later, and Tomu often spoke of his family in Niue. These connections are strong and lasting. Strangers can be welcomed as families, and family bonds can outlast even generations of absence. Teba's family connection spanned generations after her grandfather's boat was lost at sea. During her father's final voyage before retiring as a seaman, they discovered that the island community's connection to her family remained just as strong as her family's connection to her grandfather's home island:

One of my cousins from Nukulaelae, he was on his way back on that same boat. So everybody was asking "Oh, who is that captain?" "Oh, I'm from Tuvalu, and you know my family is this." … So they were curious, the guy on the boat was curious, and he said, "Oh, is your family from Nukulaelae?" and he started mentioning, and it was exactly his nephew that he was talking to! … So what they did was they called from the boat to here, because they asked him, "Do you have any families that you know of in Niutao?' and he said "No." I mean, he knows he has family but he hasn't met anybody. So he said, "It's okay, then just call from the boat to inform these people that you are coming and for them to meet." So that's how they met… And they went up and they met him there and they brought him home.

The family was flabbergasted and overjoyed to have these long lost relatives return to Tuvalu. Teba and the rest of the family followed, and Teba stayed on with a job conducting community assessments on the outer islands so that she could learn "how to be Tuvaluan," and to reestablish that line of the family in Tuvalu.

I, myself, have learned firsthand the welcome that is shared with family in Tuvalu. Even before I arrived, Tomu had gone to the customs office at the airport to introduce me as his granddaughter. I have been introduced as family from Niutao, and the Niutaoan family that I have met in Funafuti have often discussed their wishes for us to visit Niutao during a future trip, so that I can see the island and meet the rest of the family. During our interview during my

45

second trip, the phone began to ring. Tomu was explaining about the welcome that people receive when they come to Niutao:

TOMU: But there is one funny part of it, if you are in Niutao and you walk on the road everybody calls "Hey Michael, come, drink!" [phone rings] Answer that, the phone.

LAURA: Yeah?

TOMU: They might give you a surprise.

LAURA: Hello? Hello? Oh, I think they'll call back.

TOMU: Huh?

LAURA: I think they'll call back. They hung up. They're too surprised to hear my voice.

TOMU: Yeah, that's what I'm [Laughter] saying – once they hear *palagi* voice, "Oh, oh! Wrong phone, wrong number!"

[Laughter]

MICHAEL: "I called America, oh no!"

[Laughter]

TOMU: Now they are telling to the family, maybe that was our family from Niutao, "Hey, *palagi*!" "Where?" "Talking to the *palagi*!" [Laughter] That's one of the differences. Maybe if you have time in future you come and we go, just prove yourself that you are part of the family.

At the end of my first trip, I was gifted with a very intricately decorated woven mat, a traditional parting gift for family members (see Image 5). On the way back to home, when I landed in Suva, Fiji, I was whisked away to my waiting flight to Nadi, Fiji, with barely 15 minutes on the ground. More than a year later, I found out that Sueina and Kou, who were in Fiji at the time, had come to the airport to meet me. They asked all the passengers after me until someone told them of a palagi lady who was taken away for another flight. I did not manage to meet Sueina and Kou during that first trip, but they had come to the airport to meet this stranger and family member. This is part of Tuvalu's welcoming culture. During her interview, when Kou was describing the different types of pandanus that are available on the different islands, she described the difference by recalling to me the mat that had been gifted to me while she was away:

But you see, it's white, different from our, from Niutao. But that, you remember the one that's, I don't know because I'm not here, but Grandma told us they gave you a gift. You see, that is different. It's really white.

Kou spoke of the traditional family gift, and knew which mat had been given. She was able to use it as an example of the differences between the pandanus trees available on different islands.

Sueina explained to me that Niutao is known from all of the Tuvaluan islands as having the most heart and being the most welcoming nature. The example she gave to explain this statement was how the family adopted a man

Image 5. Woven mat for sleeping, decorated. Gift from the Sione family (Corlew, 2010).

from Fiji who had been living in a very bad situation. "We have a heart for him," she told me, so she and her husband brought him up into their apartment in Fiji to stay with them. Outside of Tuvalu, actions like this can have risk. Tuvalu is peaceful because it is so small and the communities are so interconnected. Sueina said, "But you know the Fijians, sometimes they get dangerous, because you don't know them, because you never know each other." Fiji has many times the population of Tuvalu, making the population large and anonymous. But leaving this man in need was untenable to Sueina and her husband:

> So we bring him up to our place. We feed him, we give him clothes. And also whatever he wants, he can ask us. So, we stay with him. And when the time, we're supposed to come back home, because Grandpa and Grandma [Tomu and Segali] came over and spent the holidays, and Grandpa told him, "Now we have to go back home, eh? And it's up to you, if you want to come with us, then you can come. If not, then you stay here." And when Grandpa asked him, he said "I'm going with you people." That's why we bring him here. And now he's really happy, eh? … That's why the people always said that the Niutao people, they have more heart than others… It's six years now he is with us.

Sharing resources. In the line between the guest culture and the gift culture is the sharing of resources in Tuvalu. As Vete Savaio explained to me:

47

One of the biggest impacts is the sharing...When there wasn't any money in the olden days everybody can give a bit, or what they give instead of buy, it's all what is available. They go to the bush, they worked to the farm, they feed the pig and when they kill the pig they share, you know. That is always giving, and they're very happy.

Tuvaluans share resources within their immediate family, amongst their extended family, and amongst the wider community. In Tuvaluan culture, it is expected that what is owned is shared. All resources are freely given to those who have need or want of them. Teba explained:

If someone asks you for things, you give without questioning. You help people. The giving part is quite something, that you just give without questioning. If someone asks you for something then you will give it. Whether you want to give it or not, you are supposed to give... Here, people just come and ask "I want that." It could be just out of the blue and you are expected to give.

This sharing of resources is beyond the desire to care for family. It is a sense of responsibility to the community. Early in the new year, Nalu Nia gave a recent example of how Tuvaluans share resources:

In our Christmas, we killed a pig and we shared some parts of the house, and they are not my relatives... And that house I gave some coconut, and that one I gave some coconut, that one also I gave them. They are not my relatives. That's a custom. I feel not good if I have something and I don't share.

The sharing is not only during big events or formal celebrations. Sharing what you have is a matter of daily living. Ken Sione said, "Mostly you know you'll see each other, you make some local food and then you can share it with your neighbors, and others, you know, just the other people."

Tuvalu has a traditionally subsistence lifestyle in which people fish, raise crops like *pulaka* and breadfruit, and live based on what the land and the sea can provide. In these remote and tiny islands, not only was there great value to the community at large to sharing during times of plenty, there was really no purpose in hoarding, for example, a large catch of fish. Fishing will happen again tomorrow. The men work the land or fish the sea every day. Every day there will be food available. But not every person will have a good catch every day. Not every family has enough men to work the *pulaka* pits. Cultural sharing is not only a strong traditional value, it is also good common sense. Lanieta Faleasiu remembered growing up in this culture of sharing:

From what I know from my family, it's not that you would take care of them every day for your extended family. Except for times that when he made a big catch for fishing, then we distribute the fish to the extended family. Because we are all living in our own separate homes. But at times, we do things together. We share. If they have a big catch from their fishing and they be sharing to us, so we do the same thing. When my dad had a big catch from the fishing, we do the distribution.

Sharing amongst extended family members who live in different homes could have ended when Tuvaluans began migrating more and more to work in

Funafuti and beyond. However, that is not the Tuvaluan way. Family members who are working in Funafuti or abroad will send money back to the family in their home island. In turn, family members in the home island send natural resources like *pulaka* to those who migrated for work. Nalu told me, "So there is a cousin of mine staying now in Niutao… And I said 'when you go back look, care for our lands and also the *pulaka* pits.'" Nalu is permitting access to his family's *pulaka* pits to his extended family. Even this access is a resource in Tuvalu, and is shared.

Sharing resources becomes even more pragmatic during times of scarcity, such as during droughts. Noa Petueli from Funafuti had twelve people staying in his house during the drought because some extended family members needed access to the hospital. The ration for water was two buckets per household, regardless of how many people stayed there. "It doesn't make sense," he said with a laugh. But families care for each other in this way, sharing what they have. When asked what people do during King tides when homes begin to flood, Noa explained "Some of the families have other related families in the islands. So when those things happen, they relocate to other houses."

In fact, sharing resources to care for others' needs even in a time of crisis is so far ingrained in the culture that a failure to do so is looked down upon. Nalu related a story from the 1963 drought in which his father put up signs around the well on his land telling other people that they were not allowed to use it. Nalu was so angry when he saw that his father had done that. He told me:

> And I said "Why don't allow the well? This well was not dug by your great grandfather. It was dug under the Niutao community a long, long time ago." And I said "No, no, no, no! I don't want your notice, to put up a notice and put 'no more drawing water.'" Yeah so I took the thing, cut it off the pole and tear up the pieces. I went to him, "You look foolish! Why you put up a notice for people from drawing water? Do you – can you make water? You can't! Water is from the ground. I don't like you to treat the people like that."

Fifty years later, Nalu's disapproval was still visible on him as he told the story. Selfishness is not the way of Tuvaluans, not even in times of scarcity and hardship. Especially not then.

Pity and the desire to share. During my first trip to Tuvalu, I met a woman who talked a great deal about the specific development problems faced by Tuvalu with climate change. One thing that stood out to me during our conversation:

> She told me that the biggest problem in Tuvalu is water. Gesturing to include the whole island, she said, 'Tuvalu is the loveliest place on Earth. Plenty of rainfall.' She said she feels so bad for the places that don't have as much rain, dry places 'like Africa.' Deserts. 'Tuvalu is very fortunate to have plenty of rain. But water storage is the problem.' They need one reservoir per island. The catchment tanks are not enough (Corlew field notes, 2010).

49

I've thought about this conversation a lot. In 2011, a drought hit Tuvalu that was so severe the country was days away from running out of water on several islands, including the populous Funafuti (Benns, 2011). The catchment tanks were not enough, and desalination units had to be shipped in along with many thousands of liters of water (Perry, 2011). But another part of her statement came back to me during a feast in Tuvalu more than a year later. I was speaking with another woman about how much food was prepared for feasts in Tuvalu. Every family might bring enough to feed 20 people, so that 30 or 40 people might prepare enough food for hundreds:

> She told me she felt so bad to see so much food and she wished that she could share it. 'I wish some wealthy nation would fly a plane over to pick up all this food and take it to Africa,' to feed the starving children that she sees on TV. With her hand over her heart, she becomes teary-eyed telling me how much she worries for them, and how much she wishes Tuvalu could share their feast (Corlew field notes, 2012).

I was struck that she was not wishing for a wealthy nation to solve the issues of starvation in Africa. Rather, the solution to hunger was there on the tables before us at this feast. The only problem was that Tuvalu had no means of transporting this solution. This Tuvaluan woman was not thinking of how someone else could share, only of how someone else might make it possible for *her* to share *more*. I was also struck by how strongly this woman in a poor, developing nation in the South Pacific could feel compassion for and the need to help people in another poor, developing region of the world. I heard similar refrains often in Tuvalu. There is a seemingly common sense that 'someone else is struggling more than me, and I must do what I can to help them.' Discussing the drought, Kina told me:

> It's so sad. You know, I was so sad when people with disabilities were left out by the committee [to receive an extra bucket of water per household], and that was really, really bad... Some of them came here, and I don't have water as well, and he said 'I don't have water. I didn't have my shower from the last two days.'"

This was a common sentiment, that even though the speaker also did not have water, or was also under severe rationing to maintain their water supply, someone else was suffering more. Two months after the drought, I never spoke to anyone who thought they had truly suffered from the restricted water, although everyone was concerned that others had. Kokea explained the rationing measures he and his family had taken, but then said:

> There were some families, I pity them. My daughter has to ask some of them from nearby, up the road, I remember some of those people. They have to use the water sparingly...our water cistern is quite big. When that one is full then we had to make it last. [Laughter] So I always look forward for another drought to come in like this... I can always supply, you know, for those who don't have enough water catchment to be supplied from, not for our own sake but for the sake of those who didn't have enough during that time.

50

He enjoys his large catchment tank and hopes to add more in case of a future drought, so that he can be sure he has enough supply for everyone who might need access to it.

Obligations to others. As mentioned, people share resources because they have a strong desire to do so. They want to share resources because they do not feel right otherwise. Sharing is the best way. However, there is a harder edge to this desire to care for others. Tuvaluans feel an obligation to do so. A powerful part of their cultural values is their sense of responsibility for the care of others. Asked after the biggest event of his life, Tomu did not cite any one instance, but rather:

> The most important thing is my contribution. Any contribution is like I give to my community. Any contribution that I give to anyone while I have life, survive, it's very important in my life. My contribution, anywhere to any community, or to religion, social government, my contribution is more interesting. If I don't contribute to anything, I don't help.

Teba concurred that this sense of responsibility is common in Tuvalu and harkens back to one of the oldest values relating to your responsibility to work:

> In the olden days people are so concerned with not doing work. It's like you are not being responsible. It's how they feel—if you are doing something, you're being responsible. If you're not doing anything, you're not being responsible.

Lanieta, who grew up experiencing the reciprocity of extended families, had explained that families take care of each other by sharing resources during a time of plenty. However, there are also cases in which some people have more than others, and it is the obligation of those more fortunate to look after those with less fortune:

> My dad would go out fishing every day, every day except for Sundays. But he goes out fishing to cater for the family. And not only that, he looks after us, he also has cousins who he feels that it's his responsibility to look after them. Like, they are not married, this cousin, they are not married and they don't have children, but they are old. So they are all under his responsibilities, to be taken care of.

The anonymous participant told me, "Tuvaluans should work hard, not only for yourself, but for the Tuvaluan people. It is important to enjoy your life" (Corlew field notes, 2011). This responsibility to others is again rooted in Tuvalu's long culture of caring for others through sharing resources. Kina explains that "it's a cycle of support... today they need me, and tomorrow I will need them to support me." This cultural value is strong enough that Kina invoked it with the name of the organization she founded to address the needs of the vulnerable population of people with disabilities:

> We call it Fusi Alofa... *fusi* is a belt and *alofa* is love. Actually it's a 'unity of love.' But if we translate it like... belt and love, and these people want to be in this belt, you know. And it's like unity of love then. That's the meaning of the organization. People with disability they need to be in this belt.

51

People with disabilities are cared for greatly by their families, but many are separated from the community by lack of accessibility infrastructure and disability technologies. Kina created an organization meant to extend the cultural responsibility of community support explicitly to people with disabilities. At times, it is a matter of unspoken family or communal responsibility. At other times, this sharing is part of a structured obligation process. Alamai said:

> Oh yes, in the outer islands, we still have this community giving. Like if the chief says we need to get together and we need to put in certain things and put in money and food and whatever, they still comply. They still have that obligation, traditional obligation to comply.

The chief may call for the community to come together to put on a feast or *fatele*, to contribute manual labor to build a community structure, or to give food or care for a family who is in need. But structured or unstructured, this obligation to care for others is very strong and can be relied upon by Tuvaluans.

Monetary contributions. Tuvaluans tend to be highly involved in their communities. They belong to churches, to church groups, to women's groups, youth groups, island groups, and others. Every group requires a contribution of time, energy (sometimes manual labor), food, and/or money. Functions that bring the community together do not spring from nothing, but must be organized and carried out by these groups, requiring contributions from their members. Additionally, in Tuvaluan culture there is an obligation of the people to care for the church leaders. This privilege of care was previously the right of the *aliki*, or chiefs. However, when Christianity came, the *aliki* passed all of their traditional privileges to the pastors, where they still reside today. Tomu explained:

> That was when the Western civilization was introduced. There's a time when the *aliki*, the high chiefs of all the islands, stood up and [gave] the protocol or privileges to the pastor … Privilege is, you have a servant, you have a cook, you have cleaners, right? You have a servant. So they give you servants. One is your cook, one is doing something else. You know, those are the privileges. One is preparing your food, the other cooks, so they cook the food for you on behalf of the island. Like the President – does the President in the United States have servants like us, yes? … that's what the high chief has in those days."

Members of church groups continue to contribute to the church to maintain these privileges to the pastor, who has a very high status in Tuvaluan society. People must also contribute to their other community groups, must contribute to their own family, and must pay school fees for their children and/or other family members. These numerous contributions add up and can put a financial burden on families who often have few working members. Teba says:

> They have obligations, but I just don't know how people meet these things, dependent only, asking people for money. That's one thing about being a Pacific Islander, you can rely on other people. Which is in a way good, but in another way it's bad because you are a burden to that person. And that person because of the traditional way of life can't say no to you and yet he is actually suffering because of it.

This same cultural system of obligation that supports Tuvaluans through times of scarcity can also perpetuate financial struggles with their cumulative burden. But regardless of any hardship Tuvaluans face, they will maintain this responsibility to others and to the community. Alamai says, "That's why we really faced hardship, because we have obligation to our family, our immediate family, our distance family, our community, the church, our island. We still contribute." In Tuvaluan culture, there is no question of either giving or receiving that support. Tafue Lusama explains that:

> Poverty does exist here. I have come across a lot of cases where people are in need of finance, who were in need of land. But the good thing is that ... the Tuvaluan way of life is very communal and very family based. So you'll look after the other and the other will look after you. If I don't have money now, I'll walk out and go to a cousin or a brother or a sister or whoever and "Okay, I need so much for this." They will definitely give. Because the next time they are in need, they will walk into my house "Okay we want this." And I'm obligated to give, because we believe in the saying that there is no one who can stand like a mountain, cannot be moved, in that sense. We all come to a moment of need and someone is in need now, you might be tomorrow.

Contributing physical labor. With this desire and responsibility to contribute to the community can come amazing feats of achievement. Tuvaluan community groups (as well as entire communities) have come together for holiday functions, games, and to build structures that are needed by the community. One recent example is that of the Nanumaga youth group in Funafuti, the Talafai. Lanieta told the story of her island's youth group with a great deal of pride:

> For the first activity that they did, they helped the Lofeagai people [a settlement on the northern end of Funafuti] build the church... And the Nanumaga youth, Talafai, they assist these people free of charge to put up their church. Without this Talafai, this church would never be able to complete because they have a very small community and they don't have that many age group, the youth group. They have only children and elderly, like 40 and up. But because of the Talafai, they were able to finish up their church. And at the end of last year, September, October, they build this preschool building ... next to the Filateli building. If you walk by, you can see they built the small classroom. The Talafai, they assisted in that. I am very proud of that. I can say that. This is really a Tuvaluan thinking of working together, you know. Nowadays it's quite difficult to know people working free of charge. People always demand for some money, money. 'While we do this work for you, you'll give us money or you feed us.' But I am very proud of this when my youths are doing this kind of work voluntarily.

The Talafai were not working in a vacuum to make these two projects happen (see Image 6). When they agreed to help the Lofeagai settlement build their church, the Nanumaga women's group realized that the settlement would not be able to provide food to take care of the workers every day they worked. So the

53

Image 6. Preschool built by the Talafai, Funafuti (Corlew, 2011).

women's group organized themselves to prepare food and other logistical support for the youth group. This is the way that Tuvaluans work together. If the Kaupule decides to hold a function, the women will organize the food preparation and the logistical arrangements to make sure the function happens. The men will slaughter a pig or harvest the pulaka so that the women will have food to prepare. All of the groups work with each other to contribute to these major community events.

Another powerful example was the Queen's visit in 1982, a few years after Tuvalu's independence from Britain. Kokea was working in government at the time and was tasked with organizing community contributions and actions to give Queen Elizabeth II a royal welcome. He said:

When everybody was ready [on the Yacht Britannia], here everyone was ready [on Funafuti]. Nobody had to wear shirts like that, we all wore local dress. If you don't have garlands [for your head], you have that one around your neck. I have to use a walkie-talkie from the police to shout out [Laughter] ... the Queen travelled back on it ... All our canoes were decorated, you know. All garlanded, our boats, our crew, even the canoe I was travelling on, they have a chair made and decorated before the Royal Yacht Britannia came to Tuvalu.

These preparations were a long time coming. A welcome of this magnitude required an extremely high level of contribution from the community. Of course, with Tuvalu's strong guest and gift cultures, community members were happy to contribute. Feue painted the scenery of the preparations:

> The government at the time relied on the support of the island communities, including the resources of the island communities. And as soon as the government made the announcement that they would like island communities, they had meetings and all that. In one voice, the island communities all agreed and all supported the initiative. And they all came together and they provided food stuff, provided entertainment and everything! The people to serve, and it was beautiful. Sometimes you really feel it, you know. With no question of whether they would get paid or not – it's just an obligation they feel that they have to contribute. They all came together. And you don't see this in the Western world.

Speaking to others/speaking for others. Tuvaluans value participation in these big events as well as in regular community group meetings and activities. During my first trip, I asked one woman if everyone was involved in community groups. She looked at me as though I had asked a strange question and thought for a moment. "She said, 'Well, I would have to wonder about someone who was not involved.' She seemed to be indicating that something must be very wrong with that hypothetical person" (Corlew field notes, 2010). I know from many conversations since then that there are enough instances of people keeping to themselves that others show concern about it. The acts of being involved in the community, of visiting with family and neighbors, of spending time talking with one another, of attending community functions – and for elders, speaking at these community functions – are all connected by the Tuvaluan value to give of oneself. By participating, people share their time and show an openness to community connection.

Speeches are very important in Tuvaluan culture. Any function will provide an opportunity for many speeches by elders[18] and other opportunities for community members to actively engage. Dancing, singing, and drumming during a *fatele* are some opportunities, but also serving food or spraying others with perfumes. Teba related the story of her first feast during her first trip to the outer islands with her job. Her boss asked her to join in spraying perfume, but Teba was shy and decided to sit it out. Only at the end of the night did she come to find out that by not spraying the perfume, she was now required to give a speech or to dance. She didn't speak Tuvaluan very well yet. She said:

> And the next thing I know I was told to stand where I was the last person, I have to stand there. And I said "What for?" and she said, "You stand there, you have to dance." And I was saying "Oh my god, I do not know how to dance" [laughter]… She said "No just follow the moves" and I said "Okay" and you know I was dancing. I was like "Oh my god" [laughter]. So when we finished it and we went and sat down,

---

[18] Typically male elders, but at times speeches from others are appropriate.

55

she explained to me "You know that is the tradition. If the community is going to have a function too, it's out of courtesy that you go and participate in what they're doing."

By giving speeches, by dancing, or by spraying perfume in a *fatele*, Tuvaluans develop a shared community connection. As with all things, it is expected for people to give. When someone doesn't give a speech during a function when they are expected to do so, there will be talk in the community about why that person did not get up to speak.

It should be noted that speaking to people is different than speaking for people. Tomu talked to me a great deal about how he strongly believed that the only way to be a politician is to be *of the people* – to be involved in community activities, and to always seek out the will of the people before making any decision by oneself. Tomu said:

If you want to serve your people, come stay with the people, you eat with the people, you laugh with the people. That's the way to become a politician. If anything happens, you're always there. You go along with the people. You start in poverty, you starve somewhere. People always look at you. But don't say the words that you like to become a politician, and then you work overseas. That's not the way…some of my colleagues said, "Tomu, when you became Governor General, is it a hard job for you?" … I said "No, it's not very hard." "Why?" And I said "My technique is always ask. If I am doubt with anything, I ask my superior, those who have been there before, and who advised me on that. That's why I am not lack of anything, because I ask."

Metia Tealofi, who also spent a large part of his life working politics, echoed this need to always seek the knowledge and the will of your community before making any decisions. Similar to Tomu's disinclination to speak for others in making political decisions, Metia exhibited a complete lack of desire to speak for others – even hypothetical others. When asked if he had any words of wisdom to impart on Tuvaluans of the future, Metia paused for a very long time before saying:

METIA: There is a problem too. Some people very, very dislike, or they will, if you talk or tell them something at you. Very, very [Laughter] very, very hard for them to answer or to give any idea or any good answer or something like that.

MICHAEL: Yeah, a very difficult question.

METIA: Very difficult, very difficult question. Because people, only when you talk to them something that they really like, that they agree, and then they support and they're, 'Oh, yes, we like that one, we like that one.'

What is reflected in this statement is a very strong desire to reach a consensus with others rather than speaking to them from a position of assumed wisdom. What is not reflected in this transcript is that Metia's speech became so slow as he considered what to say that these few sentences took nearly two minutes to say. This is a very powerful disinclination to speak for others without knowing their will.

Speaking well of people. In Hawai'i, we have a saying, "It's a small island." This saying is meant to convey both the happy assurance that people will meet again, and a warning that people will meet again. In island communities, people tend to get along much better than they do in continental communities. This is true according to the stereotypes of island living. This is also true in my experience. When the community is small, people develop a desire to get along with each other because tension and struggle takes up too much room. When there are few places possible to go to avoid someone you do not like, you have a strong motivation to learn to like everyone. Explicit efforts to show respect may be intended to ensure no offense is perceived when none is intended (Cohen & Nisbett, 1997; Cohen, Nisbett, Bowdle, & Schwartz, 1996).[19] Explicit respect is also highly correlated with collectivist cultures (Triandis & Gelfand, 1998; Triandis, McCusker, & Hui, 1990) and particularly with indigenous and island peoples (see, e.g., Schoen, 2005). In highly collectivist cultures, particularly with small and active communities, explicit respect not only reduces accidental offense, but increases smooth community functioning by actively promoting the welfare of others. I have seen this in small towns in rural Tennessee. I have seen this in Hawai'i, and I have seen this in Tuvalu.

There is a man in Tuvalu who everyone tells me is crazy. Specifically, they tell me that he is "mad" while they circle their fingers around their ears and cock their heads to one side. Adults tell me this. Children tell me this. Whenever he appeared, anyone who was nearby felt compelled to warn me that this man was mad, so that I would know not to take him seriously. However, most adults who spoke of him to me would immediately qualify their statements with examples for which they also hold him in high regard. "He's mad," they might say, "But you know, he lives a happy life." When he wants to travel, he hops on a boat and goes to another island. He knows multiple languages. He talks to everyone. He tells stories and jokes and sings. I have watched rooms full of people scoff at him as though he is a misbehaved child and warn me that he is mad as soon as he enters. Within minutes he will have everyone laughing hysterically or singing. He plays an important role in the community, bringing people this joy so effortlessly. When people warn me that he is mad, they often follow it up with a compliment (Corlew field notes, 2011).

There is another "mad" man that I never met. Some ladies I was speaking to one night were giggling in Tuvaluan. "Oh," one of them translated to me, "It is about this mad man." He went to college in Fiji, where he "smoked

---

[19] An important caveat to this point is that Cohen & Nisbett's studies on the "culture of honor" also revealed cultural elements that were **not** apparent in Tuvalu during this study, i.e., heightened levels of aggression and quicker escalation to violence after offense. It is therefore unlikely that the sole or predominant motivation to speaking well of others is merely to avoid offense.

pot and went mad." Once again, the description of this person was immediately qualified to show respect. "But he is quite clever," the woman amended quickly. He had been a scientist (Corlew field notes, 2012).

I was chatting with yet another woman one afternoon, running through the list of people we had met across the island. When I came to one name, she seemed to draw back. "Oh," she said. She confided to me that he was a practitioner of black magic. "He didn't give you anything to eat, did he?" she asked me. Once again, this negative statement was almost immediately amended with the comment, "But he's a good man. He goes to church" (Corlew field notes, 2012). There seems to be a strong desire to see the best in people and to speak well of them in Tuvaluan culture. In a small country where guest and gift cultures are so integral to sustaining community connections, it is no wonder that people actively and automatically seek to sustain these community connections in their minds – that is, in their own regard for others. Tuvaluans on a whole are genuinely kind and caring. They are welcoming and giving. They value community connections. It is no wonder that they would shy away from negative thoughts of others, or that they would temper negative thoughts by also recognizing what is good. During my first trip to Tuvalu I had the following conversation:

> I met [a man] and we discussed violence and crime in Tuvalu. The crime rate is very low compared to other places, but things will happen. Drunken men get into fights often enough. [The man] tells me, "There is one man in the jail for life. For murder. But," he adds quickly, "It was a long time ago and he was young, so it doesn't mean anything." A mistake of the past, even a terrible sin, should not affect my overall opinion of this man; there were good things about him as well. I thought about the gangs I used to work with in Chicago, and I understood what he meant (Corlew field notes, 2010).

Chapter Summary

This chapter explores a major facet of Tuvaluan culture that interacts deeply with many if not all aspects of Tuvaluan life: the guest/gift culture. Tuvaluans share their time and resources with others as a matter of cultural desire and responsibility to care for their families, their communities, and guests to their communities. This responsibility for community participation and caretaking manifests in the family, in community activities and events, in an obligation to give resources including labor, and in a desire to create consensus and to think and speak well of others. Interview participants and others with whom I interacted in Tuvalu provided myriad examples of the collectivist nature of Tuvaluan communities.

Chapter 3

3.1 The Outer Islands as a Group

Tuvalu is made up of nine islands and atolls that are often conceptually divided into two groups, Funafuti and the outer islands. The outer islands continue to be the predominant spaces in Tuvalu for traditional island living, while Funafuti is the space for business and modernity. People from Tuvalu identify strongly with their home island, regardless of where they are currently living or where they actually grew up. As Feue told me:

> We may have general commonalities between certain aspects of the culture, but there are also unique cultural norms to specific island communities... Culture is important because it sort of identifies whose home, you know, the importance of their island communities. Take that away and you'll have no land, no home, nothing.

If a person's family is from an island, that person belongs to that island. On Funafuti, community groups and many community functions are divided along island lines. The sense of connection to one's island and island community extends beyond migration for school or work, and can even extend beyond generations in cases of children raised on Funafuti or abroad while their parents worked.[20]

Although every island has its own unique cultural identity, dialect, and way of life, there are a number of overarching themes that are common amongst the outer islands. In Funafuti especially, people will talk about the "outer islands" as a group, as a general place in which a foreigner like me can see Tuvaluans living a Tuvaluan way of life. Teba moved to Tuvalu as an adult to learn her grandfather's culture:

> LAURA: Speaking of culture, you said earlier that when you first came here you wanted to spend time on the islands and learn what it means to be Tuvaluan. So what does it mean to be Tuvaluan?
>
> [Laughter]
> TEBA: There are a lot of things. But I think knowing the families, knowing the different cultures, you know? This is what Tuvaluan people do, this is the way they live. Traditionally this is what they do. They do *kaleve*. They have *pulaka*. Women are supposed to do this. Women are supposed to learn how to weave, supposed to learn how to do mats. You're supposed to learn how to do the *fatele*, you're supposed to learn how to dance... It's not things, it's, you know, practicing it. That's how it is. You learn. You know your relatives. You share things without asking.

---

[20] See Appendix B: The Outer Islands for a brief introduction to each of the outer islands' unique cultures, histories, and identities.

These practices and values make up what it is to be a Tuvaluan. There is a perception among Tuvaluans that the outer islands are stronger in these practices than Funafuti.[21] There is a further perception that although each island is very unique in many aspects, these common practices and values bind them together as Tuvaluans. This section will discuss some of these common practices that are viewed as important to the Tuvaluan cultural identities in all of the outer islands.

Connection to home island. Ironically, a strong connection to one's individual home island is one of the commonalities that unites all of the islands in terms of Tuvaluan culture. Lanieta explained it:

> This is the only place where we practice it well. Here on the land, with the people, with the language, with the land. This is the only place where we can practice the Tuvalu culture well. And for me, as a Nanumaga person, Nanumaga is the only place where I practice my Nanumaga culture very well. Not here on Funafuti. It may be a reflection of the Nanumaga culture, what I do here on Funafuti, but I still can do it better if I do it on the mainland.

In the outer islands, people have access to their lands, their family, and their community. This access enables them to maintain daily cultural practices and language in a much stronger and more consistent fashion than when they are surrounded by people from many islands and cultural backgrounds in Funafuti. The connection to one's home island therefore has a very practical component: when people are there, they are most capable of enacting their cultural identity in their daily lives. However, there is also an intangible component to this connection. Tuvaluans' identities are deeply ingrained with their island of origin. There is a strong psychological sense of attachment to the home island that is mental, emotional, and spiritual. Tuvaluans' sense of self stems in part from where they are from, and where their family is from. When asked, "Can you tell me about Niutao?" Vete began by saying:

> Niutao, that's my island. My mom is from there. My dad is also from there, and we are really indigenous. We hardly have any other components from other islands. We mainly – my dad and my mom are all very indigenous to Niutao.

This connection can give Tuvaluans a stronger sense of their ability to enact other cultural components. For example, I spoke with Kina about the different language that is spoken in Nui, the "pidgin Kiribati." During my first trip to Tuvalu, I was told that people from Nui often have a harder time learning Tuvaluan[22] than they do learning English, simply because the Micronesian structure of the Nui language was so different from the Polynesian Tuvaluan language. Kina told me she did speak the other Tuvaluan language in addition to the Nui language. I asked, "Was it hard to learn?" She responded:

> No. It's not hard to learn because, well, my grandfather is from Nui. My grandfather from my mother is from Nui. And my grandmother

---

[21] For further discussion of this topic, please refer to 3.2 Funafuti, below.

[22] Funafuti Tuvaluan, or Tuvaluan from one of the other islands than Nui.

from my mother's side, that is my mother's mom, she's from the other island. And that's why I really don't have any problems with my Tuvaluan language. Because my blood is quite mixed [Laughter].

Tuvaluans maintain this connection to their home island even after migrating to another place. I have met adults who grew up in Funafuti after their parents moved and who have spent very little of their lives in their home islands. They maintain their home island identity, even when they admit that they cannot tell me very much about life on the island. Regardless, they speak the language and practice the unique cultural traditions of that island, practiced in gatherings with their family and home island community. Across time and generations, these connections remain.

Housing. Modern, Western-style housing is becoming more and more common in Tuvalu, both on Funafuti and the outer islands (See Image 7). Of this structure, Jopeto explained:

JOPETO:	That's the local house, it's like an *umu*. The lady from the back, she makes the kind of local, I don't know what's the name, the local mat made of coconut leaves.
LAURA:	Is it like a wall, or like a shade you pull down?
JOPETO:	Yeah, yeah. When it's raining…
LAURA:	Do you spend a lot of time there?
JOPETO:	Yeah, because it's windy and fresh air.
LAURA:	Do you sleep out there sometimes?
JOPETO:	Yeah, sometimes when it's really hot inside the house.

The houses are typically built up off the ground. The area beneath can be used to store equipment or copra. As modern houses become more common, these

Image 7. Local-style house with hanging woven mats, Funafuti. (Major, 2011).

61

traditional structures remain. They may be the primary structure for a family, or they may built in addition to a Western-style house. Many families continue to have outdoor structures for cooking because they are cooler. Similarly, sitting or visiting areas may be constructed in the traditional style because the absence of four walls makes for a breezier space to spend time with loved ones (see Image 8). In modern times, these structures may be constructed with local or imported goods (e.g., thatched or corrugated tin roofs). However, the shape and function of the structures remain in the traditional style. Many Tuvaluans, especially the elders, much prefer the traditional structures to the modern houses. Teba related conversations she has had with elders on the outer islands:

> They have very nice houses to stay in. But they are staying in their own local thatched roof, open, everything is open. They love it there. And yet they have a house that is just something like this, modern, everything is so bright. They don't have to stay there. They would rather stay in their own thatched roof. So I used to ask them, "Why do you stay here when you have a very nice house?" She said, [Laughter] "What's wrong with my house – what's wrong with my house?" "No, I mean, I'm not, I'm just asking." She said, "No, because this is where I was born." Sometimes it's their house, that house is where were brought up as a child, and they got married. So when their children

Image 8. Modern Western-style house in Funafuti (background, right) with traditional-style outdoor kitchen (foreground, left) with thatched roofing (Corlew, 2011).

build houses for them to stay in, they don't want to stay there. The memories of that place hold more many meaning to them than the money spent on that house.

Modern houses are very expensive. Materials must be imported to build the house. After a few years, when repairs are needed, new materials must also be imported. Trading ships arrive more frequently in Funafuti than in the outer islands. The price of modernity is high, which is another contributing factor to the outer islands maintaining the traditional structures to a greater extent than Funafuti. Metia said:

You can build your house on your own. You don't depend on anybody or the money. In the life in Tuvalu, you build your house by your own... you go and cut your materials, cut trees, cut things, pandanus leaves. You don't use the roof or the sheet [metal], you use the pandanus leaves, that local one. Make the strings. Everything ready to build the house, very easy. The poles you cut the trees, you come and put the poles, no money cost to do that. But if you want to build a house, European, if you have money you can buy it. But if you don't have it, you can't buy it. You can't put your European house roofing. You can't.

Local foods. On the outer islands, Tuvaluans rely less on imported goods and more on local foods. Imported foods have been coming to the outer islands for generations, at least as far back as World War II. However, imports continue to be limited enough and land continues to be abundant enough that Tuvaluans on the outer islands eat much more of the traditional foods than in Funafuti. The staple crop is *pulaka*, a giant swamp taro that is grown on each of the islands. Tuvaluans also eat a lot of coconut, breadfruit, pandanus, and banana, as well as fish, birds, and pigs. Nalu said,

You know, cutting toddy, farming the animals like pigs – pigs we have in here. No other animals like in your big country, yeah. Only pigs and going out fishing... We used to eat the *pulaka* roots. That's our main food. Even the breadfruit. We planted those trees. And the coconut trees, we also plant those.

Children learn from a very young age how to grow, gather, fish, and hunt traditional foods. On the outer islands, everyone has a role to take care of in the family. These roles began as soon as a child was physically able. Metia recalled:

METIA: I think when I cut toddy, I was about eight and nine years... Climb up the tree and cut toddy, and also I can climb the tree to make coconuts for the family, something like that. So when I went to school, I climbed the tree, long one, no worry about climbing the high ones, the trees. So these are those things my parents or my teacher, father always teach me about the life.

MICHAEL: Yeah. What about cutting copra? Did he teach you that?

METIA: Ah, yeah, those times only my father, when I was young. So we went to collect the copra.

Coconuts are of particular importance to Tuvaluan culture. The flesh can be eaten, the water can ease thirst, and the copra can be used for cooking fires. But in addition, Metia explained that people used coconut oil in their hair and rubbed it on small babies who developed a rash. He explained that the coconut is:

Oh, very useful thing. Coconut, the coconut tree. The trees of the coconut, the tree body is very useful. You can use the body for poles or anything for the house. The leaves, very useful to make the mat, like the mat in the floor for sitting, the leaves of the coconut. The shoot makes the toddy that comes, the toddy. Very useful thing, the coconut.

In addition to fishing (and now, raising pigs), Tuvaluans also catch birds for meat. This is typically done on the small islets of an atoll, or otherwise away from the main human settlements. Ken explained that to avoid scaring the birds, the hunters go just before dark to set up before the birds come out. They do not wear any sort of perfumes or deodorants. They crush leaves and rub in on their bodies so as to mask the human smell. And they must be very quiet at all times. They use a large net that is affixed to the end of very a long pole (see Image 9). It looks like a giant butterfly net (Image 10). Ken said, "You climb up

Image 9. Bird-catching nets at the end of two long poles propped against a tree (Corlew, 2012).

64

Image 10. Bird-catching nets detail in the tree branches (Corlew, 2012).

with that kind of thing I showed you… It's a light one, the stick is very light; you hold it for one hour or half an hour." The net must be very light because the hunter must hold it up for such an extended period of time. The hunters go in pairs. One climbs up to the top of a tree and ties himself to it so that he doesn't fall. Ken told me:

KEN:	So you stay there for a bit, it comes dark, and then you start to whistle for the birds… So when he catches one, the other thing is to kill the birds and then throw it down. Just do it in two, and then throw it down.
LAURA:	You just like, break the neck.
KEN:	Yeah.
TOMU:	[Calls from across the room] Laura, you must pass your, you must talk like a bird. You fly like a bird. And then you can do it.
LAURA:	[Calls back] Yeah. Yeah, I wouldn't be able to do that. I can't whistle.
KEN:	[Laughs]
TOMU:	Eh?
LAURA:	I can't whistle [Laughs]. So I wouldn't be able to do that. I'll stay on the bottom and catch the birds when they throw them down. That's all I can do.

KEN: Yeah, I was thinking that if you guys were longer here, someday we go out to the woods. The thing is, though, you can't take a camera.

The flash from the camera would scare the birds just as surely as perfumes or loud noises. The Tuvaluan hunting, fishing, and growing traditions are based on many generations of knowledge and skill.

Weaving and handicrafts. Tuvaluan handicrafts are another commonality of the outer islands. Each island has its own unique style of mats, baskets, fans, garlands, *tui misa* (shell necklaces[23]) and other crafts (see Image 11). Baskets are made from coconut fronds, cut straight from the tree and woven into shape while still green. These baskets are pieced together quickly as a disposable carrying case on the way out to the bush to collect coconuts, breadfruit, or other foods. During the next trip out, a new basket is created. Weaving mats is a much more intensive process. Ken says, "I would think it's very hard to make the mats. There's a lot of things you have to do." The local mats are made from pandanus leaves. The pandanus leaves are collected and then cleaned with a sharp edge. They are dried for about two weeks, at which point they will be beaten until they become soft and smooth. Only after this long

Image 11. Local woven mat made of pandanus leaves with a stack of *tui misa* (Major, 2011).

---

[23] *Tui misa* are gifted to people similarly to the flower leis in Hawai'i.

process can the weaving began. A very skilled weaver can make a large mat in a day at that point. Weaving is very important to Tuvaluan cultural living. As shown earlier, a version of the mats can be used as a shade from the rain. Most commonly, mats are laid out on the floors of houses or sitting areas, or on the ground for outdoor spectators of games or other gatherings, for a comfortable and clean place to sit or sleep. I have been told that plain-colored mats are used for sitting and visiting, whereas decorated mats are for sleeping. These mats are a very high quality. They are sturdy and beautiful. Tuvaluans are known throughout the Pacific for their mats.

Protecting and maintaining culture. Certain aspects of Tuvaluan culture are to be protected within an individual family. The knowledge that is special to a family is passed from parent to child, and is not to be shared with the wider community. Although Tuvaluans seek to maintain their cultural practices, this type of knowledge is protected internally and is not currently maintained by the community. Feue told the story of a proposal that was once put forth to develop a Tuvaluan cultural museum. There was a lot of support behind this proposal:

> But then I asked him the question, do we have things to put in the museum? Do we have specific spots or places in the country where we could pinpoint and have photographs and say these are important historical sites in the islands? And we did the survey in terms of artifacts of historical specific significance. And we basically came up with virtually nothing. [Laughter] So the question is where did all these things—where did they go to? But we recorded a number of the fighting sticks, the magical rainmaker balls and all, but these are sacred possessions that the respective families wouldn't allow us to [Laughter] have.

The museum proposal died at that point. Since that time, several *maneapas* (including Funafuti and Niutao) have included displays of cultural artifacts into the decorations of the halls so that they are maintained as community knowledge.

Other aspects of Tuvaluan culture are maintained in functions, community gatherings, and other cultural events. Ken showed me a video of a local style of "martial arts" on Niutao called *lima* (five) in which one man with a long, pliable staff made from coconut fronds faces off against rows of men with shorter staffs. They come forward in choreographed movements, taking turns against the man with the long staff. The video we were watching of this demonstration was decades old. I asked Ken if they still did this in Niutao. He said, "Yeah. Well, now they have it if there is a function or Independence Day or something like that… if there's a new chief, then he makes this kind of thing. But not for every day."

Feasts, *fateles*, and games are other traditions that are communally maintained. Tuvalu's main traditional game is called *ano* (see Image 12). *Ano* is played with two teams made up of one or two throwers, a point person up front, and a crowd of other players behind. Two heavy, dense woven balls are in play simultaneously. Both teams' throwers hurl the ball as deep into the other team as

67

possible. The players volley the ball forward to the point person without the ball falling to hit the ground. If one team is able to move the ball forward quickly enough, their thrower can hurl the ball immediately to the other team, causing two balls to be in play on the same side.

Parliament and Kaupule. Each island has representatives in the Tuvalu House of Parliament for matters of national law. Metia explained that in traditional campaigning, candidates would not campaign to everyone. Rather, "You campaign to the old men in your family, because you really know each one." These interpersonal relationships make up the heart of the political system in this small country where an MP knows and is known by everyone on their island. For that reason, matters of State are brought before the island to solicit feedback before votes are cast on national matters. Metia said:

> I think that the job of the member of the Parliament. You go to your government, for your island, for the whole island there. Before the conference, you go to your home island. You go and ask them what they want. And then you express your opinion to them.

Image 12. One team during a game of *ano* by the Niutao community on Boxing Day, 2011, Funafuti. The judge/score keeper sits on the airstrip, watching closely (Corlew, 2011).

For local matters, the *Kaupule*, or town council, is the primary governmental structure. The Parliament enacted the *Falekaupule Act of 1997* to support a modern variation on a system of traditional rule. Prior to colonization and the arrival of Christianity, the *aliki* were the ruling power of each island.

68

After colonization, a Western governing system was enacted with three branches of government: Executive, Legislative, and Judicial. The *Falekaupule Act of 1997* established a system of local ruling bodies. Each island has its own *Kaupule*. The *Kaupule* can write local by-laws that apply only to that island; these by-laws are then approved or overruled by the *Falekaupule* which sits above all of the *Kaupules*. Tomu told me, "Today, the modern day, the only place that you can prove our traditions and our culture is the meeting hall." Each island has different rules guiding the functioning of their *Kaupule*. Teba explained:

> Some islands don't allow women to speak. The only two islands are Nukufetau and Nui, they don't allow women to speak in the *Falekaupule*. And the age range is anybody who is 50 years up, they are allowed to speak in the *Falekaupule*. And anyone below that, you can attend, but you cannot speak, and you have no say in that house… In Nanumaga, it is head of clans, it is by head of clans and by age group, but it includes men and women. In Funafuti, in Nukulaelae, it is by head of clans… Niutao, it's 40 years up, anyone who is 40 years above, men and women, they can have a say in that traditional meeting. Vaitupu, is 40 years. For Nanumea it is 50 years. With Niutao, Niutao is 50 or 40, I am not sure, I forgot.

The *Kaupule* and the Parliament are the governmental local and national leaders. The chiefs and the elders still maintain a role in the community as non-governmental leadership, although they have no official say in the government or legal actions. The pastor is often looked to in terms of counsel on morality issues, but he too will have no official say over matters of government.

Penalty or punishment. Penalties or punishments (the terms are interchangeable in this sense) play an important role in maintaining Tuvaluan culture. On Boxing Day, Michael and I attended the Niutao program in honor of the students, from primary school through college. We gathered in the morning for prayer and feast, and reconvened in the afternoon for a feast followed by speeches and a *fatele*. The day closed with a game of *ano* for the Niutao community. Tomu told us ahead of time that during the afternoon program, everyone would be required to wear traditional Niutao clothing and adornments, including the *palagi* family members. He said that if people failed to dress appropriately, they would be punished and would perhaps be required to provide the pig for next year's celebration. When preparing for the afternoon program, the family provided us with clothing, flower garlands for our heads, and banana leaves to drape around our shoulders (see Image 13). Tomu said, "Laura, now you are a Niutao lady." In the morning after the feast, every corner of the maneapa was required to have one person stand and give a speech to the gathered community. One of the corners did not have anyone stand up. The Master of Ceremonies announced that the people from that corner would be penalized. They were required to bring the perfume to the afternoon ceremonies. When afternoon came, the women were instructed to spray everyone where we sat (See Image 14). Sueina sat next to me as several women moved past us, spraying us generously with different perfumes. She nodded to a woman coming

69

Image 13. Laura and Michael Corlew, dressed in the Niutao fashion, Boxing Day 2011, Funafuti (Corlew, 2011).

Image 14. Women spraying perfume at the Niutao program, Boxing Day 2011, Funafuti (Corlew, 2011).

toward us and told me the perfume she had was her favorite. The smile she wore was that of someone luxuriating in a cherished indulgence.

Penalties such as those described above are designed to maintain Tuvaluan culture. If someone fails to participate in the requirements of a community function, they are then punished with a requirement of extra participation in the next event. This serves to encourage people to participate always in community, but it also serves to protect against people slipping away from the community. If they do not attend to cultural requirements, they are not allowed simply to fade away from the cultural life. They are singled out and brought back in for an even higher level of participation.

However, punishments include not only additional cultural requirements, but can also include actions that would more closely approximate an American use of the term. Teba explained that although extreme punishments are not as common anymore, a tradition of strict punishment remains on the outer islands. "Maybe you have to do a clean up, something like that," she said, depending on what the offense was. In earlier days, corporal punishment was common for offenses that threatened the wellbeing of the community. For example, Teba said:

> In Nui they used to have very, they still have very bad punishments, very severe punishments. Especially if people would drink. You drink on Sundays. You're taken to the *falekaupule* house and men would do the punishment. I think it is not practiced anymore, they do a corporal punishment. It's really, really bad. But now they don't do that anymore because of the various human rights things that came out.

If the *aliki* or the *Kaupule* calls for an action to be taken by community members, and someone fails to do it, that person will be called in to the *maneapa* to receive their punishment from the leadership they have defied. Tafue explained:

> We have certain rules where if you disobey, you end up in the middle of the community hall with all the elders … and I've seen people who were brought into the community hall because they disobeyed a certain rule and the elders decided to punish them. And their punishment was to be, literally translated "uplifted." But it means that the young people come take you by the hands and the legs and throw you up and leaving you to fall down to the floor. [Laughter] And you'll suffer for weeks. Because they will say your punishment is that you'll be uplifted ten times so they have to throw you up ten times. [Laughter]

In small island communities, maintaining order can be among the most important goals to maintaining community wellbeing. In a small community, if someone is drunk and disorderly, or violent, or causing other problems with the smooth functioning of community life, the impacts of their behavior can very quickly ripple out to cause strife among their neighbors. Punishments will help restore order and right wrongs that have been done. Similarly, if people fail to participate in culturally proscribed activities, the culture and the community could quickly fall apart. Punishments should therefore restore the order of the community and emphasize the priority of culture.

71

3.2 Funafuti

The urban center of Tuvalu. Community members from the outer islands increasingly migrate to Funafuti for work or for school, and they come for medical treatment at the hospital, or en route to other places through Tuvalu's only airport. Two Air Pacific planes a week land on Funafuti from Suva, Fiji, on Tuesday and Thursday. During the rest of the week, the airstrip is open as the largest communal gathering space on the atoll. In the afternoons and evenings, a dozen games or activities may take place up and down the airstrip. Funafuti is a thriving center of activity. Noa, who is from Funafuti, said:

> To be from Funafuti is very exciting for me because it is the capital of Tuvalu. Growing up in Funafuti is very different than growing up in the outer islands. In Funafuti there is a chance for you to get a good education and have a good life. It is easy to connect with the outer world. We have the airstrip here, and the wharf. To be here in Funafuti is very fascinating, exciting [Laughter]. You see more of the exciting things like airplanes and things.

Funafuti is the political capitol of Tuvalu and houses the tallest building in Tuvalu, the new three-story Government building (see Image 15). The Tuvalu government is the largest employer in the country, increasing Funafuti's status as a hub for gainful employment. With the airstrip and the wharf, Funafuti is also the center of trade with the outside world. Ken said, "The Government Building is here, everything is here, planes and also the ships. So yeah all the people, I think, from all the outer islands, those come here to work." Funafuti is also a hub for education. In addition to Nauti public primary school (see Image 16) and the Seventh Day Adventist private primary school (see Image 17), Funafuti is also home to one of Tuvalu's two secondary schools, Fetuvalu high school (see Image 18). The University of the South Pacific (USP), based in Fiji, also has a Tuvalu campus on Funafuti (see Image 19). The schools and the general public are supported by the Tuvalu National Archives (see Image 20). Students from each of these schools will go to the Tuvalu national library because, as Jopeto says, "This is more, eh? They have more high standard books, reading books."

Funafuti is also home to the one hotel in the country (see Image 21, Image 22). Jopeto tells me that "Vaiaku Lagi means, *lagi* means 'the sky'. Vaiaku Lagi Hotel." Vaiaku is the name of the village in the central portion of the island where the hotel, the Government Building, and the airport all reside (see Image 23). Tuvalu radio broadcasts out of Funafuti. Funafuti's main nightclub is located facing the airstrip (see Image 24). Jopeto says:

JOPETO: That's the night club. The only night club here in Tuvalu still going on. And you can still see the seawater from the high tide. And that's the Matagali Bar.

LAURA: Is it open every day?

JOPETO: No, only from Thursday until Saturday...The bar is inside and it's small. And it's strict for you to take alcohol inside. They have to buy alcohol from the bar inside there. And it's kind of small dancing floor inside also. And people, they like it. There are other nightclubs, but they love Matagali Bar... the meaning of Matagali is the Nice Wind... because it's located on the side where the wind is come from.

Image 15. Government Building, Funafuti (Major, 2011).

Image 16. Nauti primary school, Funafuti (Major, 2011).

Image 17. Seventh Day Adventist church (foreground) and primary school (background, right), Funafuti (Major, 2011).

Image 18. Fetuvalu high school, Funafuti (Major, 2011).

Image 19. University of the South Pacific, Tuvalu campus, Funafuti (Major, 2011).

Image 20. Tuvalu National Archives, Funafuti (Major, 2011).

Image 21. Vaiaku Lagi Hotel, Funafuti (Major, 2011).

Image 22. Vaiaku Lagi Hotel, Funafuti (Major, 2011).

Image 23. From left to right, the Vaiaku *maneapa*, the Government Building (back), the airport, and the Tuvalu National Bank (far right). In the back, the Tuvalu Broadcast Center tower can be seen, which is across the street from the Vaiaku Lagi Hotel (Corlew, 2012).

Image 24. Matagali Bar, Funafuti. There are gaps in the stone wall to allow the breeze to come through. Also notice the water in the foreground. This is off-season flooding from the high tide (Major, 2011).

New Tuvaluan language and identity. Because Funafuti is a hub for government, commerce, and education, Tuvaluans have been migrating to the island in increasing numbers. Although all islands experience immigration due to marriage, Funafuti is the only island with such a large percentage of inhabitants from other islands. In fact, Funafuti is home to people from all of the islands.[24] Over time, an interesting process has begun to take place in which a new "Tuvaluan" identity has come to exist that is an amalgam of the cultural identities of all of the islands. Alamai said that in Funafuti, "It's like there is no really clear identity. It's a new identity that's being formulated here. But if you go with the outer islands, it's still unique. So you still can identify that originally it is theirs." On Funafuti, even people who strongly maintain their home island traditions are exposed to the traditions and values of other islands. Over time, this exposure causes their own cultural identity to begin to shift as the cultures combine to form something new. This Tuvaluan cultural identity incorporates the values and lifestyles of the outer islands as well as the traditional and modern components of the Funafuti lifestyle. The new Tuvaluan identity is apparent in the language spoken in Funafuti by the people from these diverse

---

[24] With the possible exception of Niulakita at any given time, since Niulakita's population is so small.

backgrounds. The ability to speak one's native language can powerfully influence one's cultural identity (Wynne, 2010). Lanieta explains:

> I speak a Tuvaluan language. [Laughter] I call it Tuvaluan because it's not the Funafuti language. It's not the Vaitupu language. Because I've been to Vaitupu for years. And it's not the Nanumaga language... what I speak here is different from the language that is spoken in Nanumaga. Even though I claim that I speak Nanumaga language, it's not. It's different... it's quite different. I can hear the difference.

Crime, vice, and garbage. Unfortunately, as the urban center of the country, Funafuti is also home to the negative impacts of modernity and overcrowding. Compared to the United States, Funafuti is a quiet and peaceful place. However, by Tuvaluan standards, Funafuti is facing many social ills. Although I have been told by many people that drugs do not exist in Tuvalu,[25] Teba tells me that recently some youth have been found "smelling benzene" from the motorbikes.[26] Others have told me that drinking is an increasing problem among the youth and adults. Although drinking among women is becoming increasingly common, the over-consumption of alcohol by men has long been an issue in Tuvalu. Another growing social problem is gambling, in the form of Bingo. Adults, and especially women, have been known to take any earnings to play Bingo in the hopes of turning small amounts of money into large sums. Men and women are spending increasing amounts of money on drinking and gambling to the point of family financial crisis. These problems are often noted by community members when discussing modernity issues, and even compelled Sir Tomu Sione to write a song about the need for parents to avoid these vices and save money to pay for their children's school fees. In June, 2010, Tomu and I translated this song into English:

> *"My dear mommy, please can you buy me a ruler*
> *So that I can use it in school?"*
> *And mommy said, "Sorry, my daughter, I have no money.*
> *I finished it up playing Bingo."*
>
> *"My dear daddy, please can you buy me a pencil*
> *So that I can use it in school?"*
> *And daddy said, "Sorry, my son, I have no money.*
> *I finished it up in the bar."*
>
> *"Daddy and mommy, please save some money for school*

---

[25] Illegal drugs like marijuana would be difficult if not impossible to import into the country, as Tuvalu is off of the main trade routes and has few possible points of entry, which are relatively easy to inspect.

[26] "Huffing" is a highly dangerous practice that has been known to cause brain damage and many other health problems. For more information, visit http://www.mayoclinic.com/health/inhalant-abuse/HQ00923.

So that we can get some benefit for our family."
"Yes, dear son and daughter, we have saved something for you.
So go to school. We can pay the fee."

"My dear parents, we have gone to school.
We thank you for saving the money for the fee.
My dear mommy and daddy, here is our gift to you.
We give the school certificate to benefit our family."

When discussing life in the capitol atoll, Ken said to me, "I think it is a bit different, because here there are a lot of people... Here the crime rate is a bit high." Funafuti is home to Tuvalu's prison (see Image 25). When I first visited in 2010, Ken told me they were seeking funds to build a fence around the prison. On a small island where everyone knows everyone, there is of course nowhere to escape to and no point in leaving the prison when everyone knows you should be there. The fence that was built before my return trip in 2011-2012 instead serves more as a marker for the boundaries.

Image 25. Funafuti's prison, after the fence was installed (Major, 2011).

Funafuti must also deal with garbage in a way that Tuvalu has never faced in the past. The traditional subsistence lifestyle did not create waste anywhere near to the degree that industry and the use of imported goods are now creating waste. Although there is an official dump, many people opt to dispose of their garbage at the ends of the islands (see Image 26). When asked why

80

Image 26. Garbage dumped on Funafuti (Corlew, 2010).

people dumped there, Jopeto suggested it might be easier than going through the waste management system. She said:

JOPETO: There's a hole there, somewhere there. I don't think there, but they said there's a hole there, it's good to dump the rubbish there because then people won't see it.

LAURA: But if they dump it over with the waste management?

JOPETO: Well, you know, maybe they are ashamed to dump their rubbish there. If people can look, then, "Oh that family has a lot of rubbish to dump here." That kind of thing.

Garbage may also be burned, which Jopeto says causes a "polluting of the air. Really affecting the environment, and even the trees too" (see Image 27).

Tuvalu's Waste Management Department is working hard to address the large issue of waste on this small island. One project includes a community composting center (see Image 28), where Jopeto says "the Waste Management Department locates their biodegradable rubbish… They put in there to decompose for fertilizer and other kinds that can help the useful plants and plantation." Garbage is a problem that is recognized across Funafuti. Even away from the large dumping sites, garbage will often accumulate where there is no development, which further reduces the available green spaces on the island (see Image 29). Jopeto says:

81

Image 27. Garbage burning on Funafuti (Major, 2011).

Image 28. Tuvalu Waste Management Department biodegradable recycling facility (Major, 2011).

So for the people of Tuvalu, they should minimize the dumping of rubbish there. And they should cover the place with some sand or build up some block houses for people to live. Because it's a small island, Funafuti. So it's good for that land to be clear to build a house there or something so that people can live there.

Funafuti faces many issues from development. With so many people moving to the island, more and more space is being developed into housing. In the central villages, many of these houses are built in the modern, Western style and may be subdivided into two or three flats as we see in the United States. Even toward the outer ends of the island where families often build their own housing in the more traditional style, the population density remains high with large numbers of small houses built closely together and serving as home to extended family members. Jopeto gave the example of an area toward the north in which the natural environment was developed to make space for families moving in (see Image 30). She said, "This is where the people live from Nanumea… It's the mangrove side, but this time there's no longer mangroves there."

Image 29. Green space with rubbish. This digital photo has been digitally altered for brightness to highlight the garbage in the foreground. See Image 54 for original version (Major, 2011).

Image 30. Development in Funafuti where mangroves once grew (Major, 2011).

Funafuti is for working/money. Tuvaluans from the outer islands move to Funafuti to find gainful employment. They need money to financially support their family on their home island, to pay their children's school fees, and to afford the expenses of an increasingly modern Tuvalu. Jopeto told me, "You use money. Everything's money here in Funafuti." Because the opportunities for employment on the outer islands remain few, family members who can work will move to Funafuti. Kou said, "In Niutao they don't have any jobs or they don't have any money, so they ask this, the people who are working here, the families who are working here, to pay that amount of money." Once one or more family members are established on Funafuti with a job or a place to stay, often other family members will join them for short or long periods of time, all living under the same roof. Teba said:

> Here it is not much houses. It's very congestive... there's a lot of extended families here. It's a lot more here than it was in other islands... Heaps of people. People coming from outer islands to stay with their relatives here. You look for work, or come for medical, social, or just here for education. So there's a lot of extended families. The whole family here, there's a lot of them. I don't know how they could stay in one house. And there's only two bedrooms, so they have an extension put on the house. It's just a small house. I think you would know, at Tomu's place, because they've got a lot of people.

An extended family living together under one roof can provide each other support, including financial support. As it is a strong Tuvaluan value to care for and provide for one's family, no one will be left out of this care regardless of

84

their ability to find work. When several members of a family are employed, the family's finances will be quite comfortable. However, there are plenty of short- and long-term cases in which only one member of a household is employed, and that one salary is providing for the needs of many people. This is the Tuvaluan way. No one will be left homeless or hungry. Furthermore, there is an expectation that family members who live in Funafuti are meant to be earning. Their role in the family becomes to provide money to those who live with them, and those back home on the outer island. Lanieta explained that, "You cannot survive here on Funafuti without a job. So the division now is no longer with how much land you own. It's now how much you earn. Money, how much money you earn." Coupled with the value for providing for one's family, many Tuvaluans will stay in Funafuti to work even if they would like to return to their home island. Stronger than their desire to reconnect with their family, community, and land, is their desire to provide for their family, especially the children in their family. Kina explained that she has chosen to stay on Funafuti:

> Because I'm working and that's the other thing. I decided to live here instead of staying in Nui because I have an opportunity here. I have a job... So, I decided to stay here rather than going back to my home island because I think if I stay here I'll earn. I'll have an income that I can support my family. And I also look after the two children, like, one is my brother's daughter and the other one is my sister's that passed away. She got one son, and he stayed with me as well. So I would rather stay here working and support them.

Sentiments like this, the highly valued desire to provide for one's family and children, is the reason that drives migration into the capitol atoll. Of the people from the outer islands, Metia said, "They know, going to Funafuti to find the job over there. And that's why there's now so many people." The promise of job opportunities drives the continual population growth in Funafuti. On the outer islands, Noa says:

> They cannot offer more jobs than here... On each island they have their own local government, so the jobs are not for everyone. It is a limited. The posts are limited. In everyone's home they have their own duties. So to get a chance to earn monies, they come here to the main capital to find jobs. On Funafuti there are many jobs. Many shops, Chinese shops. They are creating many jobs for the locals, I think.

Employment is not the only source or obligation for income in Funafuti. Island community groups, church groups, women's groups, and youth groups will often turn their efforts toward raising money to provide for group activities or for church donations.[27] Kou explained to me that there are many types of activities that her women's group will become involved in to raise money:

---

[27] For more discussion of donations, please refer to 5.1 Christianity.

Like, we have to sell [handicrafts, etc.]. Or we have our tea parties. Like that, eh? To bring money to our community. To build up our community. That's all our things to do. Oh, after this we have to go to the government and ask for some workshops. So we make our food and take it there, and the government, they pay us. That's our thing to do here, for our community here. Always, always money. We look for money [Laughter]. So we make our own things, like we go and we have our tea parties and all those kinds of things. So I go and invite two friends to come. So my friends, they are coming here and eating here, and eat for a good party. So if you come, you give me like ten dollars.

Handicrafts are also fashioned and sold outside the airport on Tuesdays and Thursdays when the plane comes in. The *tui misa* (local shell necklaces) are sold to tourists as well as to locals, who gift them to loved ones who are leaving or returning to Tuvalu after a journey (see Image 31). Necklaces, fans, mats, and other handicrafts are sold at individual displays behind the airport, as well as at the Women's Craft Center, which sells wares from all of the islands. Jopeto shared the pictures and stories of two women who use their handicraft skills for income on Funafuti. This woman (see Image 32) showcases the fans she is currently in the process of constructing. Like many women, she receives regular income from handicrafts on Funafuti. Jopeto told me:

That's the kind, of what I was talking about before. People who stay in Funafuti have to get money because they live in Funafuti. So that old

Image 31. The author, adorned with *tui misa* before leaving Tuvalu (Corlew, 2010).

lady, she's doing local fans and selling them out for money. And she said that the fans are so expensive. It's like $40.

Another woman crafts the *tui misa* (see Image 33, Image 34). Jopeto explains that "She's been selling those when it's plane time, when it's flight time, when it's the day where the flight comes. She comes here and sells them. So she's doing that every day." She collects the shells from around the island to construct these crafts.

Although people migrate from the outer islands to Funafuti for work and to raise money, there is a sense among many that the situation is only temporary. Living in Funafuti will only last as long as one is young enough to continue working. Ken told me:

Mostly, I'm just here because I want to work to pay, help for the family, buy things. That's why I want to stay here. But you know the time is coming, I'm getting older, and I'm going to go back to where I was called, my home island.

After spending the working years providing for the family and children, many people wish to retire back home on their home island where the stresses of the crowded urban setting will be left behind, and they can reconnect with their family, community, and island. Lanieta said that many parents will work hard in Funafuti to pay for their children's school fees and give them every opportunity that can be afforded. "Once the child is working, the parents can sit back and relax. Like, 'he is fine he can, oh my child is doing good and he is now working.'" At that point, the rush to earn money in Funafuti will be gone, and people can settle back into their traditional way of life.

Image 32. Woman crafting fans in Funafuti, Nui style (Major, 2011).

Image 33. Woman on Tuvaluan mat with *tui misa* (Major, 2011).

Image 34. Detail of *tui misa* being crafted (Major, 2011).

Expenses and access to resources. People move to Funafuti to find work. The other side of the coin is that life on Funafuti is very expensive. Kokea told me, "Well, living on Funafuti to me is, you have to have a job here in order to live in Funafuti." Those who move to Funafuti but fail to find work will struggle financially. Unfortunately, people from the outer islands who live on Funafuti do not have the same access to natural resources for subsistence living, and therefore *must* work in order to support themselves. On the outer islands, there is always the opportunity to work the land for food, construction materials, and other natural resources that can be used for daily life. However, every inch of Tuvalu is owned by Tuvaluans. Funafuti is owned by people from Funafuti. People from the outer islands do not own land, and therefore cannot work the land to provide for themselves and their families. Even more than food, there are many expenses for people living on Funafuti. Kina explained:

KINA: What life is like on Funafuti? Oh, life here is very expensive. Is there anybody mentioned that life is not expensive?

LAURA: [Laughter] Nobody had said that.

KINA: Yeah. [Laughter] Life is very expensive in Funafuti because as a person from the outer island, I didn't have a home. You know, I don't have – I don't even own a house here. I don't have a land. So I'm renting. So, when it comes to food items, I don't have a breadfruit tree or a garden, a pulaka pit. I don't have it. So money everywhere. I have to pay for the rent, buy the rice from the shop, you know. Sometimes my brothers can go fishing so we'll save some money from that. Everything is so expensive. Electricity. When it comes to drought, we have to buy the water, pay for the water. And transportation. Yes, you have to have money.

Electricity and transportation are heavy expenses on Funafuti. Since the assignation of the domain name .tv, much of Tuvalu has been connected to a power grid, telephone, and internet services. However, Funafuti is the only island that has 24 hour access to electricity. Similarly, much of Tuvalu now has paved roads to ease travel. Cars and motorcycles are becoming more and more prevalent. But Funafuti is congested with this traffic (see Image 35). Of the space in this photograph, Jopeto says:

That's the Vaiaku side of Funafuti. And the important thing there, I just want to talk about the vehicles that are so plenty there. There are so many vehicles there. The gas from those vehicles affects the environment. And so I wanted to take the picture, and I just wanted to show the picture to the people that we have to minimize, you know? Reduce the number of vehicles in Tuvalu because of the effects of gasses.

Image 35. Vehicular traffic in Vaiaku village, Funafuti (Major, 2011).

The petrol for cars, motorbikes, and motorboats is a heavy financial burden in Tuvalu, where gasoline is quite expensive.[28] Lanieta said, "There are more people here. More bicycles, more motorbike, more cars. When I personally think we don't even need those." Funafuti's main islet is about nine miles long. However, traveling by foot even within the smaller area of the central villages can be physically taxing in the equatorial heat. As the convenience of motorized transportation becomes more ubiquitous, the expense is simultaneously added to the regular costs of living.[29]

Along with the expectation that people in Funafuti will have access to money is the obligation that they will then provide this money to family and community groups on Funafuti and back home. People from Funafuti do not need to pay rent for their homes because they own the land, although other expenses remain. People from Funafuti must also provide funds to their church and family, and must also provide the school fees for their children. They receive income from renting their land to families from the outer islands and to the government. Government structures, including the Government Building, the

---

[28] In 2010, gasoline was over $2.00 AUD per liter.

[29] I compare this to the ubiquitous and expensive cellphones that have become "standard" in the United States. People rarely question the necessity of adding $100.00 or more to their monthly expenses for an item that was recently considered a luxury.

airstrip, schools, etc., are not owned by the government. This land is leased from Funafuti families.

Tomu explained to me one day that the leasing process can be very similar to that of the American Eminent Domain laws. In the United States, in certain circumstances, the government can compel people to sell their land to the government for the purpose of constructing highways, buildings, or other spaces for the public good. Tomu explained that in Tuvalu, people may be compelled to lease their land. They retain ownership and are compensated yearly, but a family from Funafuti could not choose to discontinue leasing the land under the airstrip. Tomu's mother was from Funafuti, and so his family owns the land they live on, along with the stretch of land that extends across the road, airstrip, and sports grounds to the ocean (see Image 36). When asked if the disparity of expenses and income between Funafuti families and families from the outer islands may ever become a problem in Tuvalu, Tomu replied:

> It's a problem. It's always a problem. Not here, but in other countries they have the same problem. Urban area is a problem. And also the one – the urban area is the one who faced poverty, like in India. But even though we are small, but there will come a time, there will come a time.

Thus far, disparities in expenses are obvious to Tuvaluans living in Funafuti. People from the outer islands must pay more to live. However, I did not come across a sense by Tuvaluans that this disparity has yet resulted in class differences. Funafuti families have less expenses and more income, but the difference is not strong enough that Funafuti families are considered wealthy compared to families from other islands. Life in Funafuti is expensive regardless, and everyone struggles with finances. One reason is that while Funafuti families technically have access to land for natural resources and food crops, the reality is that much of this land has been developed and is not used for growing. Noa said:

> Most of the places have changed to me. Especially the place we used to play around. Big trees have all fallen. They have been replaced by buildings... Back in my grandparents' house, now there is a supermarket built on our land. But before there used to be a great scene over there. Big trees. The thing that I miss the most is the shade of the big trees. It helps us with all the dust.

The "big trees," he explained, were breadfruit trees that are now gone. What is left behind is a place to buy imported foods. Similarly, the *pulaka* pits are not as expansive or highly utilized as they once were before Funafuti's development as the urban center of Tuvalu. Jopeto told me:

> People who are from Funafuti manage only with *pulaka*, with this space here near the bank [where the *pulaka* pit is located]. They protect it from people. It's restricted to go there; you have to ask permission for something. But it's not as much as the other islands. It's only like you can harvest only two to three *talo*, I mean *pulaka*. So difficult.

The result is that all people in Funafuti must rely on imported foods. Funafuti receives regular shipments of foreign foods (see Image 37), including the rice and bread that are becoming the replacement staples to pulaka. These foods are

Image 36. Sir Tomu Sione at his house with a view of his family's land, which extends behind him through road, airstrip (where the man in the red shirt is walking), and sports grounds (by the tree line) to the ocean beyond (Corlew, 2012).

more expensive in terms of financial cost, but they are less expensive in terms of labor and land, and are therefore much easier to access in Funafuti for all Tuvaluans regardless of their home island. Traditional foods are also shipped in from the outer islands. Kou told me that while people living on Funafuti are expected to send money back home, the families remaining in the outer islands are expected to provide local foods to those in Funafuti. Kou told me:

> Living in Funafuti is good, but the bad things, because we don't have any coconuts, any foods. Because here we depend on money... only the Funafuti people, they have the land. They go to the breadfruit, they get it, because they are from the island... every boat, our family in Niutao, they bring our coconuts, the breadfruit and *pulaka*. After we finish that... we don't have any things [local foods] to eat... That's a hard thing for us here.

The lack of access to natural resources also means that traditional activities can be difficult or impossible to do. Creating the flower garlands for celebrations requires efforts to gain access to the flowers growing on the island by paying a fee to the Funafuti *Kaupule* or accessing the flowers through a family. Sueina says:

> It's not allowed to go and pick the flowers. If you pick the flowers for doing the garlands, you have to go and pick from your lands, not from

any other spots. If they found you doing that without paying a fee, then you have a penalty from them.

Community traditions maintained, but adapted. During my first visit to Tuvalu, I was told that in Vaitupu, the women's group will weave or make other traditional handicrafts. However, in Funafuti where accessing pandanus leaves for weaving is difficult at best, the Vaitupu women's group buys cloth and thread to sew pillowcases. Kou agrees that weaving is not really an option on Funafuti, however, she said, "Here you can see during the plane time, here you can see all the women sitting there with their necklaces." Shells can be gathered to make *tui misa* or other crafts. The process of gathering for community group meetings and activities remains the same, even if the specifics of the activities themselves must change. In this way, island community groups maintain their home island traditions despite the need for adaptation. The obligation of people to participate in community gatherings and functions remains intact. Alamai says:

> In Funafuti, all these people here, they sometimes contribute too. If the people of the island said "we need this kind of assistance or we are doing this and we need this much money," those people here will contribute. Sometimes they said there's an upcoming event and everybody contribute this certain amount, all these people contribute. Everybody.

Image 37. Shipping containers at the wharf signal the growing rate of imported goods (Major, 2011).

93

When asked if the people from the Niutao community on Funafuti often saw each other, Ken said:

> Yeah. Lots. Obviously, my friends are here and my family's here. We work together, and everything. And also functions. To invite the family, I call up and then come together and have a small feast, to talk about, and some other.

Kina agreed that there are plenty of instances on Funafuti in which an outer island community will gather together, including "functions and family commitments, you know, funerals or weddings, birthdays." Family members come together for such celebrations, as well as for community group meetings and island community meetings. For example, the Niutao island community meets once a month in the Niutao *maneapa* on Funafuti to discuss different activities or events or other pressing issues that the community as a whole is facing. Island-specific women's groups and youth groups also meet to help maintain the islands' sense of community on Funafuti. Also, Sueina says:

> If there's a Niutao person that works at the government, if he retires, we always have a feast for him, him or her, just to thanks him for everything that he makes for the community during the time he was still, or her, was still working, eh? So we always have a feast for those kinds of people. So we always meet like four times a month, or it depends if other programs are going on.

Programs and community gathering events can be related to a specific celebration, such as a retirement party, or can include more general types of activities, such as fundraising or sports. Lanieta said:

> The women's group, in most cases, they are the main supporting group of the whole community. So whenever this Nanumaga community wants to do, the women community is the most supporting group who support whatever is there to be done... [Community groups also] get together for social activities like maybe a dance in a club. They go out playing. They have, every Friday night, they have outdoor games, maybe volleyball or some other sports down the court. Yeah, they celebrate their annual day together in June.

Sports gatherings include both unofficial games of casual play (see Image 38) or organized sports events. Jopeto tells me:

JOPETO: There's the Tuvalu games here on Funafuti. Every year is the Tuvalu games. It happens every year, so that happens. That's islands versus the other islands.

LAURA: So it's like a week or two weeks and all the islands play against each other?

JOPETO: So Nukufetau now is the champion, is leading the islands, three times now leading.

LAURA: Oh wow.

JOPETO: But Nukulaelae is the first island to take the reigning of these games. Nukulaelae opened the first champs.

But, Jopeto tells me, people gather informally as well, "Just go riding, telling stories and things, joking. Yeah. Normal things." Despite expense, lack of

94

Image 38. Kids playing at the site of the old airport at the northern end of the airstrip. Also note the puddle in the foreground, a result of off-season flooding with the high tide (Major, 2011).

access to resources, or indeed physical distance from the home island, communities on Funafuti maintain their gathering traditions and sense of community identity.

Chapter Summary

This chapter explores life in Tuvalu. Although participants and others are clear that each Tuvaluan island has its own cultural identity, they also speak of the "outer islands" as a space in which these individual cultural identities are best maintained. Funafuti, on the other hand, is the modern, urban center of Tuvalu where people come for work, education, and other opportunities. Although living on Funafuti necessarily means that the daily practice of island cultures is changing, participants discussed in great detail the ways in which they maintain their culture by adapting to a changing context.

Chapter 4

4.1 Cultural Changes to Daily Life

In Funafuti and the outer islands, Tuvaluans are facing changes to their cultural identities, traditions, and daily activities. Some of these changes are quite recent results of modernity and the sudden development Tuvalu has experienced since being assigned the domain name .tv. Other changes have been slowly and incrementally occurring over many decades through colonization and independence, as Tuvaluans interact with other countries in more complex political and economic relationships. Participants expressed worry about some of these changes, and great pride in others. Throughout discussions of each of these issues, however, one thing is clear. Tuvaluans highly value their cultural identity. Despite any adaptations or cultural shifts that are occurring, they remain strong in this identity. In this section, I will discuss past and current norms and ideals regarding family relations and gender roles. I will discuss some of the changes that have been occurring over the past century in Tuvalu regarding food, school, and migratory work. Finally, I will discuss how certain cultural changes are now becoming more immediately apparent in the lives of the younger generations.

Family. Family traditions are a major part of Tuvalu's cultures. Historically, each family would have a role that it served in the community, called *pologa*. For example, Alamai explained:

> A certain family does the massage, a certain family does the fishing, a certain family is really good in making the houses. You know, those kinds of things. It's like when you need to build your house, you go to this one. When you are sick, then you go to this one. When the community is having a feast then these people go and do the fishing.

When *pologa* was commonly practiced, it was not that only one family in the community knew how to fish. Rather, that family held a particularly high level of skills and knowledge regarding fishing. In matters of fishing, everyone would turn to this family as both the leaders and the experts. Tafue explained:

> The different families have their own expertise. There is a family who looks after the sea... there is a clan who looks after the coconut trees, what they called the *uaniu*. There is a clan which looks after the plantations and the pulaka pits. And there is a clan who are responsible for the dancing entertainment. There is, you know, they have different expertise which contributes to the wellbeing of the community. So unless the clan which is responsible for the sea, unless they say 'we go fishing tomorrow,' no one will go – in a community way. You can go by yourself. But unless this family calls the community together and says, 'we go fish on that part of the island' no one will do that.

This family knowledge is passed down from father to son. The information is guarded even from the female children, because when they marry they join other families, which could cause the family's knowledge to be spread around. This would cause both a diluting of the knowledge and a reduction of its value to the community. Tomu told me:

We pass word by word and by mouth and not the written documents…
we pass it by mouth, talking, story tell. So from the olden days, like
what we have talked before[30], the way skills are passed down. Because
we don't like other families to know. Just passed by mouth. In the
evening we talk, talk, tomorrow we talk again. Not written in the paper,
otherwise the people – if the other family found our paper, so our skill
is going by, they took our skill. Something like that. So we always
preserve. [Laughter]

These days, *pologa* is not practiced to the extent that it once was. Some families
have not passed down their knowledge to the younger generations. Some
families' younger generations are not living full-time in their community, as
they have migrated for school or for work. It was proposed to me that the 2011
drought might not have affected the islands so severely if families were still
practicing their traditional roles to the extent they were practiced "before." In
the 1963 drought, the families mobilized to protect the land and the community
according to their expertise. The *pulaka* family directed which roots to harvest
and which to leave so that the pits would maintain viability. The coconut or
pandanus or breadfruit families used their knowledge to protect the trees, etc.
Although the 1963 drought was severe, this elder reported to me that it did not
cause the same level of damage as the recent drought because the families
activated their knowledge to protect the islands and the communities.

Tuatina, adoption, and providing for children. Throughout most of
Tuvalu's history, each island's population was small enough that an extended
definition of 'family' meant that everyone was related by blood or by marriage.
Tuvalu therefore developed highly structured rules for the relationships among
families to guide issues of land rights, family knowledge, marriageability, etc.
One of these structures is called *tuatina.* Feue explained:

This is the relationship between a man and his sister's children or a
man and his cousins. Now let me explain this because these are very
important Tuvaluan cultural aspects. In Tuvalu of course as you may
have known there is no word for cousin. There is only one word for that
relationship, be either your real sister or your first cousin, second
cousin, and the word is *tuagane*, everybody is *tuagane*… During the
old Tuvalu history, this is the explanation for why there is that sacred
relationship between the man and his sister's children. In the olden
days, if you go to war, the first people that would die for you would be
your sister's children. No question. They will offer their lives for you…
Now, in the olden days it's common knowledge that my children and
my brother's children can live either with me or with my brother.
There's no distinction. And my brother will treat them as his own.
Likewise, if they are my sister's children they can live with me. Now
this is all to do with the sharing of scarce resources in the land and I

---

[30] Regarding passing the knowledge from father to son and not through the
female children.

97

think it is a neat arrangement. There you are. Those are important cultural aspects.

Because of the *tuatina* relationship, people will show especial love or care for the children of their sisters or cousins, from early childhood on into adulthood. This relationship makes clear the close family bond of relatives that may live distantly or who may not otherwise interact with each other closely and regularly.

In Tuvalu, the responsibilities for child caregiving are much more complex than those seen in modern Western cultures. In Tuvalu, adoption within families is quite common. In cases where an adult with children has passed away or works a migratory job, it is common for other adult family members to care for the children. Adoption is also common if adults do not have their own children; they will adopt from within the family. These adoptions may be legally recognized or simply accepted by the family. Caretaking responsibilities and relationships extend beyond the parent or main guardian. Tomu told me:

> You know in our traditions, you always live with your grandmother and grandpa. You forget your dad and mom. These are the people, your guardians, your grandfather and grandmother. They are the ones looking after you. Even today, all kids we have, grandfather and grandma is always looking after them. It's the local rules, local traditions, because the grandfather and the grandmother they love more the kids than the boy, the son.

Children may spend very extended periods of time living with their grandparents on either side of the family. During my first trip to Tuvalu, the caregiving relationships were incomprehensibly complex to me. It seemed as though a child spent the night in whichever family member's house he or she happened to fall asleep in. Although I still have only a very limited knowledge and understanding of the family relationship structures that have evolved in Tuvalu over countless generations, I can certainly appreciate that the nuclear family (parent-child) is not the primary or sole relationship that guides child rearing, as in the United States. Children are also legally adopted in Tuvalu. Vete was legally adopted as a child. He told me:

> Normally adoption is done from family to family, but my adoption was in the modern – they wanted to do the legal adoption. And that time my right to the land, my adopted father's land, we have the equal right as his own descendants. But in the other – the Niutao adoption, you know, it's a family thing. But I was legally adopted.

Vete said that in his case he was called the "king of the family" because of his adoption. He was not required to work hard while he was growing up:

> I just go and bring the fire and leave it to my mom to continue the fire. Because I hardly do any work with those adopted parents of mine, I don't do any work. My life is free – only eat, sleep, and play [Laughter].

In his case, the adoption set him apart in a position of honor like a guest, or he says "a pet" in the family home. Tuvaluan traditions of complex family

98

relationships and child-rearing hold a place for both legal and family adoptions. When naming off his family members to us, Noa finished with:

NOA: And our younger adopted brother, the one that I mentioned last time. His name is Alex. He was named, you know that movie, Alexander the Great?

MICHAEL: Yes.

NOA: My grandfather named him [laughter].

MICHAEL: That is a powerful name.

Connected to the family relationship structures and adoption traditions, Tuvaluans hold a strong value for providing for the children in the family, regardless of whether they are one's own children by birth. Grandparents, the parents' siblings and cousins, even older siblings of the children will take on the mantle of responsibility of providing care and financial support. Of her own childhood experience, Kou said:

I have an uncle from overseas, they bring some money to our family and we get some from the shop, we can buy things from the shop with money. When I go to school, my parents pay for my school fee. But that time, my oldest brother was working for the police and also can help to pay my school fee.

Parents and older relatives care for the children and their advancement both in terms of economic support and as Jopeto says, "encouraging us, the children, for a better future." In the olden days, Tuvaluan parents would have encouraged their children in the family traditions and educated them in cultural practices throughout their youth and young adulthood. Over the past century, Tuvaluans have become more focused on providing education opportunities to their children "for a better future." Nalu told me:

[Parents] just know how to save the money, how to use the money. See, my youngest daughter went to Fiji. I paid everything, airfare go and back, and fees, everything. So most of the Niutao people they just open their eyes – what is better for them to do for the future of their children?

Discipline and respect. During my second trip to Tuvalu, my host family was eagerly awaiting an upcoming trip to Niutao. The boat would depart soon after I left. From my conversations with everyone who would be traveling, they were greatly anticipating this trip back to their home island. Unfortunately, as the date of travel got closer, it became obvious that the weather was turning sour. The wind was coming in from the wrong direction, signaling bad weather and rough seas. Tomu made the decision to postpone the trip until the wind had returned to normal. When Tomu told me this, I was unsure if he meant that he and Grandma Segali would remain in Funafuti, or if everyone would. When I asked Sueina if she would still be traveling, she said with a laugh, "No, we go where the boss goes," waving her hand back toward the house where Tomu sat (Corlew field notes, 2012).

Tomu is the 'old man' of his clan, literally the oldest and therefore the head of the clan. He is the patriarch of his family. In Tuvaluan culture, the elders are treated with great respect. During feasts and other functions, there is always

99

time for the elders to give speeches. When the *Kaupule* system was created, it formalized into modern government a long tradition of leadership by the elders. Along with the respect that elders receive is a responsibility to guide the family by making decisions about the lands and mediating family disputes. The family roles are structured differently on each island. Tomu explained to me once that on Niutao one person will serve as the head to decide whether a house could be built on the family lands, whereas on Funafuti, multiple people will decide together. On Funafuti, if I wanted to build a house on my family's land, I would need to get the permission and agreement of all of my siblings. Otherwise, I cannot. In Niutao, I only need to convince one person. The head of the family therefore maintains responsibility for the entire family's wellbeing. Tomu told me, "The custom still exists... to give respect to the old men and ladies, or your superior. But sometimes the young generation doesn't like it, you know... their parents are not teaching them to always respect old people today." The systems of providing discipline and paying respect are changing as Tuvalu becomes more influenced by outside cultures. For example, the penalties previously discussed are no longer likely to include corporal punishment, although that was common enough in the olden days. In addition to these changes to the punishments allotted to adults, the disciplinary systems for children are changing. Kina told me:

> When I was young I was always disciplined by my parents... with all my life I was thankful for this ... And nowadays, if you do the same discipline that we have from our parents you find out that the kid will shout back to you and then you will end up in court... They might say that the parents are trying to kill them.

However, it is not only a matter of the children no longer accepting punishments from their parents. The norms surrounding the discipline or punishments of children are changing in multiple layers. The expectations for discipline are different among the parents as well, and therefore shift the ways in which the community approaches the discipline of children. Tafue explained:

> In the olden days, the other thing was the mutual respect of the elders of each other. In the olden days I have seen a father or a grandfather or a mother or grandmother beating up someone else's kid because he or she was doing something wrong, and then sending that kid back to the parents or the grandparents and they would come and thank them for teaching the kid the right way. Now you [Laughter] you give them one stick, you end up in court. That kind of attitude of working together and respecting each other's, you know, has disappeared. Even if you don't beat them and you talk to them, you try and teach them, they will end up coming to you and say, 'What the hell did you do to my kid? Who told you to do that? What right do you have?' ... Now it all changed simply because of this modernization idea and the impact of globalization on these things.

There is a sense among many Tuvaluans that with the changes in disciplinary practices comes a necessary (and apparent) shift in level of self-discipline and respectfulness of the youth who are on the receiving ends of these practices.

Teba told me that many young people "grow up not knowing how to be responsible" because their parents are not teaching this sense of responsibility for one's family. The discipline is gone and so the respectfulness is also fading. In addition, young people are exposed to foreign cultures when they travel for school, and they can bring these influences back with them in negative ways. Jopeto told me that:

> With the influence of other cultures, people who come here, the interactions of the Tuvalu young people, it's easy for the young people to take in. They're taking the young girls and the young boys. They're out drinking at the club, smoking. Even they can fight with their parents, and too much influence.

Marriage. In Tuvalu's cultural traditions, the decision to marry is one that is made as a family. The person to be married is able to share their preferences, but the parents and elders will also be involved in this decision, divining what they know of the potential spouse and their family. Will this person work hard? Will this person behave responsibly? Are they a good match? Young men and women may not know each other at all or very well prior to marriage because of traditions of respect and segregation among the genders. There is no cultural system for an extended period of dating in which potential partners get to know each other like there is in the United States. I asked Kou about how she made her decision to get married:

KOU: During 2004 when I came here from Niutao to study at USP, then that was when we meet. I met him there, and it's not a long, we didn't have any long – We meet, just like only one week.

LAURA: Oh yeah? Just one week?

KOU: Yeah. I finished, that's why I think to get married, because he's from Niutao. It's good. Because I'm not going far, I'm staying with Niutao. That's why I want to marry him. And also, because he's already working, but I'm still schooling. So that's why I think, 'Okay.' Because with him, it's '79. No, it's '78. You're '79.

LAURA: Yeah, I'm '79.

KOU: '78. Six years between us. Myself, I'm '84, and he's '78. But the funny thing is, because we are neighbors. I stayed there on the other side. If you stand there [She points], you can see that house. Because my uncle is staying here, so I come from Niutao and I stay with him. It's where we start... my auntie said, 'No, it's good. It's okay. You can get married. Because it's good, he's from our island. You don't go far, you just stay here.'

LAURA: So then it was one week and then you got married?

KOU: So then, because I came from Niutao on Feb or March. And then I started my school at USP. I didn't

> finish. I started. Then I got married. On 24 of May,
> then I got married.[31]

The traditional decision process may happen over a short time period, but it involves the input of family in a systematic way. In the olden days, it would be almost unheard of for a couple to decide to get married without going through their parents and elders. It would certainly have been a scandal. But perhaps even this, too, is changing. Kina told me:

> Life changes... like in terms of wedding. You know, they really have a protocol – propose, the man should propose and then they decide when to get married. The family will decide on it. What I have seen now, these two young people they want to get married and they just stand up and go... they can just let up, go to the *Kaupule* and do it. They just decide like that. Not like before. Before... if I have a son, my son will come, 'Mom, I want to get married to that lady.' And then we will decide. 'Oh, let's go and propose to the family.' And then after that, these two young people, the couple will listen, when the family will decide on it... they have to get a lot of things prepared for the wedding, and it would be a big wedding. But now some people, they still use to do that and some they [Laughter] – they're just, 'Oh, tomorrow let's get married. Let's go.' And I think that is because of financial problems, you know. No one wants to get married and then spend a lot of money on the wedding... If they do it in our culture, very culturally, we'll do it like that, still the same thing. But the only difference is the money spending. They will spend more if they do it nicely and respecting the cultures and everything and if these two just stand up and go to the Kaupule then it will mean the same thing. They are together.

Gender. Tuvalu is a patriarchal and patrilineal society. While all elders are revered for their knowledge, in most cases, it is the elder men who are called upon to give speeches to teach about culture. Although women are assuming more positions of authority in government offices, even today the highest positions in government are all filled by men. In the home, men and especially the male patriarch will lead the prayers and direct family decisions. Women play an important role in this society. As with many societies around the world, in Tuvalu women are the purveyors of culture. Men may lead the ceremonies, but women organize the events, gather the people, and facilitate the functions. Men may lead the prayers and direct the families, but women spend the most time caring for the children and teaching them 'how to be Tuvaluan.' The roles of men and women are different, but are intertwined. If the elders decide the community will have an event, the women do the cooking and the organizing. The men slaughter the pigs, do the fishing, and harvest the *pulaka* so that the women can accomplish this. In their daily lives, males and females perform

---

[31] Later, Kou laughed that I should ask her husband the same question about how and why they got married, because his story was different. Ken laughed and said, "Whatever she said is right."

102

different functions in the home and community. Alamai said that an average morning will follow a predictable pattern:

> So in the morning the girls will be sweeping the surrounding and make tea. We used the open fire, so the boys have to collect the firewood for the fire. Everything is being cooked. And we don't have the electricity. We have the pressure lamps. But now when you go to the outer islands, they have electricity, they have the gas stove, they have the videos, all these things. We can find this kind of thing anywhere. But before that, the girls will be waking up in the house, make tea and breakfast, serve it to the elders. And the boys will be going to feed the pigs and cut toddy and heating the oven. And then the girls will boil the toddy over the open fire. So the cooking is all traditional, open fire.

In such ways, the lives of men and women are separate, but intertwined. I have also been told that although women defer to the men during community meetings, that is not to say that the male leaders do not listen to the women and are not beholden to them. I have been told that the wives of the male leaders will often bring the concerns of the women to their husbands in the privacy of their homes. In such ways, the cultural structures of gender dynamics and roles fit together to maintain Tuvaluan cultural activities and knowledge on a day-to-day basis, as well as to sustain the culture across generations.

The rules for guiding male and female interactions are changing in Tuvalu. One example of this that was brought up many times was the restricted interactions of cross-cousins. Cross-cousins are siblings or cousins who are different sexes. Feue said, "There are also *tapus* that had been placed in the relationships. For example, on Niutao, if you are a third, fourth, fifth cousin, there is a *tapu* there." This *tapu* also includes siblings and first cousins. The language that unites these family members is the same, since the Tuvaluan word for both sibling and cousin is *tuagane*. Alamai explained that:

> Before, especially cousin, cross-cousins, like me and my cousin brother, if my cousin brother will be coming this way and I'll be coming opposite direction, then we make sure that we don't cross each other and that we don't speak. And that shows respect. But now it's changed. This same cousin, we can speak and we can joke and tell jokes anytime.

She explained that this relationship *tapu* was not only for young adults, but for adults and elders as well, regardless of marital status. Family members showed respect for each other by diverting their paths and by not speaking freely. Cross-cousins would spend very little time together outside of family gathering contexts, and even then they might not sit together. When Teba first moved to Tuvalu after being raised in the Rotuman culture in Fiji, she came to learn of this custom quickly:

> The funny thing is… when my brother and I came, people thought that we were married because we were always together, you know, everywhere I go he is with me. And we do things together and that's the way we were brought up. And plus it is just the two of us and it brought us really close… [Laughter] So we didn't realized it until later on when

we hear people, like one of the girls I used to go with, people keep asking "Are they?" in Tuvaluan I don't understand Tuvaluan. So people ask and then when they ask, "What they are asking?" and she said "They are asking, you know, are they married?" and I said "What?!" [Laughter] "They are asking if you were married" and I said "Why? For God's sake, why?" [Laughter] And they say, "Oh, it's because you guys are always going together," and I said "And so? Don't you people do that?" So that's one of the differences in our cultures. Tuvaluan males really separate themselves from the females, whereas with us, the close kins are very close.

The way that cross-cousins used to show respect for each other by diverting their paths is now relaxing in Tuvaluan culture. Many Tuvaluans I spoke to during my two trips explained this change to me, including nearly every Tuvaluan I spoke to who was over the age of 50. I gained the impression that this was a change that had happened during the last few generations, but I learned this was a mistaken impression. Teba explained to me that this new ability for cross-cousins to speak and joke with each other developed since she moved to Tuvalu, "Only these last ten years." The tones of voice, facial expressions, and body language I witnessed when older Tuvaluans explained this change to me indicated that the easing of this *tapu* against talking with cross-cousins was perhaps unexpected, but is not entirely unwelcome. To a person, everyone who told me of this change would smile and laugh when they said they could now joke with their cousins. It seemed as though their eyes lighted with recent memories of funny conversations that could not have occurred ten years ago.

Men and women continue to retain different roles in the home and community. Ken told me, "I think the men and female are in a bit different roles, men will work hard and the females, the same, will do the house work." I clarified, "They work hard but different work?" Ken nodded, "Yeah, but different work." Sueina said:

We just do the cooking. Like men, when they wake up, sometimes they like to go fishing in the morning. And when they came up they go to the *pulaka* pit and do some work in there. And after that they rest, wait for the evening, they go and feed the pigs.

Women are the members of the family who hold the primary responsibility for caring for the home, looking after the children, cooking, cleaning, and making sure that the household continues to run smoothly. In Tuvalu, I was told by many people that 'without a mother, there is no home, there is no family.' In informal conversations, people would refer to specific cases of households whose mother died, or to a father and child that had migrated to Funafuti for work and school but the mother was not there. These and other similar cases were spoken of with pity because the home was not functioning properly. The family was not well-maintained. The complexities of caring for and organizing a home and family are more than the sum of its parts. Tuvaluan men know how to cook food, know how to rock a child to sleep. But the complex orchestration of tasks and people that is required to conduct a household represents knowledge and skills that are passed down through Tuvaluan women while the men have learned their complementary roles. Lanieta said:

> LANIETA: My mother she never, she didn't have much to do outside the house. She remained in the house and look after the kids. All the other jobs outside the house my dad is going to do it. He will do it. And my dad is never close to children, because he is out all the time, he is away. When he comes in, everyone else asleep. Yeah, that's how I spend. I never sit down with my dad because he is always out. When I wake up in the morning, he is gone. I sleep in the night, he is still out. He just come in, in late night and then woke up early and I hardly meet him.
>
> LAURA: Yeah, but your mother is always there?
>
> LANIETA: My mother is always there at home.
>
> LAURA: And the children are very close with her?
>
> LANIETA: Yes. Like me and all my other sisters, we are all close to our mother because she is the only one at home while my dad is still running around getting food for the family.

Women are also responsible for weaving the mats and creating other handicrafts for functional use and adornment. Kou said, "For the women, they have work to do. They have to weave the mats and all those kinds of things." Woven mats are placed on the floor to provide a clean place to sit and talk, to eat, and to sleep. Tomu's family home had dozens of mats that would be rolled up and stored in closets, in rafters, or propped against walls during the day while people are walking around and conducting their daily activities. When people gather to talk, eat, play games, etc., the mats would be spread out at that time. As mentioned before, the process to make these sturdy, high-quality mats is long, intricate, and difficult. The skills are taught to women from a very young age. Regarding the baskets that are woven on the spot and used to carry *pulaka* or coconuts from the bush, Ken said, "The young kids, and especially the girls, this thing they learn how to make it." The mats, however, are far more complicated and are only taught to the females.

In traditional Tuvaluan culture, women spend most of their time in their home. Younger women (unmarried women and adolescents) are not allowed to move freely away from the home without permission and perhaps accompaniment. Alamai explained:

> Before, girls' freedom is restricted. Movement away from the house is very restricted. Up to a certain age, like early teens, then that's when the parents will ensure that she is around the house, day and night, and do the house chores and what not. And the boys, when they are in their teens, the parent will, 'Oh, he's old enough to look out for himself.' So this movement is more free than the girls.

Young women in earlier days could expect that their freedom of movement would be restricted by their parents and elders. Once they were married, the complex roles required to care for their family would also require their presence in the home. Of her own experience growing up in Nui, Kina said:

> Before, when I was very little I have liked to go out, obviously [Laughter]. That is really a big, big thing. If I want to go out dancing, I have to ask permission from Monday … that is how I deal with my family. I have to ask permission from Monday, Tuesday, Wednesday, you know? And then Friday I will get the answer, yes or no. Even though I do all the own chores at home, because I want to go, but the answer I can always expect, the answer is no. You know, nowadays, now I think young girls, teenagers especially, they are really free. They can just go out. That is, what I call – what is it? It is a generation gap.

The restriction of movement also applies to what women are allowed to wear. On the outer islands these restrictions remain, although they have been relaxed somewhat on Funafuti. Ken said, "Some of culture in Tuvalu, it's humble. Like, a female can't go outside the home without a dress." Jopeto agreed that, "In Nukufetau, too, it's so strict for women to wear shorts in public. And we have to wear *sulu* and the long dress. And good t-shirts." On Funafuti, women will wear pants or shorts except for formal events where dress code restrictions apply. During Niutao's morning function on Boxing Day, I wasn't aware of the dress restrictions and wore shorts to the *maneapa*. As we arrived, Sueina gave me a *sulu* to wear over my shorts. Although women will wear shorts on Funafuti, the cultural expectations and restrictions on dress have not completely dissolved. Women will still wear their hair back in braids or buns as they conduct their daily lives. On a whole, they dress conservatively, especially when compared to the norms of my American culture. However, changes to these norms were noted by participants and others with whom I spoke. The restrictions placed on women's movement and dress are easing as more Tuvaluans are educated overseas. Expectations are changing. Kina said:

> Things our mothers cannot do when they were young like us, now we can do, we can do all those. And before, like, our grandmothers cannot wear this style of dress what we are wearing now. Before that we can – I believe that our grandmothers, they don't even wear long pants like this. Nowadays see, we are wearing these pants.

The conduct of women has a similar expectation of restriction. Women and girls are expected to speak and behave in a reserved manner in traditional Tuvaluan culture. Regarding daily behavior, Alamai said:

> If the girl is very outspoken and very outgoing, then they say that that is not a proper way of conduct of a good girl. But now we can see it's different. When somebody is really quite [reserved] and then she or he is – she is more like a loner than an outspoken one who has friends.

The understanding is that as women are increasingly joining the workforce, being educated overseas, and generally increasing their participation in the community outside of their roles in the home, they must also become less reserved in their behavior. Feue said:

> Women of course are not supposed to speak in [the *maneapa*], but this has changed a little bit, because by law those who are above 40 can

speak in the *maneapa* with the exception of one or two island communities.

Lanieta explained that in modern Tuvaluan culture, it is becoming more common for women to "get up and give a speech in a community gathering," especially in Funafuti. But this is a new development that has not yet spread to all of the islands or to all of the Tuvaluan people. For many, the expectation remains that men will give the speeches and women will remain reserved. She said:

> And here on Funafuti… they often hear advocacy about the women's right. We have equal rights as the men… So the women here in Funafuti, they have more confidence in getting up in a community gathering to give a speech. It was not like this before, just lately, just maybe 2 years ago, you can find a women getting up and give a speech in a community gathering. But you hardly find in outer islands. If you go to the outer islands, things remain the same as what was in the past. Women don't get up and give speech, except for their own women gatherings… [Nowadays] It's just when the time is right, maybe she really had something very important to say and that she will get up. [Laughter] Does it make sense to you people? [Laughter]

Feue told me a story of a trip he took with a delegation to the northern islands. Within this group was a woman who was a strong advocate of women's rights. He said:

> You know, advocating the rights for women to speak in *maneapas* and *Falekaupules* and whatever. But it was interesting because I subscribe to the notion that women should be allowed to speak. There is no doubt about that. I am all behind that… but interesting when we got to her own island community, we tried to get her to speak and she said, 'no, no, no I have to respect my culture.' See? Despite the fact that she's advocating the right for women to speak but when it comes to her own she said 'I don't want my brothers and sisters to reprimand me for.' … You have a couple of women here who are very, very strong, they're very courageous. But then again don't be misled by the fact that Tuvaluans are all against women speaking. No. It's a free for all, because I've known of many, many active women in island politics who have been nominated or appointed or elected to higher positions at local government level and they, by virtue, on their own rights, people respect them and people expected them to speak in public.

In both traditional and modern cultures, men carry a different series of roles and responsibilities. They are responsible for the leadership roles as well as for the manual labor that brings in food and builds housing and other structures. Regarding the traditional way of life, Lanieta said that "We really need strong men to do the hard work because fishing is a men's job in Tuvalu culture. Going out to the *pulaka* pits, again, will be done by men." Men are responsible to raise and slaughter the pigs, fish, grow *pulaka*, hunt, and gather firewood. In addition, when traditional-style Tuvaluan houses or other structures are built, it is the men who will gather the wood, thatch, and other materials, and men who will erect the buildings. Men are also responsible to cut *kaleve* and gather toddy from the palm trees. This pure, sweet sap is used for traditional drink and in cooking, and is gathered from the tops of palm trees. Every morning and evening, it is the job of the men to climb the tall trees and gather toddy.

In addition, men carry the responsibility of leading cultural events, meetings, and society in general. Ken told me that men, and especially old men, are expected to 'know things' and to share this wisdom with others. When the community gathers, it is the men who are expected to give speeches. When asked what these speeches are about, Ken told me:

KEN: You know, how to behave, like in work or in sport too. And especially when there was work, because there are different islands work as strong as other islands. If they do the work, then work. If break, then it was time for break. That is the words they always talked about for the boys to know.

LAURA: So if it is time for work--

KEN: Time for work, work.

LAURA: Time for play, play.

KEN: You understand what I'm? ... The old men, they know when they work, it is time for work. And that's because for a long time, years ago, they work hard and that's what they tell you to do.

Tuvaluan functions are obvious occasions in which Tuvaluan culture is maintained. Tomu told me that the *Falekaupule* meetings were "the only place that you can find, that you can prove the tradition and the culture" because the roles, activities, and behaviors of all people present are steeped in the norms and expectations that make up Tuvalu's cultures. This includes the obligations of the old men to pass along these cultural expectations to the younger generations through their speeches. Tomu said:

The women always sitting in the back, and they are the ones to pass the food to the men. And the way, when the Master of Ceremonies stood up and says "Now we allow 10 minutes for the old men to say something." And old men stood up one by one to appreciate the function, what's the meaning of the function, what's the meaning of that and that and that.

This expectation to give speeches is not only privilege of the men. It is their obligation to the community.

In traditional Tuvaluan culture, men were expected to work outside of the home in *pulaka* pits, with fishing, raising pigs, and other manual labor. As Tuvaluans have entered the local and international workforces, that expectation has remained. During World War II, men were brought in from the outer islands to Funafuti, Nanumea, and Nukufetau to work for the Americans. Metia came to Funafuti from Nukufetau to work as a cleaner for the military. Despite the fact that cleaning is traditionally the women's role in the community, Metia said "I think those times we don't care about cleaning but we really like, we're happy because we got the job, something to do." Similarly, when the phosphate mines in Ocean Island opened, many Tuvaluan men migrated to Kiribati to work in the mines. For many decades, Tuvaluan men have worked as mariners, with contracts to work on ships for eleven months at a time. Men are expected to find jobs and work outside the home, or to work the land and sea in Tuvalu's traditional forms of labor.

Even as the workforce begins to shift, this expectation to work remains. Women are working wage-earning jobs outside the home more often than before. The gender roles are shifting, but they have not been entirely left behind. Women continue to be purveyors of culture in their roles of caring for the home and family, and of organizing and facilitating community events. Men continue to lead the family and the community, and are expected to learn and pass on Tuvaluan knowledge and work ethic. The dynamic shifts in gender roles are at times pleasant, as with the ability for cross-cousins to joke with each other, but at times also create tension while Tuvaluans navigate new freedoms and responsibilities while seeking to maintain the strengths of the Tuvaluan way of life. Lanieta told me:

> Most women, they prefer working. And some women prefer to stay home, looking after the children and make most of the time with the children. And like from my case, I am a single mother and I want to stay home, and I want to work again. So it's kind of tearing me apart because I want to be with my children at home. I want to be there when they come back from school. I want to be there when they need me but I am not. And then again, I want to work. Because I want to earn money for their living, for their school… Yes, it may be different from case to case but wherever you are, do your best. [Laughter]

Other indicators of changing gender roles can be seen in Tuvalu. For example, whenever people gather to eat as a family or community, there is a very specific order for eating. Guests and elder men eat first, followed by the other men. Next, children and women will eat, followed lastly by the women who cooked. In the United States, I am used to everyone eating at the same time, and so I felt strangely singled out when I went to Tuvalu and was expected to serve myself first. At feasts, they call this "opening the table." Guests, elders, or the pastor will be the ones to open the table. However, I have heard stories about this changing. In homes, grandparents may encourage the kids to eat before them, or everyone may eat together. Once, during my first trip to Tuvalu I went to a party with a bunch of men and women in their 20s and 30s. Most of them were in the workforce, and many had spent time overseas for education or employment. After the food was prepared and served:

> We say prayer, led by one of the men, and then I and the male guest of honor are instructed to go eat first. "Then," continues the hostess, "The men will get food because we live in a patriarchal society, and then the women." The men all laugh and protest, 'No, no, the women eat first!' 'No, no, we eat all together!' In the end, the kids and I eat first while the men go out back to hang around the barbecue and continue drinking and talking. Then the women get food. The men wander back in much later to fill their plates (Corlew field notes, 2010).

109

Later in the night I mentioned this to one of the women and she laughed, saying that's their "little rebellion," to always call attention to it. It should be noted that this is the exception and not the rule. In nearly every family and social situation I have been in where food was served, the traditional eating order was maintained.

4.2 Systemic Changes

Modernity. The Tuvaluan cultures and ways of life are changing in many dynamic ways. As discussed before, "change" is inevitable for all cultures. Cultures are dynamic by nature and will shift and adapt with the passage of time and with the influences of new people and new connections to outside cultures. Tuvalu has a long history of change and adaptation. In fact, Feue told me, "On average I think that the Tuvaluans are renowned as being adaptable." This adaptability has been proven time and time again. There is, however, a sense that Tuvaluan cultures are currently in the process of very swift changes due to modernity and a large increase in the influence of Western cultures. In the past few decades (indeed, in the past few *years*), extensive shifts have been seen in many aspects of Tuvaluan culture. Some of these changes are by design as Tuvaluans embrace new values and move toward modernity. Other changes are repercussions; they were not chosen or designed, but are happening nonetheless. Also, Vete told me, "Some people adopt change with full understanding. Some people they just change, you know, just because of circumstances." The result is that Tuvaluans are having conversations about how best to balance the new ways with the old. Tomu said:

> Now the culture still exists. Every island in Tuvalu, they have their own way of preserving their customs... most of the Tuvaluan now they went overseas working in boats, you know, and they return, they have means of money to buy flour and to buy rice, not like in those days like we always preserve our local food, *pulaka*.

As increased financial means increase access to imported goods, the daily choices and activities of Tuvaluans are influenced by these imports. Corlew (2012) calls this the "market treadmill" in which Tuvaluans work so they can afford modern amenities, causing an increased demand for imports and decreased ability to live a subsistence lifestyle. Preferences and priorities begin to shift as people must make new decisions and address opportunities and responsibilities that their ancestors never faced. Vete said:

> Well, there's an impact. When they come [home from a foreign country] they want motorbikes. When they come you tell them, 'No, you don't need a motorbike.' That's, 'Oh, what about the – ?' They always think, they want a laptop, they want a – what else? – because my focus is the modern world.

The choices that parents must now make as they raise their children are unprecedented in Tuvaluan history. Two hundred years ago (and for many Tuvaluans, two decades ago), there was no choice between teaching their children Tuvalu cultural activities and sending them to a different country for education. There was no choice between working the land and migrating to

110

another island or country for paid employment. There were no decisions about owning motorbikes and laptops. The very fact that these choices must now be made influences the world in which the younger generations are raised, and therefore influences what the younger generations perceive is normal in the Tuvaluan culture and way of life. Nowadays, schooling in Fiji or elsewhere is standard practice for many. The younger generations expect to interact with people from other countries. Jopeto showed me a photograph of the Tuvalu Workshop (see Image 39), and told me it was important because:

> I just wanted to show that I think the Tuvalu Workshop ought to be more bigger than that building. You know, because sometimes the New Zealand comes here too for other kinds of programs. They come and sit in that small workshop building, and so I'm going to say that it should be more bigger.

Modernity in Tuvalu means receiving aid and programs from foreign countries, it means traveling abroad for schooling, and it means participating in international dialogues on climate change and other important topics. These things are part of Tuvaluan culture now. Vete told me:

> Where is paradise? I love Tuvalu. Why? I can sit and relax, and you know. But why I am telling my children Tuvalu is not the future? Because it will be a *palagi* life. All our future descendants, they will have to live a *palagi* life, which is, you know, for them to survive, for them to be competitive, they'll have to follow them, they'll have to go

Image 39. The Tuvalu Workshop on Funafuti (Major, 2011).

that way. If they don't go that way they will be second class. That's what I'm telling them. The way forward.

The changes that Tuvalu is undergoing with modernity are experienced most strongly in Funafuti, although they are apparent in the outer islands as well. Funafuti is a more expensive place to live than the outer islands. Although the outer islands have varying degrees of access to imports, they also have complementary access to land and therefore local foods and resources. The rising cost of daily life creates a concurrent change in the way people live. As Tuvaluans have begun to use motorboats instead of canoes, costs associated with fishing suddenly appeared. Vete said, "Anything you do for fishing in the olden days, you don't buy. Later they changed to outboard engine where you need benzene, and life started to change because of this costing more." When life costs more, people must work for wages, which in turn reduces the time they have available to invest in growing traditional foods. Growing, harvesting, and cooking *pulaka* take much more time than buying a bag of rice and boiling it. If people must work to buy benzene, then they become more likely to rely on products that are bought rather than made. Vete said:

> It creates more problems. Sustainability, the modern world in the outer islands, very difficult... The olden days, the mats are the women's thing. My mom can weave two of these in one day. If everything is ready, can just finish this one, sh, sh, sh, sh, very fast, in one day. No more, no more do they even have that. You can't find anybody who can do that, no more. Why? They want to buy this carpet, but when the carpet finished, you know [Pantomimes throwing it away; it becomes garbage]. In the olden days everything is fine, there. And you are self-sufficient.

This is not to say that Tuvalu's traditional way of life is easier. More to the point, modern life on Funafuti and a traditional subsistence life in the outer islands are considered by Tuvaluans to be differently difficult. Life working the land is easier because there is less expense and people know they will always have access to the resources they need to survive. Simultaneously, life working a wage job on Funafuti is easier because living from the land is very hard work. Both of these things are true. Jopeto told me:

> People who live in Funafuti are only those who are going to school, people who have jobs, people who live with money. Instead of living with money, you should go back to the islands and stay there. Because it's hard too, it's difficult for people to live here in Funafuti instead of living there on the island... It's easy for them to find foods, to look for foods. Like here in Funafuti it's too difficult.

The difficulty comes with the necessity to live from money and imported goods. Metia agreed that "It's very hard not to go back" to the outer islands because so many people will stay in one household with only a very few people able to find gainful employment. The financial strain is quite difficult for people. "But," he adds:

> To ask him to go back, to go home, it's very difficult for them now. It's much better to stay here than to go back. [Laughter] ... because they

112

can't work. The only thing he go back, you go and work your lands or your *pulaka* plantation, looking after life over there... so that's why now people like to stay here because a life, easy life here.

Working the land is very physically demanding, whereas many wage jobs are much less so. Having a job in an office makes for an "easy life here" even though the reliance on money and the stress over expenses also makes life difficult on Funafuti. Lanieta said that after someone has worked as a seaman:

They prefer to stay here [in Funafuti] because it's quite hard for them to go back and start all over again from the *pulaka* pits and fishing after like 30 to 40 years. He has been doing nothing but seamen's job, it's quite difficult for him to go back and start all over again. So it's easier for them to stay here and just join this casual work... But to go back to the traditional life, I mean to go back to the *pulaka* pits, no, I don't think there is anyone who's doing that.

Cultural shifts toward modernity are also causing a drain on the human resources on the outer islands. The people who migrate for work and for school are those of the younger and middle generations. Teba told me, "The ones that are left behind are the uneducated, the old, the disabled." Those who are working on Funafuti or overseas send money back to their home islands. This is both fortunate and necessary. Without young men living on the islands to work the fields, go fishing, and build structures, those who are left behind *must* rely on imports. With the money that is sent back to them, they are able to do so. In the earlier years of migratory work, the money sent back created options for local or imported goods. As migration becomes a more standard practice in modernity, the options for local goods begin to dwindle.

The previous few sections dealt with cultural changes and adaptations that are occurring throughout Tuvalu. In the next few sections, I will be discussing issues that are both causes and consequences of cultural change. These changes are the result of purposeful decisions to make change, and are simultaneously the outcomes of other, unrelated changes. These cultural shifts are among the most far-reaching in Tuvalu because they weave throughout the tapestry of everyday life, long-term planning, and community wellbeing.

Food. When I arrived in Tuvalu for the first time, one of my first lessons on Tuvaluan culture was 'how to eat like a Tuvaluan.' In this specific sense, Tomu was teaching me to discard my American misconception that a fork must always mediate between myself and my food. Tuvaluans often eat with their hands. Grandpa Tomu and Grandma Segali nodded approvingly as I became more comfortable eating a plate of fish, rice, and breadfruit with my fingers. The next lesson was to learn to eat more. Tuvaluans are Polynesian, and in general are large people.[32] Eating together and sharing food are ways to show welcome, affection, and mutual regard. I rarely ate as much as my Tuvaluan

---

[32] I say this as a small White American woman.

113

friends and family, and during both trips I became sick for a while, causing me to eat even less during those meals during my illnesses.

> Tomu says a lengthy grace. Grandma plies me with food. She and Tomu offer raw fish a lot, but my stomach is weak today and it doesn't look so good even though I know I like it. I eat from the ginormous fried fish, with a fin as big as my face. Also rice, breadfruit, stew, coconut, greens. And even when I turn down more food, Grandma puts more fried fish on my plate. And I eat it (Corlew field notes, 2010).

During both trips there was concern expressed by how little I ate, both friendly, teasing concern and true worry while I was sick. The amount of food people eat and the size of their bodies are topics open for discussion. People are freely called 'skinny' or 'fat.' In the United States, there is typically judgment attached to these words even when it is not the intention of the speaker. In Tuvalu, these words are descriptors only.

> At the party I sit in the front room with the kids while the women finish setting up the food and the men barbecue. The kids all speak English and are excited to ask me questions and tell me about themselves – dances they know, their nicknames. One girl says that I am very skinny. Another girl later asks if my husband is "like you or is he fat?" I say he is like me. They say "Ooh!" like it is very exotic (Corlew field notes, 2010).

In my host family, some of my American quirks were running jokes during my first trip. For example, I rarely drank the sugary fruity drinks available at all times because I prefer water. Before meals, someone would call out "Get Laura her water!" with a measure of mirth at my odd preference. During my second trip, my husband came as well. After a few days we learned that there had been many conversations in Tuvaluan surrounding what we ate and how we stayed so skinny. One night we were told that a number of the family members had been watching our plates, what we chose to eat and how much of it. Eventually, unable to divine the secrets to our skinniness, we were confronted with direct questions. What was healthy? What was unhealthy? How did we decide what to eat and what not to eat?

> Until fairly recently, Tuvaluans lived on a very healthy diet of local plants and fish. *Pulaka* was the staple base to every meal, combined with coconut, breadfruit, banana, pandanus, fish, crabs, and a variety of delicious and nutritious foods. Tuvaluans worked very hard in their subsistence lifestyle, expending plenty of calories and building a lot of muscle. The combination of these factors led to a very healthy life indeed. Vete told me:

VETE:	The olden days, the people are huge, huge, oh! Very big people!
LAURA:	Like very tall and—?
VETE:	Very tall and, you know, muscular, and they are strong! You know, I am not as strong as my father. Why? Because I was brought up in a free world not doing anything. My father was brought up in a way

114

where everything is energy. He climbs how many
trees a day! I think he'd climb many trees.

Slowly, slowly, after contact, more and more outside foods were introduced into
Tuvaluan society. However, in the past few decades, Tuvalu's access to
imported foods has increased dramatically. Vete explained, "Money was never
part of our society before. When we got hold of it, it started changing our lives."
As Tuvaluans have increasingly made the shift to the market economy, they
have relied more on imported foods as their staple diet. Teba said:

It's the mentality that if you have money you can buy. It makes it
easier. It's easier for them to get something from the shop and cook
rather than for them to go out and kill a chicken, and it's a lot of work.
Unless there's a community function and they need to kill the chicken
or if they need to make money out of it, they use the subsistence of it.
The economic development sort of increases the reliance on money.
That is the way I see.

Modernity has increased both the access to imported foods and the need to rely
on imported foods. When Metia was growing up, he said:

The money is very little, not much, not much. But we don't use,
because no stores. No food like the sugar now, rice, and no flour, and
no biscuit, nothing at all. We live with local one. It's very poor living
life here. We don't have any tea, we don't have any flour like in
modern. When I woke up wash, drink water, and nothing else.

Imported goods were not available in the country. Tuvaluans may access them
from time to time, for example, from the Americans who came during WWII.
But until recent decades, there was no regular access to food options beyond the
local foods. As Tuvalu's market economy grew and trade increased, this
changed. Imports began flooding the country, and the diet changed. Tomu said:

Nowadays the young kids are very hard to convince… they wake up
and they ask for a biscuit. In the olden days we are not asking for
biscuit. We don't know what biscuit means. We don't know what's the
bread is. We only ask for *popo*, *popo* tree, or pandanus, or *pulaka* or
taro. You wake up in the morning, eat, go to school or to play. Here…
when they wake up… 'What kind of thing you want?' 'Oh, tea
something like milk.' No, in those days, no milk. Only toddy. You
wake up and drink toddy, or drink coconut. You see, that's the
difference. Then living in the old time is more comfortable because if
you want that, you get it. Here, you want coconut, we have no piece of
land to plant coconut. That's the different part. We only buy imported.

On Funafuti, where there is very little access to land for growing or gathering
food (especially for families from the outer islands), it is very easy to see the
changes in food traditions. However, these changes are occurring in the outer
islands as well, even if not to the same extent. Lanieta said:

Our relatives from the outer islands, they keep asking for money or if
not money, they keep asking for food. 'Oh, the shops don't have rice,
biscuits, please do send us some biscuits or rice on this boat, yeah?' So
there is a question there. Why are these people depending on this food

when there is land? Why don't they plant potato or do some gardening while they have the land? Because here in Funafuti, as much as we want to do gardening and planting, we can't because of the limited land available to us.

In addition to the changes in food access, availability, and preference, are changes to the preparation styles in Tuvalu. Gas and electric ovens have meant a move away from open fires, not to mention appliances such as rice cookers and electric kettles. In addition, food can be stored in refrigeration units, creating a new ability to save leftovers in a way that was limited in the past. Alamai told me:

> The girls will boil the toddy over the open fire. So the cooking is all traditional, open fire. But now they also, they cook the food, the breadfruit, the *pulaka*, the banana, not this British food. But now they rely on the imported foods, the rice. During the morning they will have bread. We have vegetables, but we heated up the leftovers. Now they can put it in the fridge so they can use it in their own time.

With these modern household appliances, food preparation has become much easier and quicker than it was in the olden days. The caveat is that some local foods will still take quite a long time to cook with these modern appliances. They are not easier to cook, and in fact, may be a lot more expensive to prepare. Vete explained:

> The modern has brought rice. And rice, to cook rice is the simplest cooking you can do, rice. Clean it with water, put some water inside, put it on the oven or what, cooked very easily. You cook a *pulaka*, it takes hours and then on the firewood, Oooh it's hot! Biscuits here, they like rice, and if you put the meals here, all the young generation will go to rice. Why is that? Rice can mix easily with anything... Cook *pulaka* takes hour and energy. You will need gas to cook the *pulaka*, maybe one week, gone. That's $40.00 bucks replenishment gas, see?

Cooking before was done in an open fire or in an earth oven (see Image 40). Gas or electric ovens and appliances may be quicker for cooking, easier to operate, and offer less risk of burns, but they add to the expenses of the family as well, both in purchase and in operation. Traditional cooking practices are free in monetary cost, but they are expensive in the time and energy necessary to operate. Kokea told me:

> They cook it in the sand there and the way they cook – they put the coconut leaves, you know, these coconut leaves, the dry ones, they put the pieces in the cauldron on the beach. And that big shell, sandy and also some coral stones, but really white ones... So they cook this one and after cooking, they just put these leaves there. I think you just can see the coconut leaves, and they take out the dry ones. And then you spread them on the beach and put the fish, this sized fish and even some big ones. And they put them there and they burn the leaves. They put the fire on, and because of the wind they sort of make the thing cook quite quickly. They also turn it round, you know, because a lot of

116

coconut – they would bring so many coconut leaves here. After the first lot, they turn it round and they cook it again. [Laughter]

In Tuvalu's modern cooking traditions, cooking is still often conducted outside. Many Tuvaluan kitchens are constructed in the traditional style outside so that they are cooler and provide ventilation for the smoke (see Image 41). These kitchens may have a space for an open fire, fueled by copra, or may have a modern oven and stovetop. Where there is plenty of land available, the kitchen will be built a bit away from the rest of the housing structures for the sake of heat and smoke. On Funafuti, this is not always possible. Regarding Image 41, Jopeto said,

> That's a house, and they cook this side… It's like, a standard family. Maybe they don't have any other spaces for cooking. Almost that building will be located at the roadway. So it's like small land, eh? Small space for houses.

As is the case everywhere, food and eating traditions are an important part of Tuvaluan culture, and shifts in these traditions create obvious change. With the influx of imported foods, Tuvaluans have begun experiencing health problems that they have never faced in the past. Obesity, diabetes, and heart disease are affecting the population in record proportions. The imported foods are a major factor in this change. Of imported foods, Alamai said, "I think that's why too we have so many diabetes cases, heart attacks." Most Tuvaluans are aware that the local foods are better for them than the low quality, processed

Image 40. Woman cooking *pulaka* with burning copra (Corlew, 2011).

Image 41. Small Tuvaluan open-air kitchen with sheet metal walls, Funafuti (Major, 2011).

foods and white rice that are now abundant in their islands. However, Tuvaluans do not always have the option available to eat local foods. Furthermore, many younger Tuvaluans never developed a taste or a preference for local foods because they have always eaten imported foods. Nalu told me that his family eats a lot of rice:

> And I said 'look, if you eat more rice you will live not long. Rice doesn't make any good to your body. You better eat the local food, and that's where we were born. And also we have to drink the coconuts, eat nuts, meat.'

Alefaio told me that in Niulakita, Tuvalu's smallest island, people eat entirely local foods, and the kids there are extremely healthy. Even when someone slaughters a pig for a feast, there are no iceboxes because of the extremely limited access to electricity on the island, so the leftovers cannot be saved. The next day, everyone is back to eating local foods.

During my second trip to Tuvalu, Michael and I were asked by a lot of people what we ate, what we didn't eat, and how we maintained our health. My guess is that when I was traveling by myself, my "skinniness" was a fluke. But with two of us, we were a pattern. I was even asked to design a meal plan for one person to follow for a week. The limitations of my knowledge were immediately apparent to me. I have at least a basic grasp of nutrition, but this knowledge is based in the nutrition norms of the United States. In Tuvalu, different foods are available and the cultural eating traditions are entirely

118

different. I got online and searched for information about healthy eating in the Pacific Islands. The information that I found verified what most people already knew, but struggled to adapt into their lives because of the food options available to them in modern Tuvalu. Local foods are good. White rice is empty calories. Michael and I suggested drinking more water instead of sugary drinks, and received some very strange faces. I told Michael about the jokes from 2010 surrounding my water consumption. Perhaps in a culture that drank sweet and refreshing toddy and coconut water before importing fruity sugar drinks, plain water was just peculiar. One night he suggested to some younger girls that they drink water. They said they didn't like it; it was too bland. 'What about tea?' he said, 'You can drink tea, but just without any sugar.' What followed was a week of laughter as the story was retold in Tuvaluan time and time again, ending with the English words "Tea—No Sugar!" (Corlew field notes, 2012).

In Tuvalu, healthful dietary practices were built in to the traditional culture and foods. Tuvaluans eating only local foods lived strong and healthy lives for many generations. In recent decades, as foreign processed foods, bread, and white rice have risen in availability and popularity, the health of the people is being threatened. Simply put, the food has changed so quickly that the healthful dietary practices have not had a chance to catch up. Tuvalu is not alone. In the United States (where many processed foods are invented), our obesity rate as of 2008 is 33.8% of the population, and our obesity and overweight combined rate is 68.0% (Flegal, Carroll, Ogden, & Curtin, 2010). Modernity is leading to global changes in food consumption and availability. Tuvaluans struggle to balance these changes with their food traditions. When Sueina interrupted her interview to ask if we would be eating lunch with the family, the side conversation ended in this way:

SUEINA: [Speaks in Tuvaluan]. They worry you're not eating [Laughs, then motions to the baby]. He eats all the time [Laughs]. That's our climate change. Too much eating. Climate change here. What's your question again?

School and education. Education is another cultural change that is both a cause of changes, and a consequence of changes. Tuvaluans' access to education has incrementally increased since the first missionary schools were established. During colonization, and especially leading up to and immediately following independence, education came to be valued highly in Tuvalu. Access to education was purposefully and determinedly sought for the young people of Tuvalu. Only a matter of decades ago, advanced education was difficult for the majority of families to access for their children. Before that, only a few select sons of Tuvalu's leaders were able to access higher education beyond Tuvalu's borders. But the persistence of the Tuvaluan government and Tuvaluan families to secure aid and scholarships, and the subsequent market economy shifts that led to many Tuvaluan families being gainfully employed in wage-earning positions, has meant that nowadays any Tuvaluan child could potentially receive at least part of their education overseas. In addition to many primary schools, Tuvalu has two secondary schools and a local campus for the University of the

South Pacific. These developments were actively pursued by Tuvaluans and mark an important cultural shift over the past century, and especially in the last few decades. Feue said:

> Basically everybody believes that education is the key to have that [better life for their children], to get good jobs, good employment. So everybody is really working hard to achieve that dream, sending their sons. And I heard Vete talking about education and the fact that he has his kids in Fiji, and I told you last time that not only that, but you have many other families doing the same thing. The parents work here and they send the grandmother with the kids to Fiji, and they support their stay in Fiji, education, livelihood. It's sort of interesting because that's a new trend. The question is why. And I know it's easy to explain. That's how important education is to Tuvaluans. It's basically that. It's becoming very competitive and people realize that you need qualification to get employment.

Feue is a professor at USP in Fiji. He, himself, is highly educated and obviously believes in education since that is his chosen career path. Similarly, Nalu spent a majority of his career working in education in Tuvalu. At his home, he has a chalkboard positioned in his covered driveway with a picnic table in front of it. We interviewed him sitting at that table. He motioned to the chalkboard and said, "This is not for all the children. For only my grandchildren. Whatever they found they have a problem, I can solve with them, math, English, basic science and social studies." At Tomu's house during my first trip, one of the favorite games of the children was 'spelling test.' Grandma Segali or I would say five or ten words in English and the kids would hurriedly write them down. During corrections at the end, they would glow in the praises for correct answers, and studiously concentrate on how to fix errors. This focus on education is most likely apparent in all of the homes in Tuvalu. Education is certainly valued strongly enough to indicate that this is the case. Tafue told me, "They even composed songs for the children to sing which implies that if you don't study well, you won't have a better life. And if you study hard, then you'll have a good life." This value for scholastic education in addition to or instead of learning how to work the land has assumed a major role in Tuvaluan cultural values. Securing an education for one's children is now part of the roles and expectations for parents: Good parents will do this for their children. Feue said:

> My conviction is that everybody has to do the best for their children in terms of providing opportunities – the best in terms of securing employments, securing the best education you could afford. And that to me, talking from a religious point of view, I think it's more pleasing to the eyes of God if you really do your best. But if you fail, I mean, you've done your best but you failed. But not giving – not providing opportunities for your children, again to me, that would be a sin, so to speak. I'm not as religious as these Tuvaluans, but I would imagine all parents would like to do the best for their children.

Vete agreed that this focus on education is near-universal among Tuvaluan families (if not universal). He said:

120

And then about education, now every family is struggling to ensure that all the kids are sent to school, and it's very positive… my own perspective, I am promoting more education to my kids. Where they end, the absolute minimum qualification, is a Master's. That's what I am telling now my kids, because competition is so high. And where their future lies, I no longer tell them that Tuvalu is their future. Tuvalu is their retire home, for retirement. And the future is overseas. But your minimum key to be successful overseas is Master's Degree. And then I am telling my kids Master's Degree with double majors.

One of the major reasons Tuvaluans have for sending their children to school is to make them eligible for better employment opportunities in Tuvalu and overseas. As the economic realities of the country shift, Tuvaluans must gain wage employment to support their families and the rising costs of life. Tuvalu is a developing nation and has very few opportunities for industry with a landmass of only 25.63 km² spread out over a 900,000 km² stretch of ocean (Resture & Resture, 2005).[33] Regarding exportable resources, Tomu told me:

We have only one – human resource. We use the human resources. I think that's the only way that we survive. Send them out, educate them. If they want to work for Australia, New Zealand and America, go. But we are safe because they send some money back to their family, right? Because there's no other way of getting more money from industry. We have no industry here. We cannot establish industry.

Tuvaluans have several options available for schooling beyond the primary level. However, in most cases, the options involve sending youth away from their home island during their formative years. In Tuvalu, there are two options for secondary school: Motufoua on Vaitupu, and Fetuvalu on Funafuti. On Funafuti, there is also the opportunity for students to attend college at the University of the South Pacific, Tuvalu campus. The access to education in Funafuti is one of the driving reasons of migration from the outer islands to Funafuti. Lanieta told me:

I guess people are moving in for job opportunities and even the young people at the age of 13 to 18 are coming in for studying here on Funafuti. Students are coming into the Fetuvalu high school, as well as the secondary school leavers who are coming in to study here in the USP, Tuvalu campus. So in most cases these students come with their parents. Like, the parents come and accompany their children and support them while they study throughout the year. So, it's explained why people are moving in to Funafuti from the outer island.

Students may also be sent to other countries for secondary and college education. This is a growing trend in Tuvaluans' push for advancing educational opportunities for themselves and their children. Tomu said, "Lately we send school children overseas to get scholarships, get degrees." Lanieta agreed. When

---

[33] That is nearly the size of California, Nevada, and Oregon combined
http://en.wikipedia.org/wiki/List_of_U.S._states_and_territories_by_area

asked if she thought it was important to send children to a better school in New Zealand or Fiji in addition to or instead of education in Tuvalu, she responded "I think so. That's what I have planned to do for my two children. I want to give them the best in their studies." Students may be sent overseas for some or all of their secondary education. The thought, I've been told, is that Tuvaluan high schools are not up to the same standard as foreign schools. To offer college students the best chance of success in a foreign college, they must have at least part of their earlier education in a foreign secondary school. Feue told me:

> The parents' dream is to send their kids hopefully at the secondary level to Fiji, and then they hope that they will get a scholarship to continue on for a first degree and then perhaps a second degree. And if they really do well and I've been encouraging this, to go on for PhD... I've said 'If you do well and you work at the USP center here, there's no doubt [you'll get] sponsorship from the University of the South Pacific to continue on to PhD level.'

The other side of this coin, of course, is that when youth are sent away for education, they are spending their formative years learning about life away from their families, communities, and home islands. This is increasingly common in Tuvalu. Nowadays most youth will at the very least move to Vaitupu or Funafuti during their adolescence to attend high school, and may even spend years overseas during that time. As one example, Lanieta told me about the time she spent at and away from her home island while she was being educated:

> Otherwise I spent all my time here on Funafuti as an adolescent, and then growing up into adulthood. And spent all my childhood lifetime in Nanumaga. I went to primary school there. And then at the age of 11, I left Nanumaga for Vaitupu, to Motufoua Secondary School. And that was the last time I spent one whole year in Nanumaga, before I went to secondary school. And then I started secondary school and moved on. And then Fiji. Except for Christmas holidays – I go back to Nanumaga for just a few weeks, and I'm back to school.

Alamai told me, "When you go overseas and then you come back, then your outlook on things is different. There are things that people are not aware of, that they need to keep for their identity." Tuvaluans who are educated away from their home island maintain their cultural identity and connection to their home island, as discussed earlier. However, they may not be exposed to the community values, traditions, and activities to the same level as those who are raised entirely on their home island. Moreover, they are exposed to the influences of outside cultures. Teba said that many cultural changes in Tuvalu are happening "I think because of the amount of kids that they send to go to school overseas... they have different lifestyles there, so when they come back, they bring those attitudes." The purpose of scholastic education is to offer more opportunities to the youth of Tuvalu. This purpose has been pursued persistently by Tuvaluans. Increased education is the direct result of Tuvalu's change to strong values for education.

Another consequence of this change is *what* Tuvaluan youth are learning. When they are sent away from their home island, they do not learn the

122

culture of the home island to as great an extent. Their educational focus is on scholastic achievement, not on learning the traditional skills for living from the land and the sea. Tuvaluans have not purposefully sought to leave these skills behind for the sake of gaining scholarship. If anything, Tuvaluans highly value both. However, the reality of the focus on gaining education is that a dichotomy is beginning to emerge in which Tuvaluan youth *either* learn the traditional life *or* go to school away from their homes. This consequence of education is becoming apparent, and I suspect that over the next few generations, Tuvaluans will begin to push for traditional learning to be integrated to a greater extent into the scholastic education of their children. At the present moment, Tuvaluans seem to find themselves on a precipice of dynamic tension between their values of teaching their children the traditional culture and of offering them opportunities for education and wage employment. Tafue told his own story:

> When I was young my parents – because they were working in Kiribati, my father was an electrician – and whenever they come back they said, 'Oh, you try hard. In school, you study hard so that you can get a job and improve life.' On the other side, I was staying with my grandparents and my grandfather will be saying 'Don't waste your time on that; it will only cause you a headache. This way of life is better.' So, my grandparents and myself were staying with my uncle while my parents were in Kiribati. And my uncle and my aunt, in the morning they'll wake up, and wake the kids up, and prepare ourselves to school. But grandfather will come around and whisper to my ear 'You want to go to school or you want to go fishing?' I would say 'I wanna go fishing,' 'Okay, run down to the beach' [Laughter]. So I'll be running down to the beach. A canoe was already in the sea and my uncle will get angry, but we just turned our backs and paddled out to the sea. My parents have to, because they were transferred from that year in '76, they came to work here [Funafuti]. So they sent word to my grandparents to send me over, but they refused, they never did that. So no matter how many times the boat came, I never came. So my parents ended up asking the police to send over their policeman down there to bring me back. So, that's what they did, and put me out of the traditional way of living where my grandfather was teaching me how to live. As soon as I got here, they sent me to Fiji. That's the beginning of my education.

Migratory work. Another cultural change that can be considered both cause and consequence is migratory work. As the market economy shifts, and as Tuvaluans seek to provide educational opportunities for their children, adult Tuvaluans are no longer able to live the traditional subsistence lifestyle to the extent that they once were able. School fees, imported food, modern housing, and community and church contributions all require money. To participate in these modern cultural expectations, Tuvaluans must have wage employment. In this way, employment is a consequence of cultural adaptations. However, wage employment and especially migratory employment cause many secondary changes to the Tuvaluan way of life. Job opportunities on the outer islands are not sufficient to sustain the economic needs of the populations. Migratory employment therefore becomes necessary for many of the adults. Migratory employment exists in three separate categories: mariners who work in 11-month shifts, people who move to Funafuti for employment, and people who move overseas for employment.

A large proportion of the adult men who live on the outer islands are seamen with mariner contracts for 11-month tours on foreign vessels. The seamen return to their home islands in between contracts. However, they are away from their families, communities, and islands for very long periods of time. Seamen typically work these contracts off and on for two or three decades before retiring back to Tuvalu. They may spend several consecutive years on ships with only a month at a time at home, or they may take a year off in between, depending on a wide variety of circumstances including family needs and work opportunities. The seamen were among the first waves of Tuvaluans working overseas and sending money back home. They are a major source of income to families in Tuvalu. Lanieta told me, "A very few percentage of people have access to jobs because very few job opportunities are there. Except for the seaman. Seamen, they go out and then they bring in the money to the families." The money they sent back, Feue explains, "was quite a significant contribution to the local economy."[34] These contributions have led to changes in what families can afford to own, which in turn changes the daily lifestyle of Tuvaluan families. Lanieta said:

> Most of the changes in Nanumaga for the past 10 to 20 years are mostly from the seamen's families because they bring in the money. They build their houses and then there is a lot of change from the thatch house into the concrete house… they build their own homes and they bring in videos and freezer and electronic appliances. These are mostly the seamen that make a lot of changes around those.

Spending so much time overseas, they also develop preferences for clothing styles, foods, and gadgets that were once rarely available in Tuvalu. The seamen return with these items, thereby creating a demand that did not previously exist. Examples of these changes, Lanieta said, are "they brought new clothes for their children and their wife and families… all these mp3s, mobiles, cameras." The housing structures and appliances that are now common throughout the Tuvaluan islands are not only expensive to buy, they are expensive to use and maintain. This expense requires an ongoing income. Migratory work must continue.

---

[34] According to the CIA World Factbook, in 2007, mariner income remained a significant portion of the Tuvaluan economy at approximately $2 million. The CIA World Factbook went on to note "people make a living mainly through exploitation of the sea, reefs, and atolls and from wages sent home by those abroad (mostly workers in the phosphate industry and sailors)" Accessed 4/30/2012 from https://www.cia.gov/library/publications/the-world-factbook/geos/tv.html.

Men and women from the outer islands are also migrating to Funafuti for work. Funafuti is home to the seat of government, which is the largest employer in the country. Funafuti also has the wharf and the airport, which means that it is the hub of trade with other countries. Furthermore, what little tourist economy is existent in Tuvalu is concentrated in Funafuti where handicraft souvenirs are sold by the airport, and where the one hotel in the country and several paid guesthouses are situated. The population level in the outer islands has been decreasing in recent years with this migration[35] and, as Lanieta told me:

LANIETA: Because of the urban drift that has happened in the last couple of years. That was about 3 to 4 years ago. There's more people moving from the outer islands onto Funafuti, that's why.

LAURA: Do you know why there are more people moving?

LANIETA: I guess people are moving in for job opportunities.

Tuvaluans also migrate overseas to find permanent jobs (as opposed to the "short-term" work contracts of the mariners). Many of the younger generations who are going away for university education find employment opportunities while they are away. Kina said, "They found out that they can have more opportunities there compared to here. And that's why they moved away. They leave our place and decide to stay out in New Zealand and Australia." While it is true that there are many more job opportunities in Funafuti than in the outer islands, it is also obviously true that there are many more job opportunities out in the rest of the world. In an increasingly globalized world, Tuvaluans are seeking out their place and their future in the international arena. Vete told me:

I am telling my kids that the future is not in Tuvalu. Because the economy here, I don't think there would be a big change between now and the next 20 years. It will remain like this. The change is only minor. And I tell them get out to the world, establish yourselves, put your children into that life of competitions and then retired home, come and die home. When you are old, your energy used up, this is the best place for the future of old people. This place is only worth for the future.

Similar to the issues with education, when people migrate away from their home island for employment, they are spending time away from their traditional life and activities. For the men, this means that their lands may not be tended to for the entire time they are away from home. If they spend the majority of their adult lives working away from the island, it is very difficult to return and get the land back in working order. Spending so many years away

---

[35] According to the CIA World Factbook, Tuvaluan urbanization is increasing at a rate of 1.4% annually. Additionally, Tuvalu is experiencing a net migration rate of -6.97 migrants/1,000 population. Accessed 4/30/2012 from https://www.cia.gov/library/publications/the-world-factbook/geos/tv.html.

from local foods and activities can also influence people's tastes and preferences for what they eat and how they spend their time. They bring back with them the influences of the rest of the world. Of course, they are simultaneously maintaining the influences of their early life, their families, their communities, and their home islands that they return to. Here again is the dynamic tension between tradition and modernity in the Tuvaluan cultures. When asked if migration for school and work makes it harder for Tuvaluans to maintain their cultural traditions, Tomu told me, "Not really, not really. Because they work – they go and work overseas. They come back. They will come back. And then learn again the skills. That's the way."

Lack of experience with and knowledge of home island culture. Migration for school and work has brought with it a unique set of challenges that are unprecedented in Tuvaluan culture. These challenges did not arise immediately, but are instead part of the slow process of cultural shifts that have been occurring over the past century or more. Among these challenges is the increasing number of Tuvaluans who have not had sufficient opportunity to learn the traditional activities of Tuvaluan culture. Alamai, a Tuvaluan who was raised in large part in Kiribati, said:

> I was unfortunately not exposed to this environment where cultural things are done in the Tuvalu way. Especially like the weaving and that stuff, the cooking the traditional way, cooking of foods. Like the fish, there is plenty ways of doing it. You can salt fish. But the way you cut the fish too, is a particular way of doing it. And putting it in the earth oven to cook it, it's different too. There are skills to doing it. Like for example, cooking of the breadfruit, this way of adding the coconut tree to it so you don't get the burn in the oven. So all these things, I wasn't fortunate enough to be around for those kinds of things when I grew up.

Ken, who was raised predominantly on Funafuti, showed me a video of Niutao people weaving a basket from a coconut frond to take into the bush to collect coconuts or *pulaka*. He told me this basket weaving was still practiced in Niutao "every day." When I asked him if he knew how to do it, he said, "I know. But when I start, I don't know. But if someone will start a little bit, then I will continue on." He has this traditional knowledge, but he is not as strong in it as others who are able to practice it every day. I heard many examples from people who did not gain the knowledge of their home island to the extent to which people who were raised on it were able to learn, or who have the knowledge but have been unable to practice it to a level of expertise. Kina discussed this in great detail:

> KINA: When I see our people here, people who grow up here in Funafuti compared to those people from the outside islands, they have a very different understanding and knowledge, especially the skills that they should have. People from the outside islands know more about how to weave, and they also know how to cook in the open fire. Not here. [Laughter] Not us people who grew up here. And I left Nui a

126

long time ago when I went to school... But I still find out that I don't know how to weave a fan like that. [Points to a fan on the wall, see Image 42] That's a fan from our island. No, I spend money on that to get a fan. But people the same age as me back home, they weave those things. They weave the mats... Each island has their own way of making garlands. But I don't know how to make a proper garland or a garland from Nui, a Nui garland. I don't know. But people in my same age and they are in Nui, they know everything. They know how to make a garland. They know how to weave the fan. They know how to weave a mat, a basket, a proper basket. If we weave up the same basket, they look at my basket, it looks funny. [Laughter] You know, because I think that's like my fourth or fifth basket that I weaved, and for them it's like--

LAURA: 500. [Laughter]
KINA: --500 or more than that.
LAURA: Yeah.
KINA: I don't know, if I am still in Nui maybe I know better than my other friends.

Image 42. Kina's purchased fan, Nui traditional style (Corlew, 2012).

Migration also means that not only are people less exposed to the traditional knowledge, but they do not have access to the resources to practice it. Ken and Kina both indicated that they know how to make the baskets of their home islands, but living on Funafuti, they do not have access to the fronds to make these baskets because they do not own land. Furthermore, the wage employment that they have does not require the practice of these skills. Someone who gathers food from the bush must make a basket on an almost daily basis. This is not so for someone who works a government job in urban Funafuti. Someone who lives in New Zealand or who spends 11 months of a year on a ship may have even less access to resources and less need to practice traditional knowledge on a daily basis.

Generational changes. There is also cyclical nature to these changes. Tuvaluans have been working overseas for many decades. Migratory work is nothing new, as will be further discussed in Chapter 5. The changes regarding individuals' level of knowledge and practice with Tuvaluan activities are the result of a cumulative change over generations. Especially now, when education and migratory work occur in every family and could potentially occur for every person, these cumulative changes are being seen. Many adults today have parents who worked wage employment in Funafuti or overseas for at least some amount of time to pay for their school fees. These adults may have been raised on other islands or in other countries, or they may have been raised on their home island but were sent away for school during their formative years. Now as adults, they may be working in Funafuti or overseas to pay for opportunities for their children. These adults are less practiced in their home island's culture than their parents and grandparents were. They are away from the resources to practice these traditions. Their daily lives do not include their home island traditions to the extent that these traditions occur on their home islands. Their children are growing up in an entirely new Tuvaluan context. Lanieta says, "Their dads don't take them to the *pulaka* pits and they don't take them out fishing."

In this new context, traditional Tuvaluan culture still exists. It is still practiced daily by many Tuvaluans on the outer islands and even in Funafuti. However, not everyone practices these traditions on a daily basis. Many Tuvaluans are instead practicing modernity through educational opportunities and wage employment. Many Tuvaluans practice both – the traditional subsistence life and modernity – at different times of the year, or at different points in their adult lives. Tuvaluan youth and adults may not have the active knowledge, skills, and resources to practice the culture on their own. It is only in the context of their home island, with their island communities, with their families, etc., that they are able to maintain the traditions. The community as a whole owns the cultural knowledge. Increasingly, *individuals* within the community may not. At the Tuvaluan Office of Cultural Affairs, Alamai told me that she has been seeking to document cultural knowledge and cultural sites for several years. She said:

When they first started this one, the elders were a bit reluctant to share the knowledge that they have. But now they come to realize that if they

128

don't give the information for documentation, then if they died, then [Spreads her hands]. So they did come to realize that if they died then nobody will know that, especially the new generations.

For example, while viewing a video of Niutao men fishing, Ken and I had the following conversation:

LAURA:	Tomu told me a story of one of the old men who could say something to the hook and then the fish would jump into the boat.
KEN:	Yeah, yeah. One guy, he has a picture here.
LAURA:	He's in the video?
KEN:	Yeah, yeah.
LAURA:	Oh, show me when he comes up!
KEN:	Yup.
LAURA:	Does anybody still do that, with the words?
KEN:	Ah, I think the guy that knows that, when he died, he takes it [Laughs]
LAURA:	He takes the knowledge with him.
KEN:	Yeah [Laughs]. No one else can.

Throughout all of these shifts, there is a perception among many that the younger generations simply are not interested in maintaining the culture. They have no respect for the elders and what they know, and they have no respect for the cultural traditions. They are becoming more involved with drinking and playing Bingo. They are not respectful of the communities they live in or maintaining Tuvalu's peaceful life. Nalu told me:

How we look at the people to live in peace, and how we have to obey the local rules so that the people couldn't be, you know, to fight or whatever. And also we have to control people while using liquor. And people, the liquor people, some of them, they bring and they go home. But some, they can walk in the road, shout and talk nonsense things.

Tafue added that it is not only a matter of these social vices, but also a matter of respectful behavior in the conduct of community and cultural activities. He said:

The change in attitudes. I must say that in the past when I was young, it was very, very disrespectful for a young person, below 50, to speak in the *Falekaupule*. It is very, very disrespectful. And in those days, it was far from people's thinking that you can stand up and say something in the *Falekaupule* as young as 50 years old. Now, a 30-year-old can get up in the *Falekaupule* and shut an old man's mouth. You know, just tell him straight 'No, you are wrong, it isn't how we should do it.' It has changed.

Teba told me that the sense of responsibility for one's family and one's community seems to be fading among the younger generations. Their priorities are entirely different from those set by previous generations of Tuvaluans. She said, "This is the new millennium, you know. It's different. It's a modern lifestyle now... Migration out from here to outside and kids coming back and bring different attitudes."

Despite the outside influences and the shifts that are inherent in the culture, Tuvaluans maintain a sense of who they are. Their cultural identity is maintained. After all, many Tuvaluans are living a modern lifestyle, but many others maintain the traditional life. Multiple generations of education and migratory work, of shifts in food norms, gender dynamics, and family roles have not erased what it is to be Tuvaluan. They only add into the dynamic tension of the place and role of Tuvaluan culture in an increasingly globalized community. Tomu explained that that these influences are not enough to override Tuvaluan traditions:

MICHAEL: I've heard other Tuvaluan say that the sailors brought all sorts of technology and new ways of living, new traditions back with them. Did you notice that?

TOMU: Yeah, we noticed. Yes, we notice. But our old people, even though they brought some new technologies and new ideas, but they are not long survived. These die out in a very short time.

MICHAEL: The new ideas and

TOMU: New ideas

MICHAEL: and new technology.

TOMU: new ideas, especially new ideas to kill the tradition.

Chapter Summary

This chapter discusses the dynamic nature of cultural life in Tuvalu. Participants discussed changes they have experienced in the structure, activities, and expectations of their daily lives. Some examples include changes in family roles, discipline, marriage, and gender norms. Participants also talked about systemic changes in Tuvaluan cultures. Some of these interrelated systems include increasing modernity, changing food norms, increasing focus on education, and migratory work. Resulting from these changes are generational shifts in knowledge of and experience with traditional cultural practices among younger Tuvaluans. These cultural changes are a concern to some Tuvaluans, although there is a concurrent understanding that traditional culture continues to be active alongside these changes.

Chapter 5

Historical Drivers of Cultural Change

In Tuvalu's recent history, a number of major events have brought outside influences into the cultural traditions. Tuvaluans, as Feue says, "Are renowned as being adaptable." To varying degrees, these outside influences have impacted Tuvalu's dynamic cultures in sometimes positive and sometimes negative ways. Some of Tuvalu's traditions have been faithfully maintained, others have adapted as the context of life in Tuvalu has shifted. In this chapter, I will address several major historical events that have had a direct impact on Tuvaluan cultural practices and daily life. These include the adoption of Christianity in the county, colonization by the British Empire, World War II, phosphate mining in Banaba (Ocean Island), Tuvalu's separation from Kiribati and independence from England, and the .tv domain name assignation. I will briefly discuss the impacts of these events on modern Tuvaluan cultures.

5.1 Christianity

Arrival of Christianity in Tuvalu. Most of the recent historical events that have greatly affected Tuvaluan life are widely considered to be outside influences on the traditions and values that make up Tuvaluan cultures. Christianity certainly fits this concept by definition. However, Christianity holds a very special role in Tuvalu. It came from the outside, but was so wholly embraced by Tuvaluans as to have been interwoven seamlessly into the conception of Tuvalu's traditional values. Reverend Tafue Lusama told me, "They hold Christianity very high, and everything is done from the Christian understanding of how to do things." Other changes associated with outside teachings and influences continue to be discussed in terms of the change they brought to the Tuvaluan way of life. Christianity, on the other hand, *is part* the Tuvaluan way of life. Approximately 97% of Tuvaluans are members of the Church of Tuvalu, also known as the Ekalesia Kelisiano Tuvalu (EKT).[36] The other three percent include Seventh-Day Adventists (SDA), Bahá'í, Muslim, Brethren, and others. The Church of Tuvalu evolved from the missions of the London Missionary Society (LMS) dating back to 1861.[37] When they began to arrive on the islands of Tuvalu, they had a profound impact on the lives of people. Tuvaluans embraced Christianity. The story of the arrival of Christianity to Niutao was told in Appendix B: The Outer Islands. Below are two additional stories of the arrival of Christianity in Nanumaga and Nukulaelae. Lanieta told the story of Christianity's arrival in Nanumaga:

> LANIETA: Okay, there was [Lanieta's great great great grandfather]. His name is Tumo and he got hold of this first pastor who came on the island and protected

---

[36] http://www.tuvaluislands.com/about.htm

[37] http://www.oikoumene.org/en/member-churches/regions/pacific/tuvalu/congregational-christian-church-of-tuvalu.html

	him from the island people who really want to get him out, because they know what he is going to do, he is going to change the people. But they don't want. So this person, he kind of protected him. And so, it happened that way...
MICHAEL:	You told me a great story yesterday about how the gospel came to Nanumaga, can you repeat that story or elaborate for us?
LANIETA:	This pastor who came here from Samoa. Timoteo was his name. And he came to Nanumaga, and he was so afraid to come into the land. So he remained on the beach, for two months on the beach. He built a thatch house on the beach and he remained on the beach. So because he is harmless to the people, the people never do anything to him. They just left him there because he is not doing anything. But because he was so afraid, he just left.
LAURA:	What was he afraid of?
LANIETA:	He is afraid of the people because he knows that he is not welcome with his teaching, the gospel teaching. So he just left. But when the second pastor came, that's Ioane, he is also from Samoa. And when he came, he came right up, walked right into the land and he knew where this tree is. This tree is a very sacred place for the olden worshippers. Like, they worship evils, maybe. And you are not allowed, anybody is not allowed, it's not allowed to touch to come near the tree because it's sacred. But when this pastor came, he knows how important this tree is to this people of Nanumaga. He just cut it down one go. It lies flat on the land. Nothing happened to him. That's how the Nanumaga people believed. That's why they believed in the teaching he brought. Because they know that nothing happened to him when he cut down the most sacred tree in their lives for so many years. They have been worshipping and using this tree as a place to go to when they need help from the evil spirit. But when they saw this happened, that this pastor just cut down the tree without anything happened to him, they just believed. They just believed the gospel that he is going to teach, the power of God.
MICHAEL:	And how did things change? You went a little into that when Christianity came. Were people doing bad things before Christianity and they stopped doing, or?

132

LANIETA: Not that they kill, like that. It just that they worship
their own gods. They have their own gods. And they
believed in the dead people. When their people died,
after years they dig up their skeleton and then they
hang the skeletons in their homes, believing that
these skeletons are looking after them and they will
take care of them when they get sick. Things like
this. Yeah, so they are in their own world doing their
own things. They believed in the dead. So when the
gospel came in that's when the people start to
change. Like they believed in God. They start going
to church and the missionaries bring in the teaching –
reading and writing and yes. Small teaching like
sewing and weaving. It's all brought in by the
missionaries.

Tafue told the story of Christianity's coming to Nukulaelae:

I'm from Nukulaelae, the Southern Island. And before Christianity
came people were worshipping this god which they called the
Unknown God... So everything they do, they do in faith that this
Unknown God is looking after them. Just before Christianity arrived,
well, Christianity arrived into Tuvalu through Nukulaelae by way of a
delegation to a Christian meeting in the Cook Islands who went adrift
and they landed in Nukulaelae. But before that happened, they have the
last priestess of a sect, if we can call what they were believing in. They
have the priestess of their faith, who prophesied every morning and
every afternoon. Every time she goes into the lagoon to swim, she will
face the eastern side of the island and started calling the people, 'I can
see a light coming. That light is so bright that when it comes it will
clean the whole place up.' And, the message that this light is bringing
would come through one ear through your body and go out of the other
ear, cleaning your whole being. Just a few months she was doing that
every day, and all of a sudden there was this unknown canoe which
landed on one of the islets. Her message was one of the reasons that the
chief or the king of the island decided against killing these foreigners.
And allowed them to say whatever they want to say, and treated them
as their guests. And they started tearing up the Bible and giving out to
the people and preaching. Fortunately their language is very, very
similar – the Cook Island language is very, very similar to our language
in Nukulaelae, so they can understand in a way, to communicate.

When the missionaries arrived to Tuvalu, any initial resistance to the message
was quickly overcome. Tuvaluans embraced Christianity. Tafue explained that
the strategies used by the missionaries were "very effective." He said:

They brought Christianity and made it part of culture and a way of life
with the people. And that is why Christianity nowadays is very much
interwoven into our culture and it is looked at as part of our everyday

life. It has some very, very positive implications but it also has some very negative implications.

The Tuvaluan guest and gift cultures blended well with Christian traditions, as did the emphases on community, family, and obedience to the church pastors. However, when they arrived, missionaries saw that the Tuvaluans were living in "darkness" by worshipping their pagan gods and ancestors instead of the Christian God. Tafue was quick to note that they overlooked the aspects of Tuvaluan worship and life that were, in fact, in line with Christianity. For example, in Nukulaelae, Tuvaluans worshipped the Unknown God, who shared many attributes with the Christian God who was at that time unknown. These and other Tuvaluan traditions were not evil, but, Tafue explained, they were so intertwined with traditions that were considered evil that the missionaries banned them all without parsing the good from the bad:

> Christianity came without the people knowing and said 'No, that God is, is wrong. And this is the true God,' which is an Unknown God in reality. So instead of trying to understand what the people are worshipping, they just do away with everything. The healing methods that the people had been using throughout thousands of years before Western medicine was introduced into this country, our way of life had ways of curing all kinds of diseases, and Christianity came in and said, 'No. That was all from the dark side.' Now we are realizing that we – our ancestors – were far advanced in their knowledge of herbal medicine than the Western and the rest of the world, probably. So if only Christianity came in and worked together with our culture rather than removing aspects of culture and replacing them with present Christianity principles and concepts, it would have been much better.

It should be noted that Tafue is the only person I spoke to who expressed this point of view, that Christianity may have had a negative impact on the culture as well as a positive impact. I attribute this fact to a combination of two factors. First, as a minister, Tafue has spent a great deal of his life learning about the nuances of Christianity in his congregation, which has made him keenly aware of the spectrum of influence between religion and culture. Second, as a minister, Tafue is able to express these ideas without worry that he will be accused of failing to live up to Tuvalu's Christian values. As someone who has given his life to the church, he is obviously a man of God.

As it is, in modern Tuvalu, I have often heard stories of "the days of darkness," which is the time before Christianity arrived and brought the "light." Stories about the first people in Tuvalu are told, describing these legendary figures as "ghosts," "devils," and "half-demons." Tuvaluans refer to their pre-Christianity ancestors as having "evil" or "darkness" in them because they did not yet know Christianity. In Hawai'i, I have spoken with many Native Hawaiians who talk openly about the need to reclaim the stories, traditions, and practices of their people from before the arrival of Christianity. As Tafue says about Tuvalu, Native Hawaiians have spoken of the imprecise ways that the missionaries damned all traditions without seeking to learn about them in depth or determine if they were in fact "good" or "evil." In Tuvalu, when I explained

134

this effort of Native Hawaiians to a community member, it quickly became clear that I was making no sense because everything from "before" was "darkness." Nothing was good or worth reclaiming. The stories of the arrival of Christianity are told as stories of triumph. Tuvaluans quickly realized the goodness of the Christian way, and accepted this way into their cultural traditions.

Mission schools. Soon after the missions arrived, the missionary schools were created. Through the middle of the 1900s, the missionary schools were the primary source of education for Tuvaluans, and were the earliest steps in Tuvaluan cultural history toward the strong values for education. These mission schools were not as intensive as Tuvalu's modern educational system. Nalu told me:

> About six years old or seven, I went to a village school, a church school. The school was under the pastor... So after school takes up, and during that time, no times tables like today. No textbook like today. No pencils, nothing. It's only a big chart of, I call it, 'A for Apple' that's written in Samoa. 'E, that's elephant'... maybe one hour or one hour and 30 minutes or 45 minutes is school in session.

Tomu recounted a similar experience:

> Our school in those days is nothing, no papers, no pen, nothing to write on. And our teacher used to teach us how to count one, two three, and so. Instead of real material, stones. Eight o'clock in the morning, our teacher says, 'Go to the beach. Try to catch 10 stones.' So now in those days, I always fib to my other friend because I don't know how to count 10. So I look at some of the kid, they just pull his hand, how many inside this hand, that's 10. So like that, that boy I'm copying. So sometimes my stone is more than 10, sometimes less than 10. That's how we did in those days in school.

Other schools were eventually founded, with classrooms and school supplies and other requisite materials. The Church remains an educational entity through church services, pastoral counseling, and workshops to this day, and continues to play an important role in educating Tuvaluans on matters of culture and climate change, as will be discussed further in Chapter 7.

Literal faith in Tuvalu. Tafue told me that Tuvaluans are people of very strong faith. This faith, he said is "Very, very, very literal." The teachings and styles of the Samoan pastors prior to the Church's 1969 separation from the Samoan Congregation, are often considered to be of paramount importance when Tuvaluans judge which practices are appropriate in Christian lifestyles and worship. Tafue said that members of the Church Assembly are currently exploring the best ways to make Christian teachings more relevant to the understanding of Tuvaluans. He said:

> People talk about sheep, you know, Jesus as a good shepherd. The majority of this country hasn't seen a sheep. So, they don't understand the nature and the attitude of this animal. So how can they bring that closer to them? People talked about wine. The plant which is, they have no idea what it looks like. So these are the aspects of Christianity that we try and contextualize to be closer to the people. Bringing the

Christianity closer to the people so that they can relate to it. When having Holy Communion, Eucharist, they use the bread. They have no idea where that bread came from. I mean, they know it came from flour but where does flour come from? They haven't seen wheat in their all lives. So in that line of thought we try slowly to introduce local things, you know, because there is no difference between using bread and using green coconut flesh. Or germinated nuts... The Jesus that you believe in is not the Jesus that should come to us dressed in Western clothes. Because the Western world or whoever should not be the mediator between Christ and us. Christ came directly to us... our people think that if they do something different, that's a sin. Even if you pray without closing your eyes, that's a sin. So, these small things, you know, which the missionaries have taught the people to follow without explaining to them why they should close their eyes, stuck in the people's belief and faith and minds as if the only way, the only right way to do that.

The literal interpretation of Christian practices spans from praying with closed eyes to much large activities and events. Reverent Alefaio Honolulu told me a story of a famine that occurred on Niulakita. The famine was caused "when a boy fell in love with a married woman. The beach had no sand, only rocks. There were no birds, no turtles. When they stopped, then everything went back to normal" (Corlew field notes, 2012). Similarly, there was a great drought that affected Tuvalu in 1963. When asked about how the 1963 drought compared to the 2011 drought, Nalu said:

This one, well my old people, there they have a Pastor in our island that did something wrong. The problem was this Samoan Pastor has a wife, a real wife, not Samoan. But two of the young ladies are staying in our Pastor's house looking after a Pastor too. His wellbeing, yeah? But there is another couple, older, and they are the caretakers of the Pastor, preparing the food, and then when the food is cooked, they give the food to these two ladies and then the two ladies serve the food. But all of a sudden there was a rumor that something is wrong with the Pastor. One of the ladies staying with him is pregnant, and that's when the drought started... That's just a belief of our people.

Similarly, much has been made of the story of Noah and the flood in the Bible, and how Tuvaluans disbelieve climate change based on God's covenant to never again bring a flood. This belief will be further addressed in Chapter 7.

The role of the pastor. The pastor plays a very important role in the community. Of Nanumaga, Lanieta said, "We have a pastor who is looking after the whole island." The role of the pastor is to preach in the church, but also to bring people to worship. The pastor will also provide pastoral counseling in the home. Lanieta said:

As a pastor, he does all the religious activity. He goes around to each house, praying with the sick and preaching the gospel. When he sees this family has never been attending church for some time, he attends to

136

them, to see if there is a problem he can help with. That's what he does every day.

Through preaching and through speeches at community gatherings and events, the pastor will lead the community in all spiritual aspects of life. During my interview with Alefaio, he explained:

> At the Christmas party, for example, the pastor can share a speech. He talks about loving one another. The pastor plays the part of God for the community. He visits people, does pastoral counseling, if there is a problem in the family. They preach, visit, solve problems, and bring things from the Bible to the people in the community. The role of the pastor is to make good rules, not to punish, just to remind (Corlew field notes, 2012).

Although the pastor plays a clear leadership role in the community, he will never be directly involved with any matters of law or decision-making. His is a counseling role. He may be requested to provide guidance, but he will not make decisions. Lanieta explained:

> The chiefs now, they all respect the pastor. Not before. Like, before the pastor came in, the chief had all the say. He say the final decision. But now, no. The pastor is not interfering with the traditional activities. He remains as a pastor. He does his own religious activities. And he even respects this side of the community where the island chiefs do make decisions. The pastor will support and he is in good terms with them. They hardly make any conflict. They hardly contradict their decision. The pastor never makes decisions.

The pastor will also be involved in youth ministry. Alefaio explained that he will be in charge of bringing the youth to worship, and also conducting alcohol ministry. He explained:

> Because the youth must enjoy themselves while being young, but by the Bible. To enjoy good things, not bad things. If you fall in love with a girl, you must show your love in the proper way, not with beer – for cases when the kids are drinking to build up their courage to talk with girls (Corlew field notes, 2012).

In times of crisis, the pastor can become one of the most important people in the community when addressing the immediate response and the long-term spiritual and psychological recovery of the community (Taylor, 2000). This was the case in 2000, when one of the dorms at the Motufoua high school caught fire and killed 18 young women and their matron. Tafue said:

> I think that was the biggest thing that ever happened here in Tuvalu in modern days. Yeah, and it was a great challenge and I think that's the reason why I decided to go for further training. Because in that period of time, the whole island was in a shock. They need counseling and help and the students were there – they were psychologically affected and needed help.

The fire started when a student stayed up late studying after curfew. The electricity had been turned off for the night across the island, so she lit a candle to read underneath her covers. She fell asleep and her bed caught on fire, which quickly spread across the bunks to the roof and the entire house. The students and the matron ran to the main door to escape, but:

> The doors were locked and they couldn't open it. They said the door – to open the door you have to really push and it got stuck. And it was night so the matron tried to open it in the dark. She couldn't see what she was doing. They tried breaking it down but couldn't.

The matron's bedroom door was able to be opened. Those who went to that door for escape survived. Those who attempted to evacuate through the main door were killed. Tafue was the pastor on Vaitupu at the time. That night, he was up late talking with some of the elders. The lights went out at 10:00; they continued talking until around midnight. Soon after he went to bed, he heard a motorcycle coming into his driveway. Outside, he met the school chaplain and one of the teachers.

> They were at the door and I said, 'Hey,' I jokingly said 'Why are you roaming around while people are sleeping? You should be sleeping.' And the chaplain said 'Oh, something terrible happened.' I said 'Okay, come in'. So we walked into the sitting room, sat down and I said, 'Well tell me what's so terrible that brought you into my doorsteps in the middle of the night.' [Tafue is still using a joking tone]. And he said, 'Oh, 18 girls disappeared.' Traditionally, literally, the word he used was 'disappear' but that word can also mean 'die' or 'dead.' So he said '18 girls disappeared' from my understanding. So I said, 'Well, what's so terrible about that? It's good you came to tell me. So tomorrow I'll call the island chief and let him know, and then the community will be called, and then we'll find out where they are.' And then he said, following up he said, 'Their matron also.' And then I realized that the word he's using is 'dead' not 'disappear.' So I said, 'Now you tell me straight, have they disappeared from the school or are they dead?' And then he said 'They're dead.' 'Oh, oh, yeah, that's terrible. That's terrible. What happened?' So he explained.

Tafue sent people to call the island chief and the head of the *Kaupule*. They decided that the community should take over the arrangements rather than the school leaders. He said, "It will be treated as a Vaitupu thing." They decided to transfer the bodies to the village center, and sent a deacon to ring the church bell to announce that these deaths had occurred. There is a particular way of ringing the bell to announce a person has died. The community, asleep in the middle of the night, began to listen to the bell ringing, counting the deaths. Very quickly they decided that some kids must be playing with the bell:

> Because they counted 'Okay, one child' and then a second child and then by the third set of bells they said 'Oh this is far, this person has gone far – too much.' They started rushing down to the church to get rid of this. But when they came the other deacon was there explaining to them something has happened.

In the coming days, Tafue and other community leaders worked tirelessly to respond to the logistical and community needs in the immediate aftermath of this terrible disaster:

So straightaway we went to the principal and tried and organize things. The principal was so affected by the incident that he lost his mind and doesn't think properly, you know. Even the pastor, so I acted as the principal and the chaplain of the school at the time to organize things and to tell the staff what to do at what time and things. For 2 days, I don't know about the community, but the three of us didn't sleep for 2 days. From that night until morning and until that night and that whole night again we stayed up and worked... But that was the darkest day I believe in the whole of the country. The whole of the country. Vaitupu mourned for weeks.

The entire country was in mourning. The school and community in Vaitupu were awash in shock and grief from experiencing this disaster firsthand. To address these long-term psychological needs of the community, the government hired an Australian psychiatrist to stay in Vaitupu:

The problem is the language. So, because when he came, I've already started working with the people in my capacity as a pastor, working with the people. So he came, assisted the students, the parents, and he found out that the language was a barrier. So he decided to join forces with me. So we worked together. But it was – as I said, it was the beginning of a new vision, you know. I think we can never be satisfied until we can satisfy others and bring comfort and assistance to others.

The status of the pastor. The Motufoua fire is an example of the powerful role a pastor plays in the community in Tuvalu. Before Christianity arrived, these leadership roles associated with maintaining the wellbeing of the Tuvaluans were held by the *aliki*, the chiefs or the kings (depending on which island). This leadership role was associated with a high status and a number of privileges, such as food donations and servants. As Tomu said, "Does the president in the United States have servants like us? ... That's what the high chief has in those days." In modern Tuvalu, the chiefs are no longer entitled to these privileges. When Christianity was adopted in Tuvalu, all of the privileges of the chiefs were transferred to the pastors. Lanieta explained:

We usually give food, the best food, fish and whatever we get, we give it to our chief, our island chief. And then, when the gospel is on the island, the chief handed over this his entitlement to this pastor. And we continue from then until now. So, we no longer respect our island chief as the main man on the island. He has now handed over everything he rightfully deserves to the pastor. So the pastor now on the island is on the top of everybody... The chief remains there as a chief. But everything that we used to give to him because he is the chief, he wants the people of the island to no longer give to him, but to the pastor.

The pastors are guests to the islands on which they serve. Tomu said, "The pastors are from different islands. So because he is a foreigner to the island, the island respects or kindly offers some assistance to the pastor." Feue said, "Sometimes we refer to him as an adopted son. Now, an adopted son is in a way more important than your own siblings, your own sons and daughters."[38] However this guest tradition is only part of the pastor's status, which is much more strongly related to the privilege afforded to chiefs prior to Christianity. Feue said:

> Tradition has it that when the first Samoan pastors arrived on each of the island community, the chiefs of the island communities surrendered their status… to the pastors. And that was in a way symbolized by the handing over of the head of the turtle. Because the head of the turtle is the only portion of the turtle to be gifted to the chief. Nothing else. You know, if a turtle is caught, then it's only the head that is presented to the chief. And again, that symbolizes the fact that he is a big man and he deserves, or we owe him, the head should be given to him. And now that has gone to the pastor because the chiefs of these islands have surrendered their status to the pastors… [On some islands] as soon as the pastor has finished eating, everybody who's eating has to stop eating. You can't just [laughter]. They have to stop because the pastor has stopped. And on Funafuti here too, when the pastor speaks, when the pastor stands up and deliver a speech, that again signals that all the activities or whatever is going on has to end, because the pastor is now supposedly is the last person, the first and the last to speak. On Nanumea, same thing.

These protocols of respect in community gatherings indicate that although the pastor has no legal rule over the community, he is still held in very high regard. Feue told me these protocols are "important" because they show the Tuvaluan culture at work. The status of the pastor is a major indication of the strength of the ties between Christianity and Tuvaluan culture. Though it was introduced from external forces, Christianity is now interwoven in Tuvalu's cultural traditions and values.

Obligation to the Church. Along with other obligations to family and community, Christian Tuvaluans have obligations to their church and church groups as well. As individuals and as families, Christian Tuvaluans have roles to fulfill and activities to complete as part of their daily lives. This includes going to church services and events and conducting family devotions. In Tomu's house, every evening before dinner, the entire family gathered for nightly devotions. Tomu would lead the family in prayer and then Segali or one of the younger women would lead the family in singing a hymn. Blessings are said before meals. Holidays like Christmas and New Year's Eve are marked with family devotions. There are also rules in the community guiding behaviors according to church laws, although as with all elements of any culture, there is a variable level of compliance across people and across regions. Sueina told me:

> I think it's our culture. Because in the olden days, people used their culture, and they obeyed their culture, and now this in the new

---

[38] As an adopted son, for example, Vete had been called the "king of the family."

140

generation, they start adapting the modern styles. Like in the outer islands, we have some bells that ring for the devotion. Like in the outer islands, the first bell goes, there is no motorbike that's allowed to go around the island. But here, if the first bell rings, the motorcycles and the cars will just be moving around.

As modernity is increasing its influence on Tuvaluan culture, Tuvaluans are seeing a greater variability of adherence to church obligations. For example, when migratory workers such as seamen spend long periods of time away from Tuvalu, their habits of Christian compliance may begin to wane. When they return to Tuvalu, they are no longer accustomed to attending regular services. Different workers will then respond differently when returning to Tuvalu and the Christian way of life. Lanieta said:

Yeah, some do miss church. So when they come back, they really make it up for the time they were away. But others, 'I like it. Overseas, no church on Sunday. I can sleep in and I can get drunk on Saturday night and forget about the church the next day.' It's different, eh? We have different kinds of people. And in most cases the single ones, the single seamen, they don't mind church. They can get drunk on Saturday night and forget about the church on the next day, sleeping or still drunk on Sunday. Otherwise the other ones, like the one who are married with children, they still get back into their lifestyle. Every Sunday they go to church. There is a difference between the age group [Laughter].

Because family is so important in Tuvaluan culture, families will influence each other in terms of compliance to church rules, conducting daily devotions, and even with making larger life decisions. For example, Sueina told me the story about why she stayed in Funafuti to work rather than traveling to the Solomon Islands to complete more schooling:

I was supposed to go and study in the Solomons. I have one of my aunties there, so she arranged some papers for me. But instead, because my auntie was SDA, Seventh Day Adventist, because she married a guy from there who is SDA, but my grandfather, he doesn't want me to go there and study because he said if I go there I might be, follow my auntie. And he didn't want me to go to the SDA church. He wanted me to remain as an EKT [Laughs]. That's why I didn't go to the Solomons.

In this case, the decision was made with the guidance of the elders, as is common for many life decisions. Religion will weigh heavily in these decisions because it is such an integral part of the culture. However, Tomu indicated that there are less 'official' ways in which family will influence a person's religion and life decisions – that is, teasing:

LAURA: [Laughter] So in the United States sometimes people from different religions kind of have conflict with each other ... Do you see that in Tuvalu?

TOMU: No.

LAURA: Yeah, never?

TOMU: Here it's not. There's one of the good things in Tuvalu. The religions are not in conflict to each

141

	other. But they are laughing like brothers. Like I said, if Michael is joining the other religion, and then his sister [Makes a face].
LAURA:	[Laughter]
TOMU:	We say 'no faith' because he has changed his faith. That's what. Especially the family, but the bigger religion they don't care about. It's up to them... But in the family wise, we laugh [Laughter].

Financial obligations to the Church. Since Christianity first came to Tuvalu, Tuvaluans have been pouring donations into the Church. These donations include small Sunday donations and contributions of food, goods, or services to the pastor. They also include much larger donations of manual labor to build church structures and large monetary donations for special events. The history of these donations dates back to when the *aliki* turned their privileges over to the pastors, and to the initial building of the churches. During the period of the phosphate mines in Banaba, Kiribati, many Tuvaluans went to work to help raise funds for the church. Feue said:

> Most of the people who went to work in the phosphate industry were sort of selected to work – no, to go and fund raise. It was fund raising for church building. So they were sent to Banaba and Ocean Island for the purpose of getting funds to build the churches. And that was common in Tuvalu.

The largest donations are expected from Tuvaluans at the time of the biennial General Assembly meeting of the Church of Tuvalu. Every two years, the EKT General Assembly gathers in one of the Tuvaluan islands for a major church function. It is tradition at that time for the island community to make a major donation to the church, including food, goods, and money. The island communities put forth an enormous effort to prepare for these meetings. I've been told there's also a sense of competition among the islands as they seek to outdo each other. Of course, the islands have varying access to natural resources (land) and human resources (population/workers). Some islands are always able to contribute more. Regardless, the communities commit themselves to pooling the donation over a period of years. In 2014, the General Assembly will be in Niutao. Kou told me that preparations had already begun in 2011:

> Yeah, they are busy to do the 2014, now they are gathering for the Church members, they have a meeting there in Niutao, in 2014. So I heard it from the people, that if you're going there to Niutao, ooh, they have a lot of work to do. They have to prepare. The women, they have two types of mats, like that Grandpa has, two each per woman... The men, I heard it from those people, the men, they have to go to work in the bush and also the *pulaka* pits, because they have, I heard it from those people, they have four *pulaka* pits from one man, from the

family. But they committed the big one, not the small one.[39] So the men, they're busy, they're going, no? And gather those things up. And also they're cleaning up the island. And also the road, they're expanding it... But us here [Funafuti], because here is a working place for the Niutao people who are staying here. I think it's hard too, because the Niutao people who work here... we pay it, $1000. For this year. Now they finished this year, 2011, $1000. But for the next year, for the 2012, $500. So, here you see the Niutao, they are working here, they work for that amount of money, they have to contribute it.

Tuvaluans who are already struggling financially work very hard to achieve the donation goals that are set by the community. Each family is required to make these donations regardless of the number of employed family members on Funafuti or abroad. Family members who are living in the outer islands are required to provide material resources in the form of *pulaka* and other farmed, fished, or slaughtered foods as well as mats, garlands, ceremonial decorations, and other handicrafts. This can place an enormous burden on some families who will nevertheless do whatever they can to meet their obligations. Teba explained:

The amount of work that is put into it is just humungous. Given the fact that in the outer islands there's hardly any earning sources, and people rely on here, Funafuti, for people to send money. And yet here people depend on money to live on. And yet they are expected to contribute a certain amount of money which, for some people, they never earn in a year. They could never earn that much. Some islands are pretty much okay, they really do their thing okay. But some islands, it is just completely ridiculous, the expectations... Women are preparing mats, fans. They can't even do things for themselves, preparing mats for their own home... The conference comes for two weeks and then it's gone. They take everything that you have, everything that you do for that whole year, when you could have spent that much time doing something for your own home. Then that's the culture. You see things and sometimes it's just ridiculous. They just bring on the hardships. And I may be very critical, and people say that because I am from the outside. I mean, I've seen the way people live.

The role of Christianity in Tuvalu's cultural traditions is relatively new in the country's history, but it has become deeply interwoven into the daily lives, community expectations and obligations, cultural hierarchies, and way of life. It has been accepted as part of traditional culture. Tuvaluans speak of the Christian faith of the country with much pride. Christianity may have been considered an external influence at one time, but the stories told of Christianity's arrival and establishment indicate that this was a very short time period. Tuvaluan adoption of the Christian faith and subsequent cultural adaptation was

---

[39] There are species of *pulaka* that take years to grow to maturity.

swift and all-encompassing. There are few aspects of modern Tuvaluan culture that are not touched in some way by Christianity.

5.2 Political and Economic Changes

World War II. Perhaps no other event in Tuvalu's history had a more direct and immediate impact on the cultural and island landscapes than Tuvalu's involvement in the Second World War. In the "Battle for the Pacific," Japanese forces were tied up in the Battle for Midway, allowing American forces to establish themselves first in the Tuvaluan islands.[40] Americans set up camp on Funafuti, Nanumea, and Nukufetau. The population of Nanumea was temporarily displaced from the main island to the islet Lakena, which Nanumeans traditionally use for their *pulaka* pits. The Americans dredged the coral reefs to set up wharfs, and built airstrips on the three islands. In Funafuti, the environmental impacts remain visible. The Americans "borrowed" land from around the island and in the lagoons to fill in the land underneath the airstrip. The holes remain today and are referred to as "borrow pits" (see Image 43, Image 44). Many of the borrow pits stretch for a quarter of a mile or more, and are interspersed throughout Fogafale, the main islet of the atoll. They are filled with sea water, and as such are no longer viable for farming or building. In addition, the pits left in the lagoon eventually led to increased erosion as the land along the islets settled to fill the gaps (H. Vavae, personal communication, August 12, 2010). The lagoon currents were also impacted from this construction, causing observable changes to the beaches of Fogafale because sand is not replenished at sufficient rates (Carter, 1986).

The arrival of the Americans also changed the economic and cultural landscape of Tuvalu by introducing foreign goods, bringing wage employment to the men, and opportunities to sell handicrafts and food for the women. The Americans impacted the daily lives of the community with their presence, which was an unprecedented and exciting event. Among the elders who remember, there was a sense at the time that the Americans were protecting Tuvalu from the Japanese. Stories from some of the Japanese-occupied countries were very horrific. Metia postulated that they were just stories meant to scare people, and likely weren't as bad in reality. Regardless, life in Tuvalu was drastically different with the American presence. As a small child on Nanumea, Kokea remembered:

> The Americans, they used to leave every evening. So every evening before sundown, there is about six of them used to circulate the settlement, Lakena settlement, where the people live. They used to wave and said goodbye on their way down before sundown. So in the morning they came back. We used to, you know, us kids, we used to participate, just to count how many planes remained. You know, if there were about six of them went down to attend the bombardment,

---

[40] http://tuvaluislands.com/ww2/ww2-index.htm

144

Image 43. A 'borrow pit' in Funafuti (Corlew, 2012).

Image 44. A 'borrow pit' in Funafuti (Corlew, 2012).

they will returned four or three. They others, disappeared. They must have been caught in that [Laughter] the blood. It's – what an experience, too, when the Americans were there! Because our people, even my father was among those men working for the Americans at the main island, you know, and the main island itself is called Nanumea. So they all go every morning. They would settle on their canoes. They paddle, they go in twos or threes. So in the evening they'd come back, because sundown they arrived and they stayed in Lakena. It was really an experience for us kids, you know... They have a map where to put up the airstrip, and also to blast the passage. So their passage is still in there. It's quite an asset to Nanumea for fishing. They have access to – now they have outboard engines, you know, so that they can go easily out of the lagoon in the reef... the young boys like myself, we used to have friends with the Americans, you know. And they used to give us food and things like this, the stuff they used during the war, and they have tins. Inside, biscuits and other lollies, and things like that. So when we used to come on Saturdays they used to dish out these to the kids. So they recognize that the kids are from another culture, they used to come and, you know, see them on the wharf, and then take them to their tents.

Metia was a young man at the time of the war, and was recruited to go to Funafuti and work with the main American settlement. Funafuti was bombed nine times during the Japanese bombardment. As the story is told, during one bombing, Tuvaluans fled to a church. One of the American soldiers went after them, and evacuated them into a bunker. The church was hit soon after. The workers on Funafuti were predominantly employed as cleaners for the soldiers. Metia said:

The men arrived in the office of the, in Vaitupu, so we go there, and ask him. Luckily because, he said 'Oh, we want some young men and people to go and work in Funafuti.' 'Okay, we want to go.' They write our names and they said 'That's it,' and we leave the same day, not to stay overnight there, later that day. They said to go and pack up and then you go to the shipment, the ship is not leaving until four o'clock in the evening. That one very fast one, American, they called Torpedo Boat, something like that. Yeah, very fast, I think one hour, more than one hour from Vaitupu to here... They divided the jobs for us, they covered it, people that just arrived here. Some people, they already worked here. Now when we divided it, we work for the navy and the army. The place is somewhere near the Funafuti church where we worked, and the navy and the army, they stay over there, they stay there. So I was lucky because I worked for the commander of the army... I just, house boy, something like that, just prepare his bed, clean the place, the house. Not much that's all they did, those small jobs. So I worked for the commander and the army for more than two years... the man that divided us to the jobs, he picked up those who know some English, something like that, because during those times

146

there were not much people know that. Most of the people that come here, they don't know, they don't speak English. Because they never go to school... But I think those times we don't care about cleaning but we really like, we're happy because we got the job, something to do.

Metia said they were paid by the British Colonial Government for their work with the Americans. Though they were paid in cash, he said that when the Americans left, "I have no money at all." The reason was that although there was ample wage employment while the Americans were on the islands, there were also ample foreign goods for sale. Metia said:

METIA: There are so many new things, things were very new to me and I never have seen those things before and I never had those things, so many new things... the stores in the two big houses over there, they are all occupied by the Americans stuff. That was our first time to see, oh so many things.

MICHAEL: Do you remember buying any particular thing?

METIA: Yeah, I think it was because in those times we don't have good dress or something, we don't have trousers, we don't have T-shirt or shirts or nothing... They shared so many things with us. And people there come with their handicrafts and they buy their things. And some people they like food, some people, they like clothing. Because those times were very poor, they don't have clothes and food. They don't know, the Funafuti people got their handicrafts and they sit out here and they got the money... some of my relatives, they come, 'Please can we go and buy these things' [Laughs] and I had to get the things for them. Spending money on Funafuti people... that was quite a shock to people to suddenly have all this money where there was not a lot of money before. I think they don't know how to keep the money good at those times, because the money, the food are new to them, they don't know so much... Especially they are closing things so many pretty one, long trousers and the towels, and things like that. Because it's new to us so we are very keen to [Laughs] to see those things and we like everything. So when I was finished I don't know, I have nothing, I said 'Oh where are the things I bought now, I buy many things and I don't have clothes or the towel or the trousers, I don't know' [Laughs].

MICHAEL: Oh no [Laughs]

METIA: Yeah. Very funny, neh?

Although Tuvaluans already had experience with money and with purchasing foreign goods, they had never previously participated in the market

147

economy to the extent to which they were suddenly able when the Americans were on the islands. The troops brought food, clothing, and other items that had previously been scarce or nonexistent in Tuvalu. They also brought lots of money and created employment for men working with the soldiers, and families who made handicrafts for sale to the soldiers. The market economy shift had already been occurring over the previous decades of colonization. However, during these few years, the shift increased greatly. Telavi (1983) noted World War II as the beginning of the shift away from *pulaka* as a staple crop in Tuvalu. The large amount of imported goods to the American-inhabited islands meant that the Tuvaluan population changed their dietary and market habits as well.[41] Telavi also noted that World War II "changed the world within which Tuvalu had to live... For it helped put an end to the age of colonial rule, and brought into being a world in which colonies were to be prepared for independent nationhood" (p. 145). Furthermore, a treaty of friendship was signed between the United States and Tuvalu in 1979, one year after independence.[42]

Phosphate mining on Banaba. Banaba Island in Kiribati, also known as Ocean Island, was found to have phosphate and was set up for mining by the British. Feue told me that in 1947, they began recruiting Tuvaluans to work in the phosphate mines. Many Tuvaluan men migrated, some with their wives and children, to Kiribati to work the mines. Tomu was among the children who migrated to Banaba. He received much of his primary education in Kiribati. Feue's adopted father from Nanumea also worked in the phosphate industry, "So we were all right in terms of *palagi* goods and money" while he was growing up. With so many men working in the phosphate mines, Tuvalu was shifting further toward a market economy replete with imported goods. Feue said:

> The interesting thing was that whatever goods they returned to their island, the goods were shared. Now these people who went to work where they get ration, rations in terms of corned beef, tinned fish and all these things, biscuits. Most of them kept all these things to send back to the island. And all these goods were sent to Nanumea. They were taken to the community hall, and they were shared equally between the families. Those were the days when everything was shared. To me that was the highlights of living in Tuvalu.

Nalu agreed that while the pay was low in the phosphate mines, "They were well supplied with food. Rice, corned beef, flour, sugar, biscuits." This increased the influx of money and goods into Tuvalu. As always with change, Tuvalu adapted.

---

[41] The Encyclopedia of Nations also notes that after the war, Tuvaluans began migrating for employment to the Gilbert Islands in increased numbers. Accessed on 4/30/2012 from http://www.nationsencyclopedia.com/economies/Asia-and-the-Pacific/Tuvalu-OVERVIEW-OF-ECONOMY.html.

[42] http://www.state.gov/r/pa/ei/bgn/16479.htm

Colonization, Separation, and Independence. Tuvalu came under British jurisdiction in 1877 and was formally colonized in 1915.[43] Tuvalu was grouped with the Micronesian Kiribati islands, with which they formed the Gilbert and Ellice Islands Colony. During colonialism, many Tuvaluans moved freely to Tarawa and other Gilbertese islands, because the seat of government was located there. The Gilbertese people outnumbered Tuvaluans by a wide margin. This led to privileges being afforded the Gilbertese – for example, imports went through the Gilbert islands before going to the Ellice islands, and scholarships would be offered in number according to population rather than according to achievement. Feue said:

> For all scholarships, if there is one Tuvaluan then there should be either three or five Gilbertese students to be awarded. So if you have five good Tuvaluans and there are only five scholarships, then all the other four have to be dropped. I mean there was a lot of discriminatory sort of policies. But it's understandable because we were a colony but we were still being treated as different people.

In addition, the highest position in government typically went to the Gilbertese people while those from the Ellice Islands found it difficult to be promoted. Metia said:

> The favoritism now is something. Those in higher positions, they know that the Kiribati people always come up higher position. Their people come up, climb up. But Tuvalu, Ellice people just stay where they are. So from that, then I think that our senior servants, they decided that Tuvalu should separate.

The decision to formally separate from the Gilbert Islands was a very big decision that required a lot of negotiations with the British government as well as with the colonial authorities and leaders. Feue explained:

> The British government decided to go for a referendum. But they made the conditions for referendum so stiff, so bad for the Tuvaluans that for the sensible Tuvaluans when you read it, you would not agree to go along with the option of separation. Because a clear condition was that if Tuvalu were to separate from Kiribati, then they would not receive any of the money ... that had been invested by the colony from the royalties of phosphate. Tuvalu would not receive any of this nor get any of the island groups, Phoenix and the Line islands, nor any ships apart from one ship. The only thing that Tuvalu would get would be the infrastructure that is already here on Funafuti in Tuvalu. That's one boat. No money, nothing. Despite the very difficult conditions, terms and conditions of the referendum, the Tuvaluans, they loved it. Close to 90% opted for separation. That's how serious the Tuvaluans were. And to me that was the highlight of my life, when Tuvalu decided to take their destiny in their own hands and really moved forward, come what may. Whether we drown in the sea or we survive, it doesn't matter.

---

[43] http://tuvaluislands.com/history2.htm

What matters is that we are going to make decisions on our own accord. And to me that was a major, major event in my lifetime.

The Ellice Islands separated from the Gilbert Islands in 1976, at which time they reverted back to their traditional name, Tuvalu. Tomu, who was already a politician prior to separation, said:

We are under resolve, finally, we are separate from the Kiribati. But my appreciation and thanks to the Gilbertese in those days, especially for those who are colleagues and peers, they are supporting the motion for separation. Otherwise, if we look at some other countries, when they asked for separation or independence – bloody, fighting. But to us, we separate in a peaceful way.

Almost immediately following separation from Kiribati, Tuvalu moved to become independent from England. Feue said:

But believe me, as soon as Tuvalu separated in 1976, two years, one year later, Tuvalu decided to go for independence. And political independence was achieved in 1978, even before Kiribati got their independence. And this is how serious. The good thing about Tuvalu, the Tuvaluans, is that they have this nature, this character, they have the fortitude to march on regardless of what. And they have also the fortitude to work together under adversity.

Tomu told me the story of Tuvalu's independence:

LAURA:	So I was wondering about independence. Because you were involved in negotiating independence, weren't you?
TOMU:	Yeah, yeah.
LAURA:	Yeah. Can you tell me about independence?
TOMU:	Back in the 1978, we made an agreement with the UK for our independence conference. So we went to UK the month of February 1978. And I say it's a little bit awkward to us because we went in the wrong time, it's a winter time in UK.
LAURA:	Oh-oh!
TOMU:	February. But anyway, all our members in Parliament and members of the churches, those churches that exist in Tuvalu, the Seventh Day Adventists, the LMS, I mean, Tuvalu Christian Church, those are the two main churches in those days. So we all went to UK for that conference. Luckily, the UK accepts our independence and says 'Okay, we give you Tuvaluan Islands independence… We negotiate in February and the issue of independence comes out in October the same year, you know, to prepare ourselves for independence. Oh, thanks to the UK government… they say okay, we are our people… So we still survive now. Now it's about 33 years of independence.

150

In such a young country, there are plenty of people alive who remember life as a colony. Even in modern Tuvalu, the lasting effects of colonization can clearly be seen in the islands. For example, most Tuvaluans speak English with at least a conversational fluency. A great many Tuvaluans are educated in English-language universities and work jobs in Tuvalu and abroad in English. Tuvalu uses the Australian dollar as their currency. As a Commonwealth nation, the Tuvalu still maintains the Queen of England as the head of state.

However, Tuvalu is somewhat unique among the Pacific nations that were colonized by various outside forces. Tuvaluans were never displaced from their islands (except for the temporary evacuation of the Nanumeans to Lakena during WWII). Tuvaluan language and culture was never oppressed or criminalized. All Tuvaluans speak at least one Tuvaluan dialect, though not all speak English. Tuvaluans still make up well over 90% of the population of the country (by contrast, the 2010 census states that Native Hawaiian and other Pacific Islanders make up 10.0% of Hawai'i's population).[44] While the outside influences inherent in colonization continue to be present in Tuvaluan cultures, Tuvaluan culture has been maintained strongly in the islands. Once again, we see the adaptable nature of culture in general and Tuvaluan culture in particular.

Recent development and modernization. Over the past two decades, Tuvalu has experienced an increased rate of development, bringing both benefits and challenges. In the 1990s, Tuvalu was assigned the domain assignation .tv which the government then leased out in a deal for $40 million dollars over ten years (Lerner, 2001). During that time, the government was also busy securing aid from foreign governments, including Taiwan, Japan, Australia, and New Zealand. As a result of all of these new financial sources, Tuvalu's development began to increase rapidly. Roads were paved, the hospital and Government building were built, and telephone systems and wireless internet were installed across the country. People from the outer islands increased their migration into Funafuti in search of jobs, education, and health services.

It is important to understand that Tuvaluans as individuals do not receive a direct benefit from the .tv money or much of the aid that is entering the country. Noa said, "For me as a concerned citizen, I haven't seen the benefit of .tv." That is not to say that Tuvaluans have not benefited greatly from these revenue sources. For example, during my first trip I was told that during the past two decades, the number of water catchment tanks has grown exponentially in the country, which has made it much easier for families to get by during the dry season (see Image 45). Similarly, one woman told me that until she was a teenager, Funafuti was dark at night because there were very few electric lights in the streets and other common areas. Now, people are able to go out at night and spend time with friends and family. More jobs are available as Tuvalu

---

[44] http://quickfacts.census.gov/qfd/states/15000.html

Image 45. Water catchment tanks, Funafuti (Corlew, 2010).

continues to develop. More imports are available. Tuvalu is an increasingly globalized society.

Some impacts of this development are negative. Funafuti and the other islands have an increasing problem with garbage due to the imported goods. With added expenses, life has become expensive. A more globalized Tuvalu also means that Tuvalu is interacting with outside cultures and influences at a higher rate than before. Tuvalu is adaptable, but many Tuvaluans express concern about this rate of change. While seeking better opportunities for themselves – but more importantly, for their children – Tuvaluans also begin to think about what might be left behind. Tafue said:

> So it's in every family or in every parent's dream for their kids to get education and to have a better life. Now when I grow old and I look back, and I always questioned, you know, what better life? Because the life we had was, I believe, was a better existence. Unfortunately we cannot go back now.

Tuvalu's cultural adaptations are moving inexorably forward. Despite all of this, it has been shown in the Results Section I that Tuvaluan culture is as dynamic as it is steadfast. With these adaptations, Tuvaluans do not lose their culture, but adjust to new realities. In modern Tuvalu, there are plenty of people who no longer live a subsistence way of life. And yet, many Tuvaluans still do, and many others oscillate between traditional life and modernity. Traditional knowledge is alive and active in Tuvaluan society. New knowledge is being gained. This balance is the cultural reality of modern Tuvalu. It is in this reality that climate change arose.

Chapter Summary

This chapter follows up the discussion on Tuvalu's dynamic modern cultures by exploring some of the historical drivers of change. Christianity holds an important place in Tuvaluan culture because although it signifies a major change from the spiritual and religious practices from "before," it is regarded as a major facet of Tuvalu's traditional culture. Christianity is deeply integrated in Tuvaluan ways of life. Other historical events include World War II, phosphate mining, colonization, separation from Kiribati, and independence from Britain, as well as recent modernization and development supported in part by the .tv funds and foreign aid. Tuvaluans and Tuvaluan cultures have adapted with each of these historical changes, revealing a powerful adaptability as part and parcel of Tuvalu's dynamic cultures.

Results Section II

Te fenua ola	May the island prosper
Te fenua ke maumea	May the island be rich
Te fenua ke mau ua	May the island have plenty of rain
Te fuaga o niu ke lasi	May there be many coconuts
Mea o te lau kele ke ola lelei	May the fruit of the earth prosper
Te papa ke se tutula	May the reef have many fish
Te moana ke se tutula	May the ocean have many fish
Te sau ke to tele	May the dew fall freely
Ke makalili, ke makalili	May it be cool, may it be cool

—Excerpt, Niutaoan Blessing (Koch 1961, p. 101)

Climate Change in Context

Climate change is a global event. There is no place in the world that will not eventually feel its impacts. However, certain places will be affected more than others, and certain places will be affected sooner than others. Tuvalu is projected to become uninhabitable in the next 50 to 100 years due to sea level rise (Hunter, 2002; Mimura, et al., 2007; Patel, 2006; UNFCCC, 2005). Tuvalu is not alone in this projection: the Republic of Maldives and the Republic of Seychelles in the Indian Ocean, as well as Kiribati and the Republic of the Marshall Islands in the Pacific Ocean are also projected to be subsumed by the rising sea, as will many low-lying coastal areas of non-island countries around the world (Nicholls, et al., 2007). Other impacts of climate change are affecting and will affect Tuvalu and the Pacific region, including extreme weather events, ocean acidification and coral bleaching, more droughts, less overall rain coupled with heavier rain events, crop loss, and freshwater insecurity (Marra et al., 2012). These physical impacts of climate change will alter fundamentally the way that people live by changing the environment they live in. The ways in which people respond to and are impacted by climate change will be in large part directed by regional cultural variants in expectations, beliefs, ways of knowing, and values (Swim et al., 2010). Globally, the overall impacts of climate change will vary according to human efforts to mitigate and adapt. Increased efforts will minimize the long-term impacts while failure to act could greatly exacerbate the risk. Cultural norms and expectations will influence the actions that a population is willing to take. In this way, climate change and culture have a mutual influence on each other. Therefore, on a regional or local level, the human impacts of climate change are best understood within the cultural context of regional and local societies.

In Tuvalu, the understanding of and response to climate change is as diverse as the population (Farbotko, 2012). Participants discussed climate change in the context of cultural changes, including shifts in the market economy, increasing imports and garbage, and migration for school and work, which is consistent with previous findings on the interconnections of development and climate change in Tuvalu (Dix, 2011). In Results Section I, the dynamic cultural contexts of Tuvalu were explored in great depth. In Results

Section II, the focus will be on the current impacts and future projected impacts of climate change, within the lens of human culture. In this case, culture includes the daily lives, traditional events and activities, values, and expectations of the participants. This section will report the impacts of climate change on the weather, land, and sea, as well as reports of the 2011 drought. Following will be an exploration of participants' faith in God, belief in climate change, and the role of the church in Tuvalu's response to climate change. The section will conclude with a consideration of participants' perceptions of the influence of other countries as well as what they expect for Tuvalu's future.

Chapter 6

6.1 Changes to the Natural Environment

    Tidal flooding. For Tuvaluans, traditional subsistence life is highly integrated with the land and sea and is therefore sensitive to any climate changes. Even modern life in Tuvalu will be upset by climate changes. Changes in weather and in sea level are already impacting Tuvaluan food crops. Tuvalu has always experienced some flooding at King tides. In February or March of each year, at the full and new moon, the tides are particularly high. This can cause inundation along the shore, but can also cause flooding in the interiors of the islands. Tuvaluan rock formations are permeable, and so the sea rises up through the land. During my first trip to Tuvalu I heard from many people, including the Director of the Meteorological Office, Hilia Vavae, that in some recent years the King tides have been high to the point of damaging floods, and that over the past decade Tuvalu has begun to experience King tides-like flooding every month. As the sea rises, waves of the same height will cause greater inundation. At the August 2010 and December 2011 full moons and the January 2012 new moon, I witnessed this flooding during the high tide despite the fact that none of these dates fell during King tides events (see Image 46, Image 47, and Image 48). As these high tide events get worse, food crops are

Image 46. Tidal flooding during the December 2011 full moon high tide, Funafuti (Corlew, 2011).

Image 47. Tidal flooding during the January 2012 new moon high tide in front of the Vaitupu *maneapa*, Funafuti (Corlew, 2012).

Image 48. Sea water bubbles up through the land during the January 2012 new moon high tide, Funafuti (Corlew, 2012).

affected. Pulaka pits are increasingly exposed to salt-water inundation, which is affecting not only the current crops but also future yields. Feue explained:

> On one particular island at certain times of the year – now, all islands have *pulaka* pits, *pulaka* pits are sort of where they have the swamp taro, and they have gardens. Now this island is Nanumaga. At certain times of the year, certain parts of the *pulaka* pits would be sort of inundated by sea water. And they know that. And people have to dive to harvest their *pulaka* pits, to use of them because if they leave them, they die because the sea water has got into their *pulaka* pits. So they harvest all them to eat. Now… that is becoming more frequent.

Changes to natural resources. Although King tides have always been a fact of life in Tuvalu, the growing strategies for *pulaka* and other crops has developed for infrequent flooding events. As the saltwater floods become more regular and include greater levels of inundation, these planting and harvesting methods are becoming less effective. As the land becomes more saline, there is simply less that the growers are able to do to salvage the *pulaka*. The same is true for gardens and food trees that do not tolerate saltwater very well. Traditional activities like weaving are similarly affected when pandanus trees and palms begin to die. Flower garlands, traditional personal adornments, event and holiday decorations, and other cultural items are all impacted by suffering plant life. Coastal life is seeing similar changes in the reef ecosystems and fish populations. Feue said:

> And the reality is that things are changing, changing rapidly. Now, right now there is a complaint about the seaweed, the seaweed somehow has [Laughter] taken over our lagoon side… the seaweed is toxic. If it touches your skin you'll get itchy skin. So that's new for us and that's to do again probably because of pollution, I don't know… I used to go spear diving. I used to spear dive a lot. And there was a lot of fish and there was no problem. But nowadays if you go there all these – because you tend to know after awhile, after going diving for many months, you tend to know where you get the holes, you know, for spear fishing. And there are certain holes that we normally go to but if you go there now they are filled by all these seaweed and whatever. But that may change, I don't know, whether change for the better or change for the worse, I don't know. I have no answer for that. But the only answer I can give you is that the fish population somehow is slowly decreasing and it's decreasing rather rapidly.

Changes in access to food through crops and fishing are changes Tuvaluans have been addressing for years with shifts in the market economy. These additional environmental changes associated with climate change at the very least exacerbate a problem that is already faced in Tuvalu. At most, these environmental changes could make the islands uninhabitable incrementally by slowly (perhaps over decades or centuries) depleting all natural resources. Changes in the land and sea can also affect people on a spiritual level when historical expectations for the abundance and availability of natural resources to meet basic living needs are no longer met in reality. Tafue said:

The land and the sea are not capable of providing what they used to provide for the people's sustenance daily. People have to turn to the market for food. And then there, not everyone earned regular salaries to entertain such a lifestyle. When we plant, when we go out fishing, we go with the belief that we plant and God will give us. We go out fishing with the belief, with the faith, that God will give enough for the day. What happens if you plant and you don't get anything? What happens if you go out fishing and you don't catch enough? It will put into question your belief in God's providence. So it also impacts their spirituality and their belief in God.

Sea level rise and erosion. The largest threat to Tuvalu's long-term viability as an island nation is that of sea level rise. Regardless of what people actually believe about climate change, Tuvaluans will inevitably point to sea level rise as the major indicator. During my first trip when I visited USP, Tuvalu campus, I asked a few students what they were studying and why. Several students told me they were studying in various science fields because they wanted to learn if climate change was real, if Tuvalu was really at risk of being swallowed by the rising sea, and if so, what they could do about it. During her interview, Jopeto told me,

> The sea is getting high. Because the sea level is rising. You can see it's happening. Even global warming, it's also affecting Tuvalu... But they all know that the sea level, the olden days until now you can see the difference.

During both of my trips, a number of people asked me about the recent rash of tsunami warnings, and if I thought they were a sign of climate change. Earthquakes and tsunamis are not caused by the changing climate. They are not related to weather or climate at all. However, I began to realize that in a flat, low-lying island nation, the risks of sea-level rise, King tides, and tsunamis are all interrelated risks. The only difference is the time scale. A tsunami will occur infrequently but has the potential to bring devastatingly large waves in an instant. Tidal flooding is becoming an increasingly regular event with cumulative impacts that were not seen in the past. Sea level rise associated with climate change is the slowest event of all. Many (and given the uncertainty of climate change, perhaps most?) Tuvaluans may not live to see the most devastating impacts of sea level rise: the islands being entirely submerged or becoming completely uninhabitable. In the short term, in the practical experiences of Tuvaluans' day-to-day lives, sea level rise, tidal flooding, and tsunamis fit into the same category of risk and impact. Metia spoke of the risk of sea level rise in conjunction with the tsunami warnings Tuvalu has experienced in the past few years:

> METIA: Yeah, there is a sea level there, we see nowadays. But the time, only one knows the time of climate change. Of course, those things I mentioned, they never affected Tuvalu, they just passed by. When we heard at the news that the tidal waves or something, another thing coming in. They never hit the islands in Tuvalu.

159

They just passed by and they hit somewhere over there – And there are so many, and when we hear the news, those islands are badly damaged.[45] And I was thinking why they pass by? Because they are on their way, and they just passed by and they go away. So I think that only God now knows.

MICHAEL: Right.

METIA: I think if it just comes through, it may come. But the climate changes.

Lanieta discussed sea level rise in association with the tidal flooding:

Climate change. Since I've heard this word climate change, I am here on Funafuti. It's just like a new issue that's newly discussed by people. I don't know about the outer islands, but here on Funafuti I can see there is a change. The high tides are getting very often. And every now and then, this high tide when it's high, it's very high compared to the past 10 years. It's very high.

When Jopeto went around Funafuti to take pictures for this study, there was ample evidence of tidal flooding around the island, despite the fact that it was not King tides. There was a great amount of flooding outside the Vaitupu *maneapa* (see Image 49). Jopeto said, "It's like full of water there. It's like the sea, because the sea's full. And sometimes it can fill this roadside." Jopeto also took a picture of the Funafuti lagoon (see Image 50). She said, "That's Funafuti on the lagoon side. You can see the very high tide, and almost the sea will be next time, will be very soon to be the waves. It's so tiny." She showed me images of the grassy area to the north of the airstrip (see Image 51). She said, "Before, there was the Tuvalu sports grounds, the main sports grounds. Before, the used that side for soccer and everything they want to play." Now, the area is used to access the pigsties on the ocean-side of the airstrip, seen in the background. Tidal flooding is apparent in the foreground. Jopeto also took a picture of children playing at the site of the old airport, a location that would have been built up along with the airstrip (see Image 52). She said:

Kids are playing, and they're having fun. And you can see there's still seawater. And they're still hanging out. Before it was for, before it was the airport location, and planes will stop by there and passengers go and come. That was the airport before. But now they use it for the play area. The play court.

Finally, she took pictures of the Matagali Bar (see Image 53). She said, "you can still see the seawater from the high tide. And that's the Matagali Bar." Although the flooding in these images is not very deep or disruptive, it should be remembered that this is not during King tides. In the early and mid 2000s, several King tides events flooded roads, homes, businesses, and the airstrip. The

---

[45] Tonga, Samoa, and American Samoa during the 2009 tsunami disaster, and the tsunami warning across the Pacific associated with the 2010 Chilean Earthquake.

Image 49. Tidal flooding in front of the Vaitupu *maneapa*, Funafuti (Major, 2011).

Image 50. Funafuti, lagoon side. The island is very close to sea level (Major, 2011).

fear at the time was that in every subsequent year the flooding would become increasingly worse. However, many factors influence the King tides, and the past few years have been relatively minor. This monthly flooding, however, has been persistent. Sueina told me:

SUEINA: Climate change, I only know because of the rising of the sea level. Like those places they have waters, if they have high tide, all these areas are flooded with water.

LAURA: Oh yeah, yeah.

SUEINA: But those who are staying here for a long time, they said that they can tell the rise of sea levels. They can tell from those waters. Because before they said that there is no water coming from those places. But now, if it is really high tide, it can rise up to your leg. Before, it's only down. But now. So we think maybe, how many years until the water will be up to our body [Laughs] and we'll be drowning [Laughs].

In addition to increasing rates of tidal flooding, the rising sea is also causing erosion. Tuvalu is experiencing multiple types of erosion, including massive erosion during extreme weather events, and slow, cumulative erosion eating away the shores. Kina said:

Image 51. Northern end of the airstrip where there is access by foot or motorbike to the pigsties (background at the tree line) with tidal flooding (foreground, right), Funafuti (Major, 2011).

162

Image 52. (Also Image 38) Play court and former airport location, with tidal flooding (Major, 2011).

Image 53. (Also Image 24) Matagali Bar with tidal flooding (Major, 2011).

What I noticed from my island, it's really – there's a lot of changes. Because when I was a little girl, I used to play at the seaside. Now, in regards to climate change, there are the points that really washed away some of the places there. And there're so many changes that I've seen even where the land, some of the land has gone. Maybe, because I haven't been there for so long that I can't see all parts of my island, but from the places that I used to be, I used to play at, or I used to stay with my siblings and all my friends, they're all gone. They've been washed away. [Laughter]

Jopeto also talked about land that has eroded away in only a few years. She said:

Before, we used to stay in the other house from where they are. Before, that was in 2006, 2007. I can see the stones. There are rocks and sand. You could see sand, but now it's gone. And the stones are changing and gone, and the sands were, you can't see any sand there anymore, yeah. So maybe that's destroyed by the sea. It's been destroyed by the sea.

Niutao recently experienced an extreme storm event that was accompanied by a heavy storm surge. In one fell swoop, the storm surge washed away a large piece of land, including houses and other built structures. Ken said:

Since when I was a kid in Niutao, I see the beach is very close to the sea, and now sea is coming up, take all the sand... I think that's a little bit of climate change. And also here on this island, there was change of the island.

On Funafuti, incremental erosion has led to the loss of coastal areas, including those that were overgrown with trees and plants. The roots systems were insufficient to sustain the trees. As the sea erodes the coast and salinizes the tree roots, they will be washed away. Noa said:

Climate change. I think Tuvalu is affected by climate change in a bigger way. For me, when I was growing up, some places I used to see, used to play on, are not around anymore. Where we were staying when I was a boy, I used to stay in my grandparents' house, and we had a nice view on the beach. But now, it's just, there's no beach anymore. We used to climb on, there's a tree. It's not a breadfruit tree. I don't know what it is. It's a big tree. Our land is near to the new hospital. So we used to, when there was a high tide, we used to climb on this tree and jump to the water. We kind of made a string, like in Tarzan: The Movie. Swing to the sea. But now we can't swing anymore because there are rocks, you know? No more sand. So the land is like, it's being eaten or taken away by the sea. So left with rocks.

Feue also discussed ways in which climate change is having an impact on people's land in real and sometimes disruptive ways. His parents were compelled to move their home inland because of the threat to their property near the shoreline. He himself does not have that luxury on his narrow strip of land on Funafuti, and therefore had to construct his house differently to adapt to the changing sea. Feue said:

Now, climate change, whether or not it is caused by carbon emissions or increased carbon emissions or whatever, you know it's a science in itself, but climate change to people here also means that, it's to do with the fact that maybe homes have been destroyed by sea level rise. And my parents' home on Nanumea which was, in the '70s, in the '60s, it was by the ocean side. Now we moved that inland because at one point there was a great surge in the sea and the sea water level rose up and really went across the island. So my parents decided to relocate. And they relocated inland because they are scared that – because what happened was the wave took everything, everything... And I would imagine that you have gone to the other end [of Funafuti], yeah? You will see how narrow the strip of land is, and you will see houses there. One of the houses is mine. And every time I stand by my house looking towards the ocean, toward the sea side, I have that sort of funny, feeling that [Laughter] a wave could – because I have been all during King tides. There have been waves that came ashore and went under. I build my house on poles, so a wave came under but it went under. But it won't be before long that there is proof of climate change, but there's a lot of changes happening. A lot of changes. I was staying here before I went to Fiji and it was quite noticeable that when it is low tide, it was extremely low tide. When it is high tide it was extremely high tide. And that's interesting. It was sort of new to us, many of us. Again, whether that was a part of the cycle or whether that was caused by other means, I don't know. And to me, you can learn the science, but what is more important is the reality in the realm.

Some Tuvaluans are already adapting to climate change by displacing themselves more toward the interior of their island if possible or by building their houses up to prevent flooding from invading their homes. The reality of the rising sea is that development issues that have existed in Tuvalu for some time are now exacerbated. Funafuti has always experienced flooding at King tides. Since the Americans came and dug out the borrow pits to build the airstrip, the flooding in those parts of the island became a larger issue since they are perpetually filled with sea water. Now with the rising sea level, tidal flooding spills over from the pits into nearby areas and homes, and erosion has increased. Lanieta said:

LAURA: Have you seen any impact with the ocean or sea levels?

LANIETA: Yes. Especially places down there at Lofeagai, you can see the erosion where the sands are being taken out by the sea. And you can see the roots of coconut trees are coming out, no land covering them. Especially those places. And even the level of the sea, as I said before if it is high tide, it's really high. It's really high. Even though people stay next to the *taisala* [borrow pit] the water can really come into the homes. So most people who stay close to the *taisala*, they elevate up a bit, maybe by 1 meter. That's the impact of climate change.

The flooding impacts people living or gathering on different parts of the island with different levels of flooding. During the extreme King tide events in the past, spectacular levels of flooding occurred on multiple parts of the island, along with more manageable levels of puddling and flooding across Funafuti. Noa said:

NOA: But the only time I think about climate change is when there's King tides in February. It's like the tide is very high.

MICHAEL: How high would you say the tide normally gets? I know it got especially high in 2006. What is it, like knee deep? Ankle deep?

NOA: I think it's like knee deep.

MICHAEL: Knee deep. Pretty much all over the island, yeah?

NOA: Yes. But where the Nui community gathering place is, their *maneapa* hall... The tide will rise up to the steps. But when you look at the Nui building, their community hall, it's a bit higher than the ground level. The foundation is very high. So they have to make steps. So you have to climb up to it. When there's high tide, that place is flooded over. All the younger kids are going swimming over there [Laughter]. They can paddle their canoes over there. That's how high the sea would rise.

People and the government intervene to address the flooding and the erosion. On their own land, people will sometimes build seawalls in an attempt to prevent their property from slowly being swallowed by the sea. The government has tried this as well on a larger scale. Noa said, "I don't know which year, the government came with this idea to make a seawall. [Laughter] They put up blocks of cement. But to me, it doesn't help. It's making it worse."

Weather changes. The participants also talked about recent changes in the weather. These changes included short-term weather events that were unusual (e.g., a rainstorm during the dry season) as well as changes to larger weather patterns (e.g., longer dry seasons, wetter wet seasons, etc.). Unpredictable weather events can make fishing and seafaring difficult or dangerous for this island community. For example, when Lanieta was a child, a sudden storm came upon several men who were out fishing. Their boat was struck by lightning. Two men died and another was badly burnt. Lanieta said her father was meant to be on that fishing trip. He had stayed home to care for her. This tragedy remains sharp in Nanumaga's history. Increasingly erratic weather events pose very real risks in the lives of Tuvaluans. Unpredictable weather patterns can also make growing more difficult because growers rely on knowledge of established weather patterns to decide when to plant what, when to harvest and how much, etc. Metia explained some of the changes in the daily lives of Tuvaluans that have occurred in recent times due to the changing weather patterns:

I think we noticed that past years the weather is different to what it is now, very different. Even we ask why it is different now, I think people can say that because so many things, new things now happened in the world out there. In the olden days, the weather – there are certain times you know as the bad weather time. There is a good time for the weather. In the olden days the people, they know, they really know. 'Tomorrow might be bad weather. Tomorrow or two days' ... A bad weather in the olden days, if the wind comes from this side, at the end of the year, November, December, people know [there will be] bad weather in those islands. In those island months, people know that bad weather. Never miss... And now change, very changed. Some years, they don't have bad weather, they don't have, they change now to coming in the middle of the year. Raining and strong wind, just like as I said at the end of the year, the bad weather. And now coming in the middle of the year ... But before, people knows that. Before, people prepare something to prevent a wind to their home, put like a fence. Each home, you can see it, they put the leaves[46] outside the house just to make, because they know that bad weather is during that time. And now, you don't see anything like. At the end of the year, nothing, the house is clear, just leave like that. But before, you can see. Especially those houses in the end of the island there, to prevent the wind because they know there is long storm wind during those times. That's why now people are saying the weather now is changed, not like before.

Around the beginning of 2012, I heard a lot of discussion from people about how strange the weather was. Specifically, the wind was coming from the wrong direction. In the past, wind coming from the west at that time of year signified that a bad storm was coming. During my interview with Ken, he said:

LAURA: Do you see differences in weather too?
KEN: Yes. Different years, you know, different years, the weather. Some years the weather is calm when it's beginning of the year then the next year it will be a big change, or many of warnings, you know, cyclone warnings. For now, I know there's a different, a climate change... When it's like this, the weather is something like this, it will be raining or cyclone warning.
LAURA: When it's like this?
KEN: Yeah. When it's like this.
LAURA: [Laughter] so right now we might have a cyclone.
KEN: And also the wind direction you know. It's like what I said to you before, yesterday, that it's direction of the wind coming from the southwest of the island.

---

[46] Woven mats and/or thatch

167

	Yes, the old man, I heard from the old man, he said if the direction of the wind blows from that side, that's a cyclone wind.
LAURA:	So it's coming from that side right now, yeah?
KEN:	Yeah.

My host family was planning on taking a trip to Niutao the following week. This plan had been in the works for months. When the weather started coming from the wrong direction, Tomu decided to postpone the trip. He told me one day that when the wind came from that direction, it usually meant a storm was coming, or rough seas were ahead. He didn't want to take the family on a ship for two days to go to Niutao because of the increased risk of disaster striking the boat. He told me he was especially worried about his wife not being able to swim if the boat sank, so it was best to be safe. When discussing the impacts of climate change, Nalu also brought up the winds:

NALU:	Well, in about 20 or 50 years back we haven't received any sort of climate like this, nothing. We always have, normally we have two seasons: summer and winter. We have only the wet season. That's the time when we get rain. See now, the wind must be there in the west...Why?
MICHAEL:	So the wind has changed directions?
NALU:	Yes. Why? ... Like in the past throughout the year, winter starting from October, November, December, Jan, Feb, March, and end of is a cyclone. And it's coming from the west.

Jopeto took a picture of the trees blowing against the sky (see Image 54). She said, "I just want to show, because the trees and the weather. We were having bad weather that day. And it's like the changing of the climate, and of course, it's windy." The day before my flight, which was also the day before the ship to Niutao was scheduled to leave, all boats were docked at the wharf due to rough seas. The wrong winds had forecast rough seas and inclement weather, just as many Tuvaluans had predicted to me. Tomu had cancelled the family trip more than a week before the boats were docked.

Historic extreme events. In addition to changes in weather patterns and inclement weather events, climate change is expected to cause an increasing frequency of extreme weather events that can cause not only dangerous ocean conditions, but also dangerous conditions on land with damaging winds and storm surges. Past extreme events give an indication of the level of destruction that could be left in the wake of future extreme events associated with climate change, as well as Tuvalu's capacity to absorb and respond to disasters. For example, the Tuvaluan government, Meteorological Office, and trade sectors are able to respond effectively to strong wind warnings, as was evidenced by their response at the end of my second visit. Lanieta explained that "They just announced this strong wind warning forecasting for the Tuvalu group and yeah, just the people to be careful not to go out fishing." Ships at the wharf were docked, and Tuvaluans with small family-owned boats received warnings not to

Image 54. (Also Image 29) Palm trees on a bad weather day (Major, 2011).

go out because of the increased risk. The capacity to issue these warnings is sufficient. Other extreme events may exceed Tuvalu's capacity to prevent loss of life and property simply because the event is so highly damaging that even a forewarning would not be sufficient protection. Regarding the storm surge that wiped away a large chunk of land on Niutao, Ken told me:

LAURA: What are some changes that you've seen?
KEN: Especially the trees. The lands, some of the houses, the old houses, they were swept away. The old houses were just gone after, there was a tsunami. Not a tsunami – there was a wave washed through a few years ago. It smashed all the houses close to the shore.
LAURA: Oh Gosh! Was it a storm or a tsunami, with an earthquake?
KEN: No, I don't know, I'm not sure, not an earthquake. Like, just wave come and swallow the houses.
LAURA: How many families were affected?
KEN: No person dead. Only few persons were injured. That was in '93, I think. It was a big wave, but not a tsunami. It come and affect all the way down. It was a big difference to Niutao, because all the houses were arranged, were being fixed. But you know on Niutao, that was a big, big difference on Niutao.

169

Alefaio told me the story of the famine on Niulakita that was caused "when a boy fell in love with a married woman. The beach had no sand, only rocks. There were no birds, no turtles" (Corlew field notes, 2012). In addition to showing the literal interpretation of Christianity (i.e., the famine was caused by God in punishment for the affair), this story also demonstrates the powerful interconnection of the ecosystems on the islands. When the sand was gone from the beach, so too did the birds and the turtles disappear. If an extreme event damages one aspect of the ecosystem, others are affected, sometimes in environmentally devastating ways. Extreme events are therefore of particular concern to Tuvaluans. Sea level rise may slowly become devastating over a century, but extreme weather events could wreak havoc long before then. In responding to disaster events, communities rely on established cultural structures and activities to cope, as well as the responsive development of new support systems, as needed (Brokopp Binder, 2012). Tuvalu's experiences coping with disaster events can therefore reveal potential future avenues for climate change response.

Tsunami warning 2010. As previously discussed, tsunamis are not related to climate change. Tectonic plates shift to cause earthquakes within a geological system that is unrelated to weather and climate.[47] When an earthquake occurs near or under an ocean body, the quick displacement of water caused by the rapidly moving earth can cause tsunami waves.[48] When tsunamis reach land, they can create extremely large and devastating floods as occurred in Japan in 2011 (Taylor, 2011), in Tonga, Samoa, and American Samoa in 2009 (Perry, 2009a), and in many Indian Ocean nations in 2004 (e.g., Soeriaatmadja & Ghosh, 2005). Tsunamis may also come ashore as very small waves that are not damaging and are perhaps hardly noticeable as was the case in Hawai'i in 2009 with the Samoa earthquake and tsunami (Perry, 2009b). Tsunamis may cause only minor flooding and shoreline damages, as occurred in Hawai'i in 2011 with the Japanese earthquake and tsunami (Song, 2011). However, because the waves in the open ocean are small, it is difficult to predict under most circumstances how they will manifest once they reach various coasts. As previously discussed, the threat of these waves is interrelated with the threat of King tides flooding and sea level rise in the practical experiences of Tuvaluans. When a tsunami-generating earthquake occurs in the Pacific, the low-lying Tuvaluan islands are at great risk. Lanieta recounted her recent experiences:

> LANIETA: Even we, in the year 2010 we had a quite a number of tsunami warnings. Two or three, which is, we rarely have had that in the past. But in the year 2010 and there one in 2011, early 2011, in January. And after that we had no more tsunami warnings. But it's quite

---

[47] For more information on the causes of earthquakes, visit http://pubs.usgs.gov/gip/dynamic/dynamic.html.

[48] For more information on the causes of tsunamis, visit http://www.tsunami.noaa.gov/.

	scary when it comes, the tsunami warning. You can see the parents running here and there looking for their children. They run to school and get their children. Here you are not allowed to ride a motorbike, three people on the motorbike. Believe me, in those times when they had the tsunami warnings, they are mother and two in front and one at back children. They get their children from school. And the people are running here into this tall building which is an office.
LAURA:	Oh yeah, the Government building? What other places did people go during tsunami warning?
LANIETA:	Me and my family?
LAURA:	Yeah, or other people, where did people go?
LANIETA:	Yeah, yes, they come into this wider land because at the end, at the two ends, is a very narrow. So, have you been out to the end?
LAURA:	Yes.
LANIETA:	Yes, it's very, very narrow. Just the road.

In the wider expanse of Funafuti where the Government building is located, there is a marginally higher level of protection from flooding than in the narrow expanse of the atoll which is only fifteen or twenty feet across at certain points. However, a large tsunami wave could potentially flood the entire country, as close to sea level as it is. Fortunately, the recent tsunamis have not been damaging to Tuvaluan shores. Regardless, the threat of tsunamis remains connected to other natural threats, including those related to climate change. Metia says:

MICHAEL:	Do you have any thoughts on climate change, any thoughts or opinions on climate change?
MATIA:	So far, I think every people now, they know or they realized that climate change is there, that there is climate change nowadays. Because before, they never see anything like this. But now when so many news are going around and they see that they might come through something like—In Tuvalu, I think few years past, a few things like Bebe in 1972.
MICHAEL:	Oh yeah, Hurricane Bebe.
MATIA:	Bebe, yeah. And a tsunami. So many things passing by. I think we heard the news about those things many, I mean in years past now, tidal waves coming up, something about the sea level that's coming up.

Hurricanes Bebe and Ofa. In 1972, Funafuti was hit by Hurricane Bebe, which left enormous damage in its wake. Lanieta said, "Funafuti was the main place that got struck by Hurricane Bebe in 1972. The outer islands, I think, were okay. They were all okay except for Funafuti." The storm surge that occurred with Bebe was absolutely massive, exceeding 3 meters (Richmond &

Morton, 2007). Of "the big wave that hit Funafuti" during Hurricane Bebe, Jopeto had heard growing up that "only a few people died and the rest they are still here. Some of them they know went missing at that time." Noa, who is from Funafuti, also grew up hearing the stories:

NOA: My grandmother used to tell me the stories when the hurricane struck. They stayed at home at that time but the wind was getting strong. So my grandfather told them they have to move to the primary school classroom. So they went there. And it was getting darker. And the classroom's roof went off. [Laughter] So my grandfather told me 'We have to make a run for the Funafuti council house.' It is that building next to the Funafuti primary school building. So they made a run for it and they stayed there, and some other families. My mother was about nine years old at the time. Her younger sister was about six or seven years old. So while they were staying there, the water was rising. Up to their chest, I think. So they had to put up cement bags to put the children on. They stayed in the water but the children and the older ladies. So they stay there until morning. They thought they were the only people alive at that time … another thing my grandmother told me, lighting and thunder. Just like, on the ground. When they on their torch, they can't see further. The torch just stays right here [Motions a foot way]. The clouds blocking them.

MICHAEL: So with the flashlight they couldn't see father than just a foot or so.

NOA: But they can't sit still inside the building. They were rocking because of the wind. They can't hear. When they are talking to one another they can't hear a word. You need to get closer to the ear. But all they hear is like someone is whistling [Whistles] like that [Laughs]. That is the sound of the wind. When the daylight comes, none of the trees are around. They all fell down. They said there was a huge wave at that time. I don't know, I was not there.

Metia was not on Funafuti at the time of the hurricane, but he did arrive soon after. The island was devastated. He said:

MATIA: I think 1972, on my way to Fiji, direct from Kiribati to here. So that's the time, 1972, I saw the islands. Very different. I mean, you can see from here to the ocean side, very clear because there's no smoke or just no bushes and everything—

MICHAEL: Everything's flat?

172

MATIA:	– clear but – yeah.
MICHAEL:	No houses, no trees?
MATIA:	Only the trees, there were some trees there, but it's very, you can see clearly from the ocean, the lagoon side to the ocean side.
MICHAEL:	Wow.
MATIA:	Very good.
MICHAEL:	How were people dealing with it when you saw them?
MATIA:	Well, I think – because most of them they went to stay in Funafala[49] and the other islets. I think the only problem is because they don't have any planting or gardens, or something like that. The trees were okay but the gardens or things like that, nothing. So I think they were in a hard situation living here. It was very hard to move, to get things. No store, only fishes, I think they eat fish and the nut – coconut or something like that.

Many homes and other buildings were heavily damaged or destroyed, as were food crops and other natural resources. In many ways, Hurricane Bebe is an example of a worst-case disaster scenario in Tuvalu because the storm hit the most populous area of the country directly, bringing high winds and heavy rains and a massive storm surge wave. Nalu was working in Kiribati at the time, but when word came in about Bebe, he was able to return the next day because he was staying on one of the small colonial ships sent for aid. He said:

NALU:	The Japanese people, oh, very sad. And also the Funafuti people, because all the houses have been blown off by the hurricane. And they put up empty drums, metal drums, put the timbers, put the hook and they were staying under that.
MICHAEL:	Really?
NALU:	Yeah... that's where they slept at. And the plane came from New Zealand to deliver, the food, the medicines, and tents. And one Indian observer in the nets, died, who is an Indian and married to a Tuvaluan lady. And one Tuvaluan passed away also, lost. And one baby. So the parent lost holding the baby and, because the waves came from the east. There were three big waves. I didn't see them, but I got this when I came and I talked to them and they told me that. They are – the field was flooded with trunks of coconut trees. Those trees were blown up

---

[49] One of the larger islets in the southern end of the Funafuti atoll.

by the hurricane. So when the water is emptied, they take off the coconut trunks so that the plane can land... So in about two weeks after, then those 2 bodies were found... they found them because there was a smell and they found the Indian and the Tuvaluan, it was a Funafuti person, both they were wrapped in the nets... Only those people 2, and one young lady, so the baby was, the body has been blown away and the father holding one hand. Because of the wave, big waves, three waves.

MICHAEL: Three big waves came with...

NALU: About 10 meters high.

LAURA: Oh!

MICHAEL: 10 meters high?

NALU: Yeah. But now you haven't seen, what, a seawall. During those three waves there was a big seawall from the end up to the other end of the island, all the stones heap up.

MICHAEL: It was created by those waves?

NALU: It looks like some machines have been involved.

That coral seawall that was deposited by the hurricane's storm surge remains on the ocean side of the island, and is in fact among the highest land in Funafuti (Fitchett, 1987). Other people I talked to about Hurricane Bebe also told stories of waves splashing as high as the tops of coconut palm trees. The flooding of Funafuti by the powerful ocean waves was massive and devastating. In 1990, Hurricane Ofa hit Vaitupu. The cyclone was not as destructive as 1972's Hurricane Bebe in Funafuti, but caused extensive damage nonetheless. Lanieta recounted the story:

LANIETA: But we have other strong winds in '90. The most destructive one on Vaitupu, Cyclone Ofa. It was quite destructive. The whole settlement went down, the thatched housed. One side of the settlement – all cleared in the next morning. All the houses are down. But nobody died.

LAURA: Oh that's great.

LANIETA: That was in February '90.

LAURA: Were you at school over there then?

LANIETA: I was in school then in Vaitupu. And we had our chapel roof blown off, two of the classrooms went off, the staffroom down, that's in the campus. But on the island in Vaitupu, one side of the whole of the main settlement, the whole side, all down. It was quite a destructive one. But we were lucky. Nobody died.

174

6.2 Changes to People's Lives

Drought of 2011. In October, 2011, Tuvalu declared a state of emergency when a drought that had stretched over six months finally depleted water to critically low levels (Benns, 2011; Whiteman, 2011). Aid in the form of desalination tanks and bottled water were shipped in from Australia and New Zealand to alleviate the crisis (Beckford, 2011; see Image 55, Image 56, Image 57, and Image 58). As the drought stretched on, plants began to die, as captured by the photography of Stephen Boland (see Image 59, Image 60, Image 61, Image 62, and Image 63). People suffered, including suspected cases of cholera (Tzeng & Wu, 2011). The drought greatly affected both the land and the community. One woman I chatted with in the community told me, "If I didn't believe in climate change before, I believed after the drought" (Corlew field notes, 2011).

Droughts are not new to Tuvalu, although a drought of this magnitude has not occurred in living memory. Nalu said:

> There was a little bit of change, especially the droughts... never happened like this in the past, you know. The droughts took only about 1 month or 1 month and 2 weeks, rain starts. But now it takes too long and I don't know why.

Droughts are expected to increase in much of the Pacific associated with the changing wind and weather patterns projected from climate change (Anthony,

Image 55. Tuvaluans gather to watch the arrival of foreign aid, Funafuti (Boland, 2011).

175

Image 56. Desalination unit at the Funafuti Lagoon (Boland, 2011).

Image 57. Pumping freshwater for distribution, Funafuti (Boland, 2011).

Image 58. Freshwater rations are distributed, Funafuti (Boland, 2011).

Izuka, & Keener, 2012; Finucane, 2010). Freshwater availability and vulnerability to climate change is a far-reaching problem that affects every sector (World Climate Programme – Water, 2006). The drought caused much of the land on Funafuti to dry out, killing the plant life. Even after nearly two months of regular rain, during my trip, the husks of dried, dead trees remained as a reminder of the recent extended lack of rainfall (see Image 64). Lanieta described the impacts of the drought on the island, particularly on the food crops and trees:

> We can see that the trees are still brown and no leaves yet. But if we were to have another drought in the next few months, then they won't be able to recover soon. They will wait for another year or so to get them fully. So those are the impacts of having droughts, especially when we have a very, very long drought when all the trees are dying out.

Recovery becomes more difficult when multiple droughts happen in a short period of time. Much of the Pacific is already experiencing less overall rainfall, including enhanced times of drought (Marra, et al., 2012). As with other weather

177

Image 59. The Funafuti sports field became a dry, dusty space (Boland, 2011).

Image 60. Tuvaluans line up for water rations amidst yellowing grass and palm trees (Boland, 2011).

Image 61. Dying banana trees, Funafuti (Boland, 2011).

and environmental impacts, drought is highly interconnected with cultural changes that have occurred in recent decades. The use and stewardship of the land is different than it was, for example, at the time of the 1963 drought when many families were reportedly able to enact their roles in the *pologa* system to protect the *pulaka*, coconut palms, and breadfruit trees, etc. Alamai also explained there has been a decline in sustainable water usage in the recent past. She said:

> I was on Vaitupu. Sometimes we go to the village, then the main road will be flooded. But now it's hardly happening. But because it depends too on how you make the road, how they make the land on the side, put some more sand and soil and stones... I can see that in the school we used to have our well, one well, where the school is. You use it for the bathing, washing. That was then with 200 students. But now it's 500 students and they have big [catchment] tanks. It is the way they used, to what is not proper use. Like for us with the rain water, we can only collect just in a cup to drink. But now they can pressure, and use it anyhow. So misuse of water, so they run out of water... Partly it's the people. It's the behavior of the people.

When the 2011 drought hit, and then continued for so long, everyone in Tuvalu was affected. Jopeto said, "in Funafuti, there's a drought that's happening here, just a few months ago, and it's like suffering all the people of Tuvalu. And the weather is changing, you know what I mean, the weather is changing."

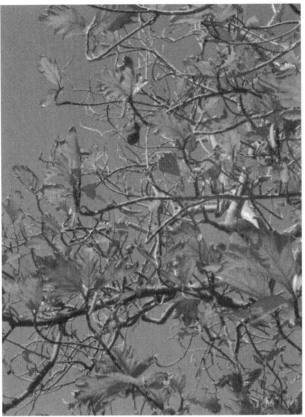

Image 62. Stephen Boland captioned this picture "Stunted breadfruit" (Boland, 2011).

The drought in 2011 extended to the point that everyone had to ration their water. This included water that may remain in their rain catchment tanks, brackish well water, and water distributed from the desalination tanks. When the foreign aid came in, families were rationed two buckets of water per household per day, regardless of the number of people in the home (see Image 65). I was told that special exceptions were made of families that had babies, pregnant women, or elderly adults living in the home. They received an extra bucket. However, Kina explained, there was no exception made of other vulnerable populations, such as people with disabilities. They instead relied on water from the other sources. Kina said:

> This office, this place, we were surrounded by those people who have wells, underground water. There were five around. So with all these five, I tasted them all, it's all the same. They're all taste salty. Because I went around looking for a place that we can use for toilet if people with disability are here. And then that's why I went around to taste this water and they were like, it's all the same here. And what else, you just

use the first available when the volunteers went, this water is salty, it's poor. Get the water from there. We can't wait to go to the other place because if we saw there are so many people staying and lining up there, with their buckets. So the first well that we went and we see that no one is around or we see that there's less people there, we get water from there. You can see during the drought people are just walking outside with their handcart full of buckets. You know, it was so sad. I don't think if you are here you are happy too. Oh, it might be an unforgotten memory.

Tuvaluans had to be strict with their water usage during the drought. Many Tuvaluans bathed in the sea or with the brackish well water rather than using precious freshwater rations for something other than food or drinking. Tuvalu's guest culture became apparent in two major ways. First, within an extended family, people worked hard to take care of the needs of others. Noa talked about his own experience:

NOA: To me during the drought my family were doing okay. We managed to budget our water. And make use of the available water reserves that the government was distributing to each house. What I

Image 63. Trees dying from lack of rain, Funafuti (Boland, 2011).

181

have seen is the temperatures, here in Tuvalu, it is very hot. Even some of the trees dying. Breadfruits and our local garden – *pulaka* pits. We are suffering from water, but the sea is very rising at that time. It is very high, the sea. I think here in Funafuti I can see the any effects, you can feel the drought is on, but no one will suffer from it. I managed to dig a well at the time, just to have the family, so we used the well. Fresh water, but not that fresh. It is a bit salty, but we don't use it for drinking, just our baths and to wash our clothes. We leave our main water cisterns for drinking and making our food.

MICHAEL: So the government ration was two buckets per family, per day. And your family has four people, no five people living at home.

NOA: At that time we had a distance family, they stay in Nukufetau, but they came here because the mother is my mother's cousin. So her daughter is pregnant, so they came here to Funafuti to deliver him in a hospital. So lots of us at the house: me, my son, my

Image 64. Dead and recovering trees, months after the 2011 drought (Corlew, 2012).

182

Image 65. Man with two buckets of water, Funafuti (Boland, 2011).

	wife, my wife's mother, her three brothers, and the people from Nukufetau came. And one of my wife's uncles staying with us at the time. It was twelve of us in the house.
MICHAEL:	So two buckets of water for twelve people, huh?
NOA:	It doesn't make sense. [Laughs]
MICHAEL:	And these are, how big are these buckets, five, ten gallons – liters?
NOA:	Maybe four gallons.

With so many family members staying together and relying on such a small amount of water, each must be careful in their water usage not only for their own welfare, but for the welfare of their family. However, these efforts to conserve and to share water were not necessarily confined to each family. The second way in which Tuvalu's guest culture manifested during the drought was the sharing that occurred from families that had more catchment tanks and therefore greater amounts of stored water to neighboring families with fewer catchment tanks. Kokea told me his experience:

We have three tanks at the back there. All the same sizes here, three water tanks. At my home I have a cistern in there, and only my daughter and her husband and their son [Laughter] ... So, when the drought was on, we were all right. Some people there too were using our – I remember my daughter was still, you know, 'Give them water, allow them to get their buckets here'... We were doing all right. Well, we take precautions, you know, in having our shower and all that. Because we have a shower, but we – because we can always rely [Laughter] on our water cistern in there... I told my daughter and her husband to stay over here, but then the drought it sort of subsided. I was going to ask the engineering carpenter whether they could provide me with another tank. If they are going to send them to households, we're gonna buy another one... But there were some families, I pity them. My daughter has to ask some of them from nearby, up the road, I remember some of those people. They have to use the water sparingly, you know... I can always come myself to supply for those who have enough water catchment to be supplied from. Not for our own sake but for the sake of those who didn't have enough during that time. So that I can have another two tanks and everybody in nearby houses can have water from here.

The increasing number of water catchment tanks on the islands through foreign aid has been of great benefit to Tuvaluan during the dry seasons in the past decade. In the recent past, a majority of houses in Funafuti had only one catchment tank, regardless of the number of people staying there. With the recent influx of aid, many households now have three to five tanks, although others still have only one or two. Unfortunately, in order to prepare for an extreme dry spell like the 2011 drought, much more water storage will be necessary. Vete has his background in civil engineering, and was able to explain:

The drought is one of our worst in history... there's been an increase in storage capacities here. Without those, oh it will be worse. But even now, this one tank per household will never solve problems. Because on water consumption, the more tanks you have the more water you're going to use. It's like looking at how much liters in America, the wealthiest person now in America is going 2,000 liters a day for flower, for gardening, for washing the house, for the mansion, the cars, the thing, the parking, everything. In Tuvalu, we still limited to 50 liters per head per day... And in terms of water, you'll never be sufficient unless you reach the highest capacity of storage you can. But water consumption will never be sufficient to Tuvalu. This is only good now for rainy days. When the drought comes for 3 months, no rainwater, the tank won't last. And it won't solve problems. And when I did my thesis, I calculated that absolute minimum storage for any Funafuti house is 10,000 gallons, 10,000 gallons for this size of house.[50] For people to enjoy life without any problems, I did the simulation, you must have a capacity of storage 10,000 gallons... With these new things, typically it's about 2,000 gallons, the average. Per house. It won't be sufficient. It won't. Because water determines your lifestyle. Water is a key to your lifestyle needs. If you have a lot of water, you change your life and then more family comes in, and they look at you how you bath three times a day, they will bath three times a day... even if you reach the 10,000 gallons, you still have to learn about water conservation... Everybody must learn how to conserve water. Because there's always dry period.

Jopeto took pictures of catchment tanks to demonstrate Tuvalu's need for these tanks and the fact that many households do not have enough water storage capacity (see Image 66). Jopeto said:

I just want to take this picture because it tells us that Tuvalu is using water tanks for water. Without these things, we suffer from getting water and we fill the tanks. It's like, they have to get more than three or more than four tanks so that if rain falls, the water can go inside... Those people that suffered much, it was because they don't have many tanks. They only have like two. Like that house, that's my house. And in the time of drought, we only have one tank half, still half. We really had to manage our water wisely. Yeah. But three to four tanks isn't enough for when it's raining time. When it's bad weather and when it's raining. It isn't enough. It should be more than five, because if it's drought, then there's a lot of water.

Every single person I spoke to about the drought in recorded interviews and casual conversations said that Tuvaluans suffered a lot during the drought, though they themselves were okay. Everyone admitted that they had to restrict their water usage and that they had to sacrifice comforts. People spoke of having to change their hygiene activities, such as bathing in the ocean instead of showering, or not being able to wash their clothes as often, or an inability to change out of sweaty clothes multiple times throughout the hot, sunny, drought-stricken, equatorial days. But although everyone made these and more sacrifices, they also explained that they and their families were fine. Other families, however, had truly suffered. Ken told me that their family was okay because "they've got three water tanks, so we use what we have. That one for drinks, cooking." Kou talked a bit more about her family's welfare versus that of other people who were really suffering:

Oh, it was really, really bad. I feel sorry for some people. They're always going to swim in the sea, because they don't have any water. But that happened, those people didn't have any water for drinking. They had sickness too during the drought. There's a lot of sickness

---

[50] Referring to Tomu's house where the interview took place.

Image 66. Rainwater catchment tanks at a Funafuti house (Major, 2011).

during that time, I think because of the sun, yeah? But for us it was good because we have three tanks here... They are full that time. This one, because we only use it for, we bathe with this, from this tank here. Those two, they kept it for us for our drink, for us to cook our food. But especially, we also go to the sea, come back. We have one bucket each. One bucket, we have two people. It was so bad.

Connected with the collectivist and guest cultural norms in Tuvalu, many people perceived the sacrifices they themselves had to make during the drought as reasonable accommodations to make sure that others also have access to water. Their perception of the suffering of others who were making similar sacrifices is connected with a strong desire to provide for the wellbeing of family, friends, and neighbors. Kokea discussed how he "pitied" some of his neighbors with fewer catchment tanks, and wished for more tanks to make sure he could provide better for others during the next drought. Jopeto also showed concern for those who had fewer catchment tanks than her family had access too. Even though she had to be very strict with her water usage, she felt she was more fortunate than those who had to make do with less. Lanieta described some of the accommodations that Tuvaluans made by using brackish well water and sea water for activities that were normally conducted with freshwater:

But during the drought we were into an extent where people bath from the well water. Like the ground water, we dig the well, and get the water from it, ground water. People use that water for washing the dishes and they bath from there, most families... it's a little salty. And

186

we'd also been warned by the Director of Health not to use that for bathing. It's not good for the skin because it is quite contaminated, but we have no choice. The people still use that water. But I think we were also lucky because we were just distributed with this green tank. If not, without that, I don't know, I don't know where we were during August or June.

Kina discussed her role in searching for water for people with disabilities, as well as advocating for a rationing exception for households that included people with disabilities. She said:

During the drought, it's so sad. You know, I was so sad when people with disabilities were left out by the committee, and that was really, really bad. At the beginning of the drought we still have water so I don't think that I can complain of that, because I can still provide them with water, and I can always bring them here. Some of them they just came in, wanting to use the shower. Yes, we helped them with that… I found out later that people with disabilities haven't had a shower. Some of them they came here and I don't have water as well, and he said 'I don't have water. I didn't have my shower from the last two days.' You know, from saying that, and I always have my shower daily, like twice a day, and I was so sad. And I said 'why?' Because they have only two buckets of water a day. That's their ration. And that's when I realized that I should stand for them and I should go and ask for them at the committee. So I decided to go around asking everybody, asking Tuvalu Red Cross… I felt so bad and I just wanted to push this through and then I started to email this committee. And I emailed them and they still give us – you know, some of them they supported, and some of them didn't. And at the end, I was happy again because at the end they – they managed to – but it won't cover all people with disabilities but at least some people with disabilities they have access to water… All people are vulnerable because if I compare myself and a person with disability, if there is no water, I can go around and look for water and this person is so suffer, because there is no water. [Laughter] No water, there will be big problems – I'll tell you.

Lanieta told the story of when the drought finally came to an end:

The past drought was severe, yes. Most people are getting worried, especially families with babies and bedridden sick. But the Lord was so good to us, he never comes late to rescue us. The first rain was in October 19, during the drought. And the rain was so soft, it just rained, no wind. It just rained, heavy rain but you know, it's really soft. And it was streaming down, like filling our tanks and our cistern. It was so good. It rained for about 2 hours from 4:00 until 6, and that morning, like, 4:00 in the morning when the rain starts, all the homes on Funafuti they put on their lights. [Laughter] No one slept during that time. Everybody outside catching every rain drops. We were so blessed with the rain. And then the rain continues afterwards. After that October 19th and then the rain continues, but it was forecasted the drought will

187

continue throughout the holidays into Jan and Feb 2012. But that was not the case, as we know. When it started raining on 19 October, the rain starts coming every week until now, until Jan. So we are blessed.

Climate change impacts on people. The thesis of this paper is that climate change is unambiguously intertwined with the lives of people. The actions that humans have taken and the decisions they have made over the past two and a half centuries have led to the current state of the climate, and continue to alter multiple interconnected weather and environmental systems. Furthermore, as is the case in Tuvalu, these climate changes are fundamentally altering the lives of people in both direct (e.g., surviving extreme events) and indirect (e.g., reduced crops translating to heavier reliance on imports) ways. There remains a high level of scientific uncertainty in the projections of climate change impacts, which affects the public perception of the reality of climate change and the best modes of response (Weber & Stern, 2011). Most of the uncertainty in the projections stems from the human unknowns – what will we as a global population choose to do to address climate change? Even in local communities, the commitment to mitigation and adaptation actions depends as much on the current physical impacts of climate change as it does on the public perceptions that people *should* do something about it, and that they *can* do something about it. Regarding the human-climate change interface in Tuvalu, Alamai explained:

> About climate change. We can see a lot of things have been changed because of climate change, but not necessarily climate change. It's the people. It's the choice of the people making changes to their lifestyle. Because if we can say that climate change has an effect on our lives, if it's so much change, then definitely we won't be having this breadfruit, no more coconut, no more fish. But it's not. You still have those. Maybe that's an advantage, because now we can see we have droughts. We have droughts a way back. But not really frequent. Here we have, I can say it's not really drought. It's drought in a way because there are too many people, you know? There are too many people and not enough supply of water. Because the catchment is limited. But the plants being affected, yes, it is because of climate change. But we still have them, it doesn't really mean that when we have a drought everything would just be gone, but it's essential of the people, it's the people themselves.

Climate change is impacting the people of Tuvalu, and thereby affecting their perceptions of climate change.

Lives affected. Due to the unique vulnerabilities of atoll nations in the Pacific Ocean to climate change (Marra, et al., 2012), the lives of Tuvaluans are already being affected by climate changes. The necessity for adaptations such as moving inland or building raised houses has been steadily increasing as the shores have begun to erode and tidal flooding has increased in frequency and severity. During the 2011 drought, nearly every aspect of Tuvaluans' daily lives were affected by the need for strict water rationing, and the longer term drought impacts on crops and other natural resources continues to be seen and felt. Feue explained:

> I have reasons to believe that there is an increased level of these activities [climate changes] happening. I don't know why, because the sciences are not agreeable on this, whether that is caused by manmade carbon emissions or whether caused by other means – it doesn't matter. What matters is that people's lives are being affected by all this.

As mentioned before, the traditional subsistence lifestyle includes a high level of knowledge and understanding about weather patterns and characteristics of the land and sea. As the patterns begin to break down and seasonal uncertainties increase, this traditional knowledge may no longer be as effective. For example, decisions about when to plant and when to harvest based on decades of experience navigating seasonal changes may be more difficult to make in the face of increasingly unpredictable weather. Even more modern activities are impacted by the effects of climate change. For example, during the 2011 drought, some program events were cancelled because so much time, effort, and resources had to be redirected to address the water needs of the community. Kina explained:

> We planned that we will sustain – maintain this. But because there are so many things around, like the drought just came in and what else. And that's all, these things, these natural disasters came out and they really stop us from our programs. That we didn't plan for.

Although Lanieta said that she did not believe that anyone had yet migrated from Tuvalu because of climate change, Ken stated his belief that the threats of climate change are already influencing people's decisions to go overseas. He said:

> The change from before, it's a bit of change here because some of the people migrate to overseas. So Tuvaluans go to New Zealand, Australia. And so nowadays the people are changing. People are looking for their future, especially for the climate change.

He explained that, as of now, he did not believe that the migration decisions were being made solely on the basis of climate change, but were rather multifaceted decisions including plans for studies, jobs, and future opportunities, with climate change contributing to the consideration. Some Tuvaluans may already be more likely to pursue opportunities overseas based on future projections of climate change.

Loss of property and resources. As previously discussed, some Tuvaluans have lost property due to incremental but steady shoreline erosion as well as from major storm surge or tidal events that washed away large sections of land in a very short amount of time. Previous disaster events like Hurricane Bebe in Funafuti and Hurricane Ofa in Vaitupu give an indication of the possibilities of property damage and loss should major storm events become increasingly common due to climate change. The impacts of these storms on built structures were immense and indiscriminate. Similarly, the 2011 drought caused massive damage to the environment and natural resources including crops and food trees, as well as the most immediately necessary resource to sustain life: freshwater. The damage to these resources constitutes another form of loss that directly impacts people's lives and livelihoods.

Tuvaluans have cultural norms that can help mitigate these human impacts. This is another case in which the cultural values and expectations of different localities will determine the extent of the impact of climate change. For example, Tuvalu is very strong with their guest culture and with care for extended family. When the storm surge wiped away homes in Niutao, affected families were not left without a place to stay. Homelessness is not an issue in Tuvalu because there are always family members, neighbors, or even strangers willing to take people in. Someone who is without a place to stay, especially someone without family, will be pitied and adopted into a family to be cared for. This is the way Teba acquired family on the outer islands. This is the way I acquired family in Niutao. In addition, family, friends, and neighbors will come together to assist with rebuilding. After Hurricane Ofa, people whose homes were destroyed received money from the government to help rebuild their homes. Alamai said, "So building their houses then, the community will help. They assist them. It's really good." Noa told us with pride that during the last tsunami warning, the Funafuti youth group organized to travel across the island in the middle of the night to wake up people and warn them that waves could be arriving at dawn. Alamai said that these youth groups also play a role in the reconstruction after a disaster. She said:

> They take turns to go and do the work. That's one way of being helpful.
> And in disaster times, especially cyclones probably, the youth people,
> the youth groups on the islands, they go around the islands for whoever
> needs the trees to cut down, or if somebody needs the needs the house
> to be rebuilt.

The same role that these groups play in the course of everyday life, they will play during and after disasters. Just as the Talafai, the Nanumaga youth group on Funafuti, built the church and the preschool, so too will youth groups and other community members come together to provide reconstruction services in the wake of a disaster. This cultural norm is a strength to Tuvaluan communities threatened by the impacts of climate change.

Ambient stress. In places where there is particularly high vulnerability to climate change, such as low-lying Tuvalu, ambient stress can affect the long term mental and emotional wellbeing of the population (Swim, et al., 2010). This is also common to communities at or near the site of toxic environments (Baum, 1987; Levine, 1982). Ambient stress stems from the understanding that even if nothing bad is happening now, a disaster could strike anytime or things could become incrementally worse as time passes. In the case of people living near toxic environments, ambient stress includes fear of acute and chronic symptoms or illnesses, cancers developing decades later, or the imminent possibility of toxic disasters. In places that are greatly threatened by climate change, ambient stress may include fears for future generations, fears of imminent disaster, uncertainty about opportunities for action, mitigation, and adaptation, feelings of powerlessness to prevent impacts or to compel powerful nations to act, and the cumulative impact of living for a long period of time (decades or more) with these stresses (Swim, et al., 2010).

In part due to the sensationalist nature of international reporting on the issue of climate change in Tuvalu, when I first arrived in 2010 I half expected everyone to be in a constant state of panic and despair regarding climate change threats.[51] This is, of course, not the case at all. Tuvaluans, like all people, have complex lives with responsibilities, roles, and relationships that must be attended to daily, hourly, immediately, on an ongoing basis. Life has not stopped with the projections of sea level rise. As previously mentioned, the majority of effects of climate change are incremental and slow. The sea level is not projected to rise a meter until the end roughly the end of this century. This type of threat is not one to take precedence over the need to find a job, the need to provide education for children, or the need to fix dinner. Life continues on. Except perhaps for people who work with climate change in their employment, I would suspect that for most Tuvaluans, climate change is added to a list of background concerns but is not a primary concern in the day-to-day. I found no evidence that Tuvaluans are in a constant state of panic and despair, not even among those who admit to having witnessed the early impacts of climate change personally. This lack of constant panic should not be considered evidence that climate change is of no concern to Tuvaluans or the world. Rather, it should be understood that climate change is not a panic-inducing acute disaster. Climate change is more equivalent to a toxic environment, which causes chronic ambient stress with periodically higher rates of stress or fear when short-term events create uncertainty or destruction.

With recent development, modernization, globalization, and Westernization, Tuvaluans are experiencing a number of changes to their culture and daily lives. These changes have brought with them a new series of concerns and stresses to face. Vete said:

> If we talk about life, the Tuvaluan life is the best… if you think like a Niutaoan, you won't die because you will have your, unless there's a drastic catastrophe that happens, like climate change, and then you cannot plant anymore, you know? You'll have to raise all the trees two meters high so that the intrusion of saltwater is not affecting the crops, then life in Tuvalu is the best, no stress. Traditionally, the Tuvaluan life is really – no stress. What we do is go fish, they come back, they go and dance and then after that they sleep, tomorrow they go and, you know. We only started knowing stress is very bad when we changed our life to the Western world. And you'll see how much stress we have gone through. Now our people are no longer as big as our old people. One of the things that is contributing to the size of people – they are going the small size – stress. It's been injected to their brain… Stress is in our life. In the old life, 'Why do you stress, are you stupid?' They

---

[51] For further exploration of international reporting, please refer to the 8.3 International Discourse on Climate Change in Tuvalu.

are happy. Everything is enthusiasm. You will contribute to the community, you'll go out fishing and participate, every activity we do, it's all very happy. Now these things are all gone. Now we're talking here and I'm thinking about my meeting at six o'clock. There's a meeting there waiting for me at six o'clock pm. [With the] Niutao way everything is, if you are late too, no problem, everything is happy, happy.

Climate change is only one of the many introduced stresses. The projections of the rising sea were made during the time of quick development and the increased focus on money in Tuvalu. In their daily lives, Tuvaluans are not faced with immediate danger from climate change. High levels of stress and fear are associated only with times of immediate disaster, such as the 2011 drought when Funafuti came within days of completely depleting their freshwater supplies. Climate change may also increase the risk of heavy storms and hurricanes, which would be likely to provoke the type of reaction that Lanieta described for the tsunami warnings:

So usually these people at the ends, they come into this wider land. And these people on this wider land, they go to higher houses like the office, like tall, first story buildings. Yeah we also have some families coming to our place. We have a double story. We have mothers with their babies coming out. But we are lucky the tsunami never hit us. You can see people praying at that time. People are just, tears are just running down our eyes, especially in mothers and babies, yes. And it's really scary when the warning comes for a tsunami. You can't do much but just be together. Everybody comes to this wider land.

The cumulative effects of ambient stress and acute fear during disaster threats may eventually manifest in a decline in the psychological wellbeing of Tuvaluans. However, again, Tuvaluans have built-in social supports with their cultural values for community togetherness and care (Cline, et al., 2010; Norris, Baker, Murphy, & Kaniasty, 2005). This cultural strength can help Tuvaluans cope with short and long term effects of stress associated with climate change.

Chapter Summary

This chapter explores how climate change indirectly and directly impacts the people in Tuvalu. As the land, sea, and weather change, Tuvaluan lives are affected in systemic ways (e.g., changes to farming and fishing practices) and direct ways (e.g., relocating homes in response to erosion). The 2011 drought is a recent example of a disaster event related to the changing climate. Participants explored the ways in which the drought altered their daily lives, and how cultural norms affected the ways they responded to the drought. The interface between humans and climate change is not uni-directional with climate change only impacting people. People respond to these changes. Participants discussed Tuvaluan responses to the climate change impacts on their country.

Chapter 7

7.1 Faith and the Church of Tuvalu

Faith in God. As previously discussed, Tuvaluans are a people of strong faith, and tend toward a more literal interpretation of Christian teachings. Reverend Tafue Lusama explained that Tuvaluans often maintain the faith that if they live good lives and follow the teachings of the church, then God will protect them and provide for them. He and other members of the General Assembly of the Church of Tuvalu are concerned that should the human-caused climate change disrupt Tuvalu's balance of Christian living and sustainable subsistence, Tuvaluans' faith could be threatened along with the land. He said:

> What happens if you plant and you don't get anything? What happens if you go out fishing and you don't catch enough? It will put into question your belief in God's providence. So it also impacts their spirituality and their belief in God.

The causes and impacts of climate change are much bigger than the choices and lifestyles of Tuvaluans. However, the Christian faith and Tuvaluan culture are highly interconnected in ways that affect some Tuvaluans' responses to the threat of climate change. For example, when I asked Teba if people talked about climate change to her when she traveled to the outer islands for work, she responded:

> Not much. You know here, to tell you the truth, religion plays a very important role in how people view things. They think – they believe in God. And we said 'Oh do you believe in climate change?' and they said 'No, we believe in God. And if God wanted to take our island, He would take it. But until such time, we will stay as long as we are able.' So it's a very religious value.

Tomu also indicated that many Tuvaluans put their faith in God in regards to climate change. His belief is that when the country must begin to make decisions about what to do next, people should be given a choice.[52] He said, "If you say that God is always there with you, thank you." That will be their choice to follow their faith. Participants of this study repeatedly indicated that faith and prayer are legitimate action steps in response to climate change. In the interface between Tuvaluan culture and Christianity, having faith that God will provide is a powerful tool. For example, Kina told me:

> [Laughter] Climate change? Well, climate change is a big, big issue. I think, because we can't do much on climate change we can – I think the only thing that we can do is just to lobby and lobby, you know to get to the place that they should take up our concerns. We can't do much on it, because it's about time, you know. It's about time and we can't. I think the only thing that we should do now is just to work hard, work

---

[52] For more discussion on this topic, please see 7.2 Tuvalu's Future.

193

together, and not forgetting to pray, you know. We should pray, knowing all these impacts.

Kokea also indicated that the protection of God is of the utmost importance in safeguarding Tuvalu from the impacts of climate change. He said:

> Well, the change in sea level rise is just a natural thing that's going to happen and we are so unfortunate in our, you know, nature put us here. So this, what the people say, God should be able to look after us. He managed to put us up here in this type of island, so God should be able to provide water, rain for us. And so far it's quite all right.

Kokea is not necessarily saying that sea level rise is caused by a natural system. Rather, he is indicating that because the sea is part of nature, any of its activities are under the power of God. Tuvaluans were blessed by God to be placed in a location that can sustain subsistence and bounty, although they are unfortunate now that the sea level is rising. However, God is loving and powerful, and will continue to protect Tuvaluans as long as they continue to deserve it. Reverend Alefaio Honolulu told the story of the famine that came to Niulakita because a boy had an affair with a married woman. Similarly, on the topic of climate change, he said:

> Regarding the drought he says, "God is love. Maybe we did something wrong, such as failing to put God first. Why point to God as the cause of climate change? Why not point to you?" When he says this, it is not to indicate that humans are causing climate change with industrialization, but rather indicating that humans have sinned and climate change is a punishment from God for that sin. He says Tuvaluans can be compared to the Israelites in Egypt in the Bible. Bad things happened to them, but God loves them still. Even if you do bad things, God loves you. God freed the Israelites and then brought them back to him. He also mentions Job in the Bible, who suffered greatly and yet his faith in God never wavered. He said, "We must accept the good things and the bad things, not just accepting the good things" (Corlew field notes, 2012).

The direct relationship between climate change and God's power of influence over natural systems is not in question for many Tuvaluans. God is capable of restoring the environment despite any damages done. If He chooses to do so, He will. Nalu gave an example of the hole in the ozone layer:

LAURA: When you look forward into the future what do you see in the future for Tuvalu?

NALU: That's another very difficult question. Well I'm not a predictor, I'm not a predictor, right? But anyway, what I think is, I think the climate, because I asked one question to one of the priests during the workshop, 'As you mentioned that the' – what do you call that one, the blanket which is covering the earth, has big in holes because of using – ?

MICHAEL: The ozone?

194

NALU:	Yeah, the ozone layer. [I said to the priest] 'So you mentioned that the ozone layer has been in holes. Why? Because of heat, the oil, burning oil. And that God didn't like his people, or God doesn't want to repair the ozone layer?' He did not answer my questions. [I said] 'I think because of you priests. You are not doing your work properly.' And they were laughing.

Nalu's tone during this story was one of playful triumph with his challenge to the priests. If God has not fixed the ozone layer, there is a clearly a reason why, and that reason clearly has to do with His displeasure at the actions of humans – in this case, Nalu suggests, tongue-in-cheek, that the reason is the failure of the priests to do their work properly.

Noah and the covenant. There is a common perception among Tuvaluans that God will protect the islands from the rising sea. The reason for this belief can be found in the Old Testament. In Genesis, 6:1-9:17 (New International Version), the story of Noah and the flood is recounted. God was displeased with the wicked ways of humanity except for Noah and his family. He warned Noah that a great flood was coming. Noah built a large ark, and as directed by God, gathered one male and one female of every species of animal into the ark. When the storm began, the great flood lifted the ark, keeping Noah, his family, and the animal couples safe while the rest of the world was drowned for their wickedness. As the flood subsided and the inhabitants of the ark came forth to repopulate the Earth, God made a covenant with Noah, promising "Never again will all life be destroyed by the waters of a flood" (Genesis 9:11). He sealed his promise by creating rainbows as a sign for future generations.

Faced with a rising sea that is projected to slowly flood their country until it becomes uninhabitable, many Tuvaluans turn to rainbows as proof that God will protect them from this threat. Feue said:

> But this other category of people, but mostly religious figures, they tend to think, and I think you'll have heard from many, that God has made a promise and the sign is the rainbow that there will be no more flood. And they said that all this will come to pass. God will keep His promise.

Metia also said that many Tuvaluans hold strong to this belief in God's protection due to the sign of the rainbow:

METIA:	Because they said that there was one flooding and after that the Holy Almighty, I think in the Bible something mentioned that's the only one. There is no more flooding, or something like that.
MICHAEL:	Yeah, God promised that there wouldn't be any more floods, right?
METIA:	Yeah, it is written that God promised no flooding. So especially the old men, I think some of the young ones, they believe that. But they all know that the sea

195

level, the olden days until now, you can see the difference.

The reality of climate change is already being witnessed, but faith remains strong amongst many Tuvaluans that God will protect their homeland. For example, Metia indicated that despite noticeable changes in sea level, erosion, and monthly tidal flooding, Tuvalu is still safe and Tuvaluans continue to live in their land. Many Tuvaluans indicate that there is plenty of time for God to use His influence over nature to protect the country.

Biblical interpretations of climate change. As previously discussed, some members of the EKT General Assembly, including Tafue, are concerned that if Tuvalu ceases to be sustainable (if growing and fishing are interrupted by climate changes, for example), that it will shake the foundation of Tuvaluans' belief in God. Any threat to the welfare and faith of the Church's people is a threat to the Church and must be addressed. The Church of Tuvalu is therefore exploring Biblical interpretations that are applicable in this time of unprecedented climate change to help Tuvaluans and other people of faith explore God's role in what is happening to the world. Tafue said:

> We have been trying to talk to the people about climate change, and they always refers back to the flood narrative where God promised Noah there wouldn't be any more flood. And that is literal, a literal understanding of the story. So, we have to go deeper into the narrative and try to explain to them that God made His promise and He is keeping it. We still see the rainbow up. Noah didn't make a promise, and who is causing this flood? I mean, who is causing climate changes? And you realize it is not God. It is us human beings who are. We are Noah in that. So we didn't make any promise to God, like, 'Okay since You promised us, so we won't cause anymore flood as well.' So, it's our fault. We are facing the consequence of our actions.

In this case, the 'we' who are at fault for climate change are not Tuvaluans. It is the human race, particularly those who come from wealthy, industrialized nations who have spent 250 years pouring carbon into the atmosphere. From this perspective, humans did not make a promise to God within the covenant that we would not create a flood. Tafue's point is that God has kept His promise, and it is we humans who had never made the promise in the first place.

Belief in climate change. Participants expressed a range of levels of belief in climate change from complete acceptance of the science to a denial reliant on faith that God would protect Tuvalu regardless. This array of climate change belief is a normal range that has been recorded in other populations around the world, including in the United States (Doherty & Clayton, 2011; Gifford, 2011; McCright & Dunlap, 2011; Swim, et al., 2010; Weber & Stern, 2011). Such ranges of belief can be attributed to faith, political leanings, experiential differences, and other diversities within each population. There is no single unified Tuvaluan belief about climate change, just as there is no one American belief about climate change. Here I will present several coexisting categories of belief in Tuvalu, exemplified by the statements of participants, to show the diverse range of interpretations of climate change in Tuvalu. First,

196

Vete expressed a belief founded on the scientific projections that the global climate is changing. He underscored his religious beliefs, but argued that his belief in science and his belief in the Bible were not mutually exclusive. Vete said:

> My view on climate change, learning science, it will happen. Scientifically, if the temperature of world has increased due to carbon emissions and if these big countries are not decreasing or doing away with emissions, then it will happen. Learning science, you know. Biblically, from the Biblical side, somebody said that God created this to happen. But not according to the – man creates his own downfall. And the forward-looking depends on man. If you wish to save the world then he has to reduce those carbon emissions. Because scientifically it's proven that if emissions are not controlled or inhibited, it will continue. The layer is depleting, it is getting thinner and thinner and thinner, and shortly all the weather will just be directly to the earth. But we still have the opportunity to decide.

Again, the actions that need to be taken to save Tuvalu are not only meant to be taken by Tuvaluans but also by "these big countries" to reduce their emissions. In Vete's Christian belief and interpretation of the Bible, when "man creates his own downfall" it is not because he is sinning and God is sending climate change as punishment. It is actually that humans are polluting the world to the extent that they themselves are destroying their ability to live in it. God is not causing climate change, people are by failing to be good stewards of the planet. It is therefore up to people to take the actions necessary to stop climate change.

Jopeto talked a great deal about what she had learned about climate change, what she had seen herself as evidence of climate change, and her belief that wealthy countries should take action to help Tuvalu address the threats of climate change. However, even these extensive considerations of climate change are couched within the practicality of daily life. She said:

> Yeah, so people are moving outside of Tuvalu just because of that. They believe it. But for us, for my family, they believe it, but they don't want to move yet. They've been building many of the houses here, doing a lot of business here, so it's like moving out. Even we don't want to leave our islands where we grew up and where we've grown. It's like it's hard to forget it.

The worst impacts of climate change on Tuvalu's land and sea are not projected to occur soon or quickly. In the meantime, life continues on in Tuvalu. From Jopeto's perspective, climate change is an important event affecting the country, but responses to climate change should be considered within the context of other life goals and responsibilities. This perspective is not a denial of climate change, but is rather a determination that the lives of Tuvaluans should not simply stop due to projected impacts.

Noa's lack of belief in climate change was based in large part on his Christian faith and his dreams for his and his family's future. With a desire to live a good life and provide opportunities to the coming generations, the projected impacts of climate change simply cannot fit. The possibilities are too dire. Noa said:

> They said it's better to live here in Tuvalu still. Some people, they just feel threatened by this climate change. But to me, as a Christian, I don't really believe in climate change. I used to imagine being a grandfather, looking at my grandchildren. Like I mentioned my, in the future, if climate change does really – yeah, it does really exist. I was thinking about, they said that climate change was being introduced in ten or twenty years here in Tuvalu. But there's little changes. It doesn't give a big indication that it's time for us to leave. But now with this kind of tsunami and things, some people are forced to leave. It's better to go and live in high grounds. For us here in Tuvalu, there are no chances here, if there is a tsunami. It's too big. But we take our chances. It's very hard to leave the place where you grow up. It hurts me, because we didn't do anything. It's like we are forced to live with somebody's action.

The current reality of climate change is only a condition of threat, not a state of destruction. From this perspective, there is no reason to accept the worst case scenario until it is the current state of events. The threat itself is hard enough to live with. When Noa considers the possibilities of flood events, he cannot make these possibilities fit with his dreams to be a grandfather in Tuvalu. It is better to focus on Tuvalu's current state and to "take our chances."

Faith in God as a coping mechanism. As previously discussed, there are many ways to cope with the stress caused by the projected impacts of climate change in Tuvalu. Tuvalu's collectivist system of family and community support is a powerful tool in addressing these stresses. In addition, faith is a powerful tool for coping with disaster events (McCrae, 1984; McGeehan, 2012). During my first field trip to Tuvalu, one woman told me that it is common when you speak with Tuvaluans to hear that they believe God will protect them from climate change. But, she said, this is not always the only thing that is true about their beliefs. Tuvalu is a developing nation with limited infrastructure. She said "People talk about their faith but they know in reality that they have no other hope" (Corlew field notes, 2010). There is one airstrip in Funafuti that accepts only two flights per week. The plane, she noted, holds only 40 people. If a disaster occurs, she told me, Tuvaluans know that they will not all be able to get on that plane. The Prime Minister and other leaders will be evacuated. In the face of a potentially high level of risk and limited ability among individual Tuvaluans to respond to that risk, faith in God is what keeps them going as life continues on. I would like to stipulate that this is a psychologically healthy coping response to a large global threat, and it is a testament to the strength of Tuvaluans' faith that they turn their prayers to God in the midst of this threat.

Connected with faith in God is faith in country. During both trips, many Tuvaluans have told me that they do not intend to migrate away from their home country no matter what.[53] When I asked Kou if there was anything she would like to tell people from other countries about Tuvalu, she said:

> [Laughs] Okay, I would say [Laughs; Picks up the recorder to speak into it] Tuvalu, it's good. It's a beautiful country. But especially for the sea level. But for me, I believe… Noah, there is no more flood. I believe it… To me, I have to stay here and die here for my country. For most of, for some of Tuvalu, they all migrate, because of the water, sea level. You heard it… But those people that are going, they don't have any faith. They should stay there in our country where you were born. Only those people going there, they don't want to die. That's why they want to go and migrate to the big countries there. But for me, Tuvalu is good. Not like other countries. For us here, if you don't have any food, you're still alive. Compared to those people from Africa. You can see it from movies, the children, they are crying that they don't have much food. And also they don't have any shelter to stay in. But here it's good… That's why it's better for you to stay here in Tuvalu compared to the other countries.

Kou said that she would "die here for my country" and that she believes that those who leave "don't have any faith." Tuvaluans have been blessed with bounty and God has promised not to bring floods to the world again. These beliefs are interconnected and inform her personal response to climate change – that she would not leave, but will instead have faith. Nalu expressed a similar belief that Tuvaluans should not be looking for responses to climate change outside of their faith. He said, "Whatever happened in the world, we can't do anything." This type of coping uses acceptance of the inability of individual Tuvaluans to effect climate change and places faith that everything will be okay regardless of one's personal power over the situation. Jopeto also expressed that she uses denial and faith to maintain her ability to cope positively with this ongoing threat so as to continue her life and work toward improving the opportunities and wellbeing of herself, her family, and her country. She said, "Some people, they believe that Tuvalu will sink, some people don't believe. But for me, I believe that I don't want to know [Laughs]. I just want to help my country."

The role of EKT with climate change. A powerful theme that arose in the interview analysis was the role of Christianity, and especially the Church of Tuvalu (EKT), in addressing the impacts of climate change in Tuvalu in two major ways. First, the Church is seeking to help Tuvaluans to understand and respond to climate change within the framework of their faith. Secondly, delegates from EKT have been active on the international stage in advocating for wealthy nations to be more proactive in global mitigation and adaptation efforts, such as their recent vocal presence at the UN Climate Change Conferences in Copenhagen (Farbotko & McGregor, 2010) and in Durban,

---

[53] For more discussion of this topic, please see 7.2 Tuvalu's Future.

South Africa (Wilson, 2012). These findings are consistent with previous research into the role of EKT in Tuvalu (Allice, 2009). In this section, I will focus particularly on the role of the Church within the Tuvaluan communities. Tafue is the leader of this movement within EKT, and explained to me extensively the role that the Church seeks to play in Tuvaluans' faithful understanding of climate changes. He said:

> To start off with I must say that the Church believes that whatever impacts the life of the people impacts the Church, and as such we should respond to the issue. So since climate change impacts the life and the very existence of our people, the Church has prioritized climate change as an issue that we should deal with, locally, regionally, and internationally. And that is why I have been active with the government delegations and the international meetings for the past years up until now. The Church does have a stand on climate change. And it is simply a call to our faith in God and what was given to us, and how should we respond to the issue from a Christian perspective.

In order to explore this Christian perspective with Tuvaluans and open a dialogue (e.g., about the Biblical interpretations of God's covenant with Noah as related to climate change) the Church has begun organizing gatherings around the country to discuss climate change. Tafue said:

> The church has run several awareness workshops on climate change. We have gone out to the other islands and talked to the communities, stayed with them for 2 to 3 weeks. Travelling from island to island, explaining to them what climate change is, what the Bible says, how should we encounter that from a Christian perspective.

Tafue is clear that the Church's role is not to interfere with political decisions or to direct community members in their choices regarding what actions they take in response to climate change. He said, "We do not go into the communities and talk about the politics of climate… We leave politics out of it. Even with the negotiations and all the meetings that we attend, we attend on behalf of the Church." During the workshops, they focus solely on understanding this global event within the context of Tuvaluan faith. Tafue said that during the workshops, the conversations have followed a similar pattern. He said:

> I'll start off with a question, 'Do you believe in climate? If you don't then tell me why.' And majority of them will always say, 'No we don't believe in climate change. Who can change the climate? God is the sole ruler of everything. If God's willing to change the climate then he will change it. But God is so loving. He won't be changing the climate just to make us suffer.' And that's the kind of belief that they have. And then, I say, 'Okay, if you don't believe in climate change what about sea level rise?' And they said 'Oh, we don't believe sea level rise as well because of the covenant in Genesis.' So, well, we prepared ourselves beforehand for this. [Laughter] So we tackled those by going back to the Bible and re-reading the story of Noah and re-interpreting it in a theological way that makes them understand the context of the narrative, and what was intended by the writer for the people to know

and to believe, and bringing that into the context of climate change and looking at the covenant from a climate change perspective. Who's causing it? Is God causing it? Because if we keep on believing that God made a covenant and there won't be any climate change and sea level rise, then we are simply blaming God. Because when the time comes, and we come to the extreme that we cannot survive here, all you can do is look up to God and say, 'Hey, I had faith in you. Why are you failing me?' Whereas it's better to open your eyes now and see who's causing it. And say, 'Oh, yes I'll stand with God and try and solve the problem' rather than denying it now and then it will challenge your faith later… they will always come back and say 'So what should we do now? If that is the case, then what should we do?' So instead of giving them directly what they should do, I tell them well, 'You know the cause of the issue now. So decide what you should do. Your way of life, how you approach your representative to the Parliament and the issues that you raise with the government or development proposals, you know, you'll have to take all these into consideration.' So the attitude started to change.

The outcomes of these island workshops were so positive that the Church decided to run national workshops in Funafuti, with representatives of different congregations outside of EKT, as well as political and environmental leaders. Tafue said:

The idea was to get together every faith-based group, listen to speakers from the government, from NGOs, from the Environment Department and from the Church on what climate change is and how does it impact our lives, how does it relate to our faith, and our way of life. And that was the idea. But it went further. The workshop went further and they proposed that they need two things. First, they wanted a document to be released from the workshop signed by all faith-based groups agreeing on what should be done and how they should act. Secondly, they proposed that an interreligious climate change committee be set up. To keep every faith group up to date with what is happening, and to organize such actions, like workshops every day. It is very, very positive and I was really happy with the outcome of that workshop. So we've been working on that. Hopefully, we can establish that permanently, the committee.

Given the powerful role that faith plays in Tuvaluan culture, as well as the role of respect, privilege, and spiritual leadership that the pastors play in Tuvalu's cultural hierarchy, it is natural that the Church leadership would become an important voice regarding climate change. The interreligious committee, the workshops, and the ongoing dialogues at the island level and the national level all indicate that the culture of faith in Tuvalu is a cultural strength in addressing climate change. The communities are able to come together to evaluate and reevaluate the dynamic state of a changing community and a changing environment. Tafue said:

But for EKT itself, we've taken up the challenge of climate change as a priority challenge to us. We believe that we are not owners of this earth. We are not owners of this globe. We are just keepers for a time, for a certain period of time. We just keep it for the others who are coming. And our Christian stewardship role in keeping God's earth, looking after God's planet is put into question if we do not perform our stewardship role well. And, you know, as the saying always goes that the worst thing to do when faced with an issue is to do or say nothing. So we cannot be silent. We cannot say, 'Oh, it's not our part, it's not our role. It's not our responsibility. Leave it to the government or the NGOs.' It is definitely our role and our responsibility to do something. And to certain meetings, government meetings and even NGO meetings, when I attend certain of them, several times I've been questioned why the Church is very active on the issue of climate change. I always give them the same response. This is not only a political issue. It is a survival issue and it is the Church's responsibility to make sure that our people survive and this planet survives.

7.2 Tuvalu's Future

Tuvalu has an uncertain future in regards to climate change. Many questions remain. Will wealthy nations reduce their carbon emissions and enact sufficient mitigation efforts quickly enough to stem sea level rise? Will they support the adaptations of developing nations to protect against the impacts of climate change? Will the Tuvalu government be successful in their international advocacy efforts at persuading the world to systematically and comprehensively address the threat of climate change? Will Tuvaluans eventually be forced to migrate, and if so, will they actually go? Will they stay together as one nation or will they be scattered around the world? There are no clear answers to these questions. It is not even clear at this time if these are ultimately the right questions or if new and more important concerns will be raised. What remains true is that Tuvaluans are living in a period of uncertainty. Tuvalu is made up of nine islands and atolls spread out over 900,000 km². They are unlikely to all experience the same changes over the same time period due to their different geography and the distance between them. Sueina said she believes Funafuti is more likely to suffer from floods and other disasters than Niutao. She said:

> I think Niutao can't go down, go sinking. Because we have a round shape, and even though during times of cyclones and bad weather. But here it can be probably washed away. Because if you see the sea over that side and the sea over that side, you can see the sea from the other side to the other side. But in Niutao, you can't see, if you stand in the middle of the island you can't see the sea from the other side as well as the other side. So I think Niutao may be a hundred years later, then we can see the changes.

Differential rates of change may (or may not) affect Tuvaluans' future responses to climate change. If one island is greatly impacted, that community may be compelled to enact extreme adaptive actions while others are able to postpone

202

adaptations. Current responses to climate change are based within the context of this high level of uncertainty. In this section, I will explore a range of responses that were expressed by participants when considering Tuvalu's future.

Drowning. The idea that Tuvaluans will drown with sea level rise was expressed by several recorded participants as well as during unrecorded conversations in the community. It is a powerful image and one that is commonly engaged in international news media headlines, such as *Call for Action on 'Drowning' Islands* (Canberra, 2006), *Global Drowning: Ocean may Soon Swallow a Nation* (Simons, 2007), *Drowning Island Pins Hopes on Clean Energy* (CNN Tech, 2009), and *Tuvalu is Drowning* (Berzon, 2006). Legitimate concerns that at some point in the future Tuvalu may be underwater were expressed by participants with a somewhat light-hearted prediction about drowning. For example, Ken said:

LAURA:	When you look forward into the future for Tuvalu, what do you think is going to happen?
KEN:	I can't explain but I think something is different with climate change, about Niutao and here. There were some places that were closed by the sea and if the year will come and this would happen, I think it is a difference, this climate change.
LAURA:	What do you think may happen?
KEN:	What I think?
LAURA:	Yeah.
KEN:	What I think may happen to here or Niutao, I think they will be closed by climate change and sea level rise. That will be it.
LAURA:	What would happen to Tuvaluans?
KEN:	I think people will drown [Laughs].

Sueina also invoked the image of drowning when she spoke the future, by comparing the predictions of sea level rise associated with climate change to the current experiences of tidal flooding in Tuvalu. She said:

> Those who are staying here for a long time, they said that they can tell the rise of sea levels. They can tell from those waters. Because before, they said that there is no water coming from those places. But now, if it is really high tide, it can rise up to your leg. Before it's only down, but now. So we think it's maybe, how many years until the water will be up to our body [Laughs] and we'll be drowning [Laughs].

Migration. Inevitably, the idea of migration arises with discussions of climate change. Kiribati is currently seeking to buy land in Fiji to begin a generations-long whole population migration to higher ground (Chapman, 2012). Discussions among low-lying island nations across the Pacific and the world include the eventual possibilities of migration (e.g., Locke, 2009; Nine, 2010). Although international media and research often place migration in the foreground of the global conversation (Lazrus, 2008), the Tuvalu national government's current policy is not to negotiate for migration at this time. This position is supported by the Church of Tuvalu leadership and many Tuvaluans

(Allice, 2009). Tomu explained to me during my first trip that the purpose for this policy is to maintain pressure on wealthy nations who are dragging their feet about responding to climate change. If Tuvalu and other nations agree now to migrate, these wealthy nations may decide there is no point to reduce carbon emissions or mitigate their globally polluting behaviors. However, if the actions of wealthy nations pose a direct and ongoing threat to countries like Tuvalu, they must address this threat. If at a later date it becomes impossible to save Tuvalu, then at that point the Tuvaluan government will make the necessary decisions. But until it is necessary to give up their homeland, they refuse to do so. What is just and what is right is that Tuvaluans be able to maintain their home. Tafue said:

> I stand together with the government and with the Church as well on the understanding that we would like to save our country. No matter how small, no matter how poor it is, it is our place, our inheritance. Like the saying always goes, 'there's nowhere like home.' I travelled the world a lot and from place to place but there's always a longing to get back. And that is the sense of belonging. If Tuvalu disappears then we – I mean, if we prefer to throw in the white towel now and surrender and go live somewhere else and Tuvalu disappears, I will have no sense of belonging at all. Because my identity as a person is linked to a place that does not exist, where it is no longer. It is good now to migrate. If I decide to migrate somewhere else, I can migrate. Any Tuvaluan can migrate as the others have done. But they migrate with the understanding that their home is there. Whenever they want to come back they can. They can come back. And the climate and sea level rise, if Tuvalu disappears, and we have to be resettled somewhere, we are simply homeless people. We lose our land and we lose our identity as a distinct people on the face of this planet. We lose everything and we simply become second class citizens of a country. And slowly and slowly through generations we will lose our culture and our way of life. We will simply assimilate into their culture and their way of life, as we have seen in New Zealand with our communities there. So, the disappearance of the country or the islands simply signifies the disappearance of the people. Because land is life and land is our identity.

Tafue spoke of the possibility of permanent migration as "Plan B." "Plan A is to save the country." Wealthy nations and donor organizations must work together with Tuvalu to build up the shores and enact every other potential adaptation to save Tuvalu before considering the possibility of leaving the country entirely and becoming a nation of people "with no sense of belonging at all."

Other participants shared this belief that migration was not the best option for Tuvaluans at this time. Some insisted that there would never be a time in which they would consider migrations. During my first trip to Tuvalu, one woman told me she would never migrate. She said, "I was born here and I will die here" (Corlew field notes, 2010). Another woman told me that many of the elders will refuse to leave, preferring to stay in Tuvalu and die rather than live without their home. Kou insisted that "I have to stay here and die here for my country." Alamai said that even under the threat of disasters with climate change, Tuvalu is no less safe a place to be than anywhere else in the world:

We can't predict the reality of all these cyclones and tsunamis, to be on the safe side. It is not really safe to be here. If we hear about the story of the recent tsunamis in the Pacific, especially Tonga and Samoa, and they got hills. We don't have those. We don't have mountains. Even this highest building, the Government building, is not that high if the tsunami is bigger and bigger. But I think it's safe, Tuvalu is safe... it's better to stay than somewhere else where you can't. But even other places too in the world there will be natural disasters.

As previously discussed, Tuvaluans are adaptable. When Kina mentioned the possibility of migration in her future, she indicated that she believes she could adapt to living in another country if it came to that, but she simply did not want to consider that as a real possibility. She said:

KINA: Yeah. Because even though there are so many problems, but we love our place. Maybe if we are, the whole of Tuvalu is moving somewhere else then we'll accept to go. The only thing, I love here because it's very peaceful. And I grew up here, that's why I love my culture. I don't know if I am adopting a new culture. I don't, I don't want to think of it.

LAURA: Yeah.

KINA: You know.

LAURA: Yeah.

KINA: And I know if I'm going to adopt new culture I will love it as well. Since I grew up here and I'm 34 years old and I still love my [culture].

Lanieta also expressed her belief that although there are surely other good places in the world, there is no other place for Tuvaluans that is better than Tuvalu. She is not ready to migrate, and is still hopeful that the most dire concerns about climate change will prove to be overstatements of the actual risk. She said:

Tuvalu is a good place to be – whatever takes, overcrowded or less job opportunities – but it's still a good place to be if you are Tuvaluan. But it's all up to them. If they find it not good, then the world is so wide. They can always find another place to migrate. But like for me, I can still find peace here. Can still remain here. Maybe climate change, maybe it's just another issue we talk about.

Ken noted that many people are considering migration. He explained that people who are already migrating are doing so in conjunction with job and schooling opportunities and may or may not be considering climate change as a driving motivation. However, when looking to the future, he said that migration may become more common for some people. Ken said:

KEN: I think the people will move, or some will, if it's the years will come. If the year comes, and also closed, I

205

	think it is better that people will move. Otherwise it
	will be very bad.
LAURA:	Would you move?
KEN:	I don't think I will move. I will move, but I don't
	know at what time.

Migration for climate change is often considered only as a last resort, and even then a very unhappy one. Even "if the year comes" and people must move or "it will be very bad," there is a strong desire to stay as long as possible if not forever. Feue explained that there are many different considerations and opinions regarding future possibilities of migration in Tuvalu. Even those who would consider migration are only considering it because they feel they must be cautious with their planning. Feue said:

> Now there are many different views that people have expressed. One view, and this is sort of more common to the old people, is that come what may they won't budge. They will stay... but the old men say, 'Oh yeah, but these [changes] are normal. But if whatever the current debate that is going on, whatever the outcome is, whether there is truth in all this, we won't go. We'd rather stay.' But there is also the other view, a more cautious view, that we have to prepare ourselves for whatever consequences that may be. And preparing ourselves basically means that we have to look for options.

These options include Tafue's "Plan B" of migration. In Tuvalu's current state of development and cultural change, migration is considered within the context of ongoing migration for work and school. Migration is a pattern in Tuvalu's history. The difference with climate change, of course, is that the migration is irreversible. But when faced with the range of possibilities with climate change, some people believe it should be cautiously considered, at least within the context of migration for job and education opportunities. The Anonymous participant I spoke with said that he believed "It is important for people to move if there is sea level rise because of so many people" (Corlew field notes, 2012). If climate changes were to become suddenly catastrophic for Tuvalu, many people would suffer. He said that people should already be looking for job opportunities overseas so that they can "Be prepared for when climate change becomes too much to survive in Tuvalu" (Corlew field notes, 2012). Vete also talked about migration within this context of migration for school and work. He has worked very hard to provide educational opportunities for his children, and has told them they should pursue schooling to a Master's level at least in order to be competitive on a global job market. The idea of permanent migration seemed distasteful to him, but he said that if every other possible solution is tried and fails, it may be the only option left to Tuvaluans in the future. Vete said:

> If it's going to be an ocean here then I think, I personally will tell my kids 'You all migrate and disappear, stay in Australia. Only come back to enjoy that last bit of it when the real time event comes.' Who on earth can stay and live and the water coming from there and there and there, you know? Of course we want to live here. We have our heart for

Tuvalu. We love Tuvalu. What are we going to do? Losing my culture, it's – if you're going to lose your culture. It's bold decision that has to be made. But this decision has to be realistic so that it will get done. If it is going to be under water then what are the remedial actions? And how much money? Anybody can give us that much money to raise all these islands 3 meters above? Protect all the oceans or when they starting to come through the land, the land will still remain? Those are the questions. If it is a reality, then life is a different thing. You cannot destroy your life. Nobody will say 'Oh, I can remain here and let the wave come and destroy my life.' If it is a reality. It's in our heart to protect the culture. We can only protect it to a certain level. We know we wish Australia give us, say, 'Oh, this is your land. You can be Tuvalu here. You will have all the right to call Tuvalu to your culture here... but when you come to Sydney or Melbourne you'll have to bear with Australia.' I don't think they can give you where you got your own passport, you got the, all this. What are we doing? We don't have any power, we don't have any – we don't mean anything to them.

The crux of the matter with migration is that Tuvaluans would be living in someone else's country on someone else's land surrounded by someone else's culture. Tuvaluans who are migrating currently have and exercise the ability to come back home and visit, or retire back into their families, communities, and islands. The culture remains intact because it has a homeland in which traditional activities are practiced right along with new cultural activities. The dynamic culture is maintained with a clear sense of the Tuvaluan identity. The fear with migration is that this identity will begin to fade away or will be absorbed into another country's national identity. Alamai said:

> Now people are becoming aware of the need to preserve their culture and they come to realize that global change or globalization and climate change are coming and having the effect to all these culture materials. And all this going overseas and coming, definitely, maybe in the near future, there will be no cultural materials that can identify, can be detected, that can be named like 'it's a Tuvaluan originality'.

Feue also discussed this fear that culture could be lost if permanent migration were to take place with climate change. He said, "Culture would suddenly be the loser, be the loser here, in terms of the fact that now with people going their own way and all that, that's clear that the culture would be the bigger loser." However, Feue pointed to the many examples of migration in Tuvalu's past in which migrants have actively maintained their culture even as they live overseas. He said:

> But as I've explained to you last time, an interesting thing is happening in New Zealand, in Auckland... there is a huge Tuvaluan population there. Somehow they decided to retain a lot of their cultural values in New Zealand, and what are these? Now they decided that in terms of their religious beliefs, they have decided to have Tuvaluan church pastors to come to New Zealand and form church... So in a way that's

an education that Tuvaluan cultural values are strong through that aspect.

These church groups sent groups of their youth back to Niutao so that they could be exposed to the Niutao culture in the homeland. Youth who were born or raised in foreign countries had an opportunity to connect with the larger Niutao community back in Tuvalu. Feue said, "Now, my first answer was that certainly culture will be the loser, but there are also trends that are going on that indicates the fact that we are not really losing all that." Tuvaluans overseas are being proactive in maintaining Tuvaluan culture. In a possible distant future if Tuvaluans are forced to migrate, they will not be able to send their youth back to their home islands to experience the culture there. However, it has been demonstrated that Tuvaluans overseas living in communities or near to each other actively look for ways to continue to be Tuvaluan. Tuvaluans have been migrating for work for generations, and recently there has been a large increase in the number of Tuvaluans migrating for both education and work opportunities. Tuvaluan culture in Tuvalu is influenced and dynamically changed by this history of migration, from trade, from globalization, development, and modernization. But despite all of these influences, Tuvaluans have maintained their culture. Tuvaluans who are overseas similarly work to maintain their culture. Tuvaluan culture and identity is obviously very important to Tuvaluans, who will do what they can to maintain this identity. When asked if he thought there was anything else of importance to say about Tuvalu, Ken told me:

KEN: Well, what I am thinking, just to people now, as you watch Tuvalu, just to keep in mind their culture. What are you thinking about, for the future?

LAURA: Yeah.

KEN: I think there is a, something I was thinking about, if you are Tuvaluan, you will keep your culture. When you look forward, you keep your culture.

Having options. When discussing the important role that faith plays in Tuvaluans' wellbeing as they consider the threats of climate change, a woman I spoke with during my first trip indicated that people are well aware of the fact that they themselves may not have many options open to them in preparation for climate change. They do not have the funds to migrate or the personal power to protect their land. Feue also stated that many Tuvaluans do not have the means to migrate even if they wanted to. He said:

You know, it's basically giving them the opportunities, providing them the means to decide. Most Tuvaluans are helpless because they don't have the means to decide. They may dream of migrating but they don't have the skills to migrate. So who's going to help them? The answer is government, but government doesn't have the money to. But this is where public policy, good public policies come into play. But I don't know. But my belief is that families, and this is including the Tuvalu government, has to come up with options and prepare for the worst. It doesn't matter what climate change, Tuvalu would be submerged or otherwise, but it's a question of giving opportunities for them to decide for their own, and the option I think, the only option that is viable is education.

Tomu, a 40-year veteran of the Tuvaluan government, also expressed his belief that what is most necessary for Tuvaluans as they look forward to the future is to have options that are available to them. In the long term, Tuvaluans should be educated about the risks of climate change, and then given the means to do what they think is right. He said:

> What are my plans, is to explain, talk. 'These are the disadvantages of this. These are the advantages of this.' You see there that, if you say that God is always there with you, thank you. There are many stories, there are many records and writing papers. The thing is coming up. It is better for you people in the Pacific to think.

Those who wish to stay in Tuvalu should be able to stay, and those who wish to migrate should be able to migrate. And if Tuvaluans are to migrate, Tomu wishes to find a space in which they can migrate as a group to stay together and stay safe, "Not giving us how many billions. Keep your money. Only take us to a safe place so that we can survive and retain our own culture. Identity, the most important thing is our identity. Retain our identity." This is, of course, a decision for the future. For now, the Tuvaluan government as well as the Church of Tuvalu and other leaders are advocating on a global scale for wealthy and industrialized nations to address climate change so that Tuvaluans can keep their country. But, Tomu said, these issues will be addressed in the future so that Tuvaluans can maintain their lives and their cultures. He said:

> TOMU: Well climate change is a one of our problems... I see it's one of our problems to look at to our future. People are in those days, when we first received the message, when the message was first initiated in our Pacific, because we get it, sometimes people are not believing. Some people don't, they are not scared of it. They said they are normal feelings. Like today now, sometimes you see the difference. Those days none.
>
> MICHAEL: No western winds like this [today now].
>
> TOMU: No western winds. People say – they say it is true, the rise of the seas come true. And then looking at your own welfare, 'Am I going to live with this kind of crisis or am I going to get some options so that they can survive when the real crisis is here affecting us?'

Plan A. Tafue explained that to him, migration was "Plan B." "Plan A" was to do everything possible to maintain and protect the Tuvaluan homeland. Even participants who believed that migration may one day be necessary indicated that at most migration should be considered a worst case scenario. Before agreeing to a measure so disruptive to Tuvaluans' lives, other options must first be pursued. Kina said:

209

I don't know what we don't know about climate change. If we can work together, nothing will make a change. But that's the best thing to do. We have to work, work and do what is best for climate change. Because climate change really affects many things. It affects people with disabilities as well.

The Tuvaluan government is quite active in the global community as a voice for comprehensive mitigation and adaptation efforts. According to a 2010 General Environment Briefing, Tuvalu is actively calling for developed and developing nations to work toward reducing their emissions (although not in conjunction with nuclear energy due to the "problems with highly radioactive waste," A.1.2), and calls for target reductions to begin as early as 2015. "Setting targets for 2050 is too far away. No government can guarantee to stick to a target so far away as 2050" (A.1.4). Tuvalu is advocating for rainforest protections without the reliance on a carbon credit market because it opens possibilities for corruption and inaction. Tuvalu is supportive of a new Adaptation Convention updated from the UN Framework Convention on Climate Change, the Convention on Biological Diversity, the UN Convention to Combat Desertification, and other global efforts that together can address the potential global impacts of climate change in a comprehensive manner. Annex 1 of this document noted, "It is important that the international community recognize LDCs and SIDS[54] as the most vulnerable countries to the impacts of climate change" (Annex 1.2.viii). This vulnerability is due in part to regional physical vulnerabilities and in part due to the lack of development and current infrastructure necessary to adequately implement climate change adaptations and protections. "Tuvalu is aiming to build appropriate infrastructure to protect people, property and livestock from the impacts of cyclones and storm surges" (Annex 1.3). The government is pursuing a range of actions that together will help to protect the Tuvaluan homeland. As mentioned in the Introduction section of this paper, the General Environment Briefing ends with the note that:

> While Tuvalu faces an uncertain future due to climate change, it is our view that Tuvaluans will remain in Tuvalu. We will fight to keep our country, our culture and our way of living. We are not considering any migration scheme. We believe if the right actions are taken to address climate change, Tuvalu will survive.

Participants of this study discussed some of the options that they have seen at play in Tuvalu to protect the country as part of Plan A. Vete, a civil engineer by education, spoke about the sea walls in Funafuti. They were designed to protect the coast from erosion and subsidence. However, he said, "The problem we faced is the funding was not sufficient for equipment." The blocks that were designed for use in the seawall turned out to be logistically impossible to install given Tuvalu's current infrastructure. Vete said:

---

[54] Least Developed Countries and Small Island Developing States

Those blocks are not supposed to be those sizes, because the adverse effects of cyclones. Those blocks can be moved by the wave. But in design you need to design to the extreme conditions. But the problem is, we don't have equipment to lift. If you make a block heavy then who's going to lift it? Very difficult. So that's why – the only things that we come up with are cubes in which one person can lift it or two people can lift it and install it, hand installation. But otherwise if we have all the funds that we need, we could come up with a solution. Designing is not the problem but the installation ... these had a lot of our limitations.

A further problem he mentioned is getting the equipment and stones to the outer islands for installation there as well. The isolation makes shipment "too costly," which is another logistical barrier to implementing adaptations. The limited infrastructure in developing nations is one of the reasons they are most vulnerable to climate change. The United States, for example, has more available infrastructure to protect its low-lying islands (like Manhattan) than does Tuvalu. Outside aid to Tuvalu needs to address not only the adaptation needs, but the infrastructure that is needed to actually enact those adaptations. Vete said:

For anybody to put in $150 million to this country, very difficult. They only come at five, three, two million because of population. How can we invest $150 million with only this population? There's no justification, economic justification with the people in relation to the beneficiaries. Well, how many are going to benefit?

One of the government's most pressing issues is to secure aid in terms of individual projects, long-term sustainability, and increasing infrastructure. Like in many other places, these projects can be considered "no regrets" adaptations – that is, they are beneficial to the health, safety, and welfare of the Tuvaluan community above and beyond their benefits in terms of climate change. Feue said:

In terms of culture and climate change, I think an important aspect is basically the understanding and the support of the donor community. Because without their support it would be extremely for Tuvaluans, for the majority of Tuvaluans to have the opportunities to go further.

Both Vete and Tafue discussed their beliefs that one of the major adaptations that should be considered for Tuvalu's future is to raise the level of the land above the projected sea level rise. Vete said, "If we know that one degree of [global temperature] increase will raise the water level in Tuvalu by 1 meter, we can lift the land above 2 meters." Tafue also discussed the legitimacy of this action:

For Plan A, I always talk about raising the level of the land. Now Tuvalu is only 26 square kilometers. Raising that is not a big problem. And it can be done. It's possible, though costly. But that is worth considering, saving the country and the identity of the people, than not doing it and leaving them to disappear.

The potential costs for this course of action are prohibitive to Tuvalu, a developing nation. Wealthy nations have this money available but so far have not expressed a willingness to spend it to protect Tuvalu from climate impacts for which they are not to blame. To wealthy nations, this plan may seem extreme. But to some Tuvaluans, it is an exceedingly reasonable course of action. Vete said:

> What's the use of doing it piecemeal? Addressing the climate change has to be realistic. They have to be realistic. We need to be realistic. If in the next 50 years everything is gone, 'Okay, Tuvalu, are you going to trust this?' 'Oh no no no, we want to stay.' 'Okay. What can we do? Raise your island by 3 meters. If they are still under water by then that is not our problem. We have given you your choice and it's your choice to go with that, to remain here.' Because there's quite a lot of people that don't want to migrate. Of course we don't want to migrate if we can protect ourselves, if we can protect Tuvalu to ensure that Tuvalu will be above water.

Protecting the land is priority number one. With Tuvalu's homeland intact, the community and the culture are sure to survive into the future in dynamic ways that are uniquely Tuvaluan. In this time of increasing development, regardless of Tuvalu's future actions with climate change, protecting the culture must also be a major priority. With the Office of Cultural Affairs, Alamai has been working with the island communities to document and store important information about Tuvalu's cultural history. She explains that like other projects, cultural preservation is beneficial to Tuvaluans regardless of climate change. However, should any disaster strike in Tuvalu's future, cultural knowledge will certainly survive. Alamai said:

> So that's why I am here within the department, to have this in place especially for the storage… Anything happened, then at least it is there. If the tsunami comes and destroys all the stuff, people still have access to it. So those are the kind of things we are trying to have in place should something happen, should people shift elsewhere, they will still have the access to it.

Activities such as this do not address the physical impacts of climate change, but rather look to protecting people and culture against the human impacts of climate change. Cultural documentation can play an important role in sustaining culture beyond Tuvalu's shores for Tuvaluans who migrate temporarily for work or school, for Tuvaluans who wish to learn more about their ancestors and cultural history, and for Tuvaluans into the future no matter what changes occur with globalization or climate change.

The role of foreign nations. Regarding climate change impacts in Tuvalu, foreign nations have played and will play a very large role. For example, the Industrial Revolution and subsequent two and a half centuries of carbon pollution in foreign countries caused climate change to threaten Tuvalu. Consequently, many Tuvaluans feel justified in expecting foreign aid to help them address the threats to their shores. Vete said, "Like the rich countries, what they're saying, and they say '*Our* people's employments, *our* people's economy.' You know, Tuvalu is sinking!" The potential impacts of climate change in Tuvalu are so much worse than the concerns of the wealthy nations that are responsible. The actions of wealthy nations to protecting developing nations against climate change should include donor aid to assist these countries in implementing protective adaptations as well as enacting comprehensive climate change mitigation efforts such as drastically reducing emissions. Nalu told the story of a message he sent to the U.S. President via a documentarian that came through Funafuti a few years ago. He said:

NALU: One time one journalist came to me. That was back in 2009. He came from the USA. He got a camera, he took me down there with a chair and interviewed me and take notes.

MICHAEL: Really?

NALU: Then he said 'Do you have any messages for someone?' And I said 'Yes.' 'What?' I told him, 'Can I talk to your new President?'

MICHAEL: [Laughter]

NALU: And he said 'Yes, you can talk. It will be with your TV.'

MICHAEL: [Laughter]

NALU: And this is what I said, 'Please, President, can you cut down because we are suffering with global change!'

MICHAEL: With climate change, cut down your carbon, yeah?

NALU: That's right. And he was laughing!

Vete also noted that the wealthy nations of the world must be the leaders in reducing emissions. If Tuvalu were to cut emissions, "Its contribution is very negligible... We don't control the emission. The superpowers, the wealthier nations, the powerful nations, they dictate."

Tuvalu is working with donors from other countries to enact protective adaptations as well as conducting education and awareness campaigns. Eco-tourism in Tuvalu is on the rise (Tuvalu-News.tv, 2006), which brings tourist dollars to the local economy and raises awareness abroad about the risks of climate change and unsustainable development. In addition, Tafue told me:

We have been working on a project which we called the Rehabilitation Eco Center... built with materials which are environmentally friendly. Everything in the house is recycled, everything. And in this center we try and rehabilitate, we try and replant corals and reefs. And we had done some studies. We've sent a couple to go to training for that in Fiji. In the center we will do training on climate change. And the center is where we will invite people, specifically small families, to come and live in for say a week or two, a month or two months, to experience the way of life within this kind of eco house, and to see for themselves what the recycled things do for their own good. I was just corresponding with one NGO in the UK who are willing to be part of that but they have something to add which is they wanted to put in place a machine that can eat up plastics. And do educational programs in the Eco Center on the negative impacts of climate change on the environment and on the unborn babies as well. So we are still in dialogue with them. So far, Eco Center has been taken up by an NGO in New York which is called the Tribal Link Foundation. I have worked with them for the past eight, nine years. And the New York Institute of Technology, the Architectural School, so they've taken that up. They've come up with a design, sent the design across, looked at it and made some comments and sent it back to them. So those two in the US are fundraising for it, and the UK, in London.

The need for such collaborations as Tuvalu moves forward is recognized by many Tuvaluans. As a former colony, Tuvaluans are aware of the support that can be gained by wealthier nations. They are also aware that they would rather live independently with self-determination than be a part of another country. This is not to say that Tuvalu wants to cut all ties. Indeed, as was discussed extensively in the Results Section I, Tuvalu is an increasingly globalized community with many ties to other countries through trade, jobs, and education. Tuvalu's search for donor aid in conjunction with climate change is an extension of the donor support that has helped build infrastructure like the hospital and water catchment tanks. In her interview, Jopeto issued an appeal to foreign countries to support Tuvalu. She said:

> I just wish the big countries could see Tuvalu, as it's going to sink, affected from the global warming and the kinds of gasses from vehicles, even from the fridge and those kinds of things made of gas. So that's affecting the air and all of Tuvalu. So I'm just hoping that friends, Tuvalu's friends like Taiwan, the U.S., Australia, New Zealand, that they help Tuvalu... I just want to tell them that Tuvalu is a very small island that we couldn't see on the map... And I just want them to know that Tuvalu is a very small island so they can help us, with Tuvalu, with this climate change and all the effects of global warming. So that's all I want them to know.

The role of foreign nations and organizations in the future of Tuvalu is integral to the survival of the country's land, in keeping the population together, and in supporting the long-term sustainability of the Tuvaluan cultural community. If Tuvaluans are forced to scatter across the globe without a home to return to, future manifestations of Tuvaluan culture will be imbedded in other cultural communities, but will be difficult to maintain as a singular entity. This possible future is abhorrent to Tuvaluans who obviously and justifiably want to keep their homeland, keep their community intact, and keep their self-determination for the future of their country and their culture. A future without Tuvalu as an intact country and community, said Kina, is like no future at all:

| LAURA: | When you look into the future for Tuvalu, what do you think is going to happen in the future? |
| KINA: | I don't know. I don't know, because I don't want to believe that Tuvalu is going to sink. You know, like what the media people have said, have been |

214

mentioning, 'Tuvalu is going to sink. Tuvalu is sinking.' I don't believe in that. I don't believe in that because, you know, we are about to reach the end of – that's what I believe in, I believe that this world will be ending, and that will be like that's the end of it when Tuvalu is going to sink. And the world is going to be ending with Tuvalu.

LAURA: So you mean that, Tuvalu is sunk then the entire world is going to end?

KINA: No, I don't believe that Tuvalu is going to sink. But I believe that there is an end. Yeah, I think if we, I don't want to leave Tuvalu. And even though my family has been migrating and encouraging me come, I don't know. I don't want to go. I'll just say 'I am staying here.' I want to see what is going to happen but I don't think Tuvalu is sinking. But we'll see if it's sinking [Laughter].

Chapter Summary

This chapter discusses the agency of Tuvaluans in responding to climate change. They are not passive victims of external forces, but rather actively explore complex reactions and diverse beliefs in their country and around the world. Participants discussed their faith in God and the ways in which this faith interacts with their belief in climate change, current responses to climate change, as well as future plans. The Church of Tuvalu plays a major role in helping Tuvaluans cope with the threat of climate change as well as in international advocacy efforts in conjunction with the government and other leaders. Tuvaluans have diverse beliefs about what will happen in the future and what Tuvaluans should do. Some believe that migration may eventually be necessary. However, nearly all participants expressed clearly that migration is not currently the best option for Tuvalu. Rather, all possible mitigation and adaptation measures that could save the Tuvaluan homeland must first be explored before migration should be considered. Participants expressed a belief that foreign governments and agencies must be involved in this process to save Tuvalu.

Chapter 8

Discussion

This is an exploratory qualitative study seeking to build a deeper understanding of the human interface with climate change. One of the most important facets of the psychology of climate change is the impact of climate change on culture, as well as the effects of regional cultures on the human response to climate change. The APA's 2010 report on the psychology of climate change noted that a developed-nations bias exists in the literature because a vast majority of the research has been conducted in the United States, Europe, and Australia (Swim, et al., 2010). In Chapter 1, I added that this also constitutes a continental bias. Indeed, the extremely thorough 108-page report only mentioned island communities in one paragraph. The current study seeks to explore the interactions between cultural systems and climate change and to address the gaps in the previous research in the field. Cultural and Community Psychology are fields uniquely suited to positively contribute to the knowledge base in the psychology of climate change because of the reliance on mixed methods, grounded theory, community collaborations, cultural responsiveness, and the mutual connections and impacts between person and environment.

This study included two major components: semi-structured qualitative interviews and ethnographic field data. Photographic imagery is also utilized to assist in the thick description of the experiences, opinions, and perceptions of Tuvaluans to increase verisimilitude in foreign audiences who may have little personal experience with Pacific Island communities. The intended audiences of this document include academics from psychology and related fields, as well as lay readers in Tuvalu, the United States and beyond. As such, all data in the results section was reported in lay language and/or in a narrative format as much as possible so that the results of this study are accessible to participants and other interested audience members. This chapter will review the research questions in turn:

(1) What is the relationship between land and the wellbeing of the Tuvalu people (sense of place)?

(2) What is the relationship between community connections and the wellbeing of the Tuvalu people (sense of community)?

(3) What is the relationship between land and community connections (sense of place and sense of community) in Tuvalu culture(s)? and,

(4) How might global climate change affect the Tuvalu community as well as the land?

In this chapter, I will discuss:

(1) Tuvaluan culture through the psychological theories of Sense of Place and Sense of Community.

(2) How these two theories are manifest in highly interconnected ways in Tuvaluan culture.

(3) The interface between Tuvaluan culture and climate change, including both the cultural impacts of climate change and the

strengths of Tuvaluan culture that will aid in Tuvalu's long-term response to the climate change threats.

(4) Recent cultural changes that have occurred in Tuvalu and how these changes can offer a roadmap for future climate change response.

(5) These changes within Activity Settings theory.

(6) International academic literature and news media to consider the current international discourse about Tuvalu and climate change, and the place of this study within that conversation.

(7) The limitations of the study.

(8) The implications of this research for Tuvalu, for other places and cultures around the world, and for future research on climate change and related topics.

Because this chapter heavily explores psychological theory, it will be written in the technical and academic language of the field.

8.1 Research Questions

Research question 1: Sense of place in Tuvalu. What is the relationship between land and the wellbeing of the Tuvalu people? As presented in the Chapter 1, sense of place is an overarching psychological concept that includes place attachment and place identity. Sense of places speaks to the extent to which individuals and communities base their conceptions of who they are as people on a locality in which they live or reside. Indigenous peoples' health and wellbeing are often intricately connected with their land due to a heightened sense of place (Oneha, 2001) which stems from multiple generations of their forebears living in that locality and practicing cultural norms that were developed across generations with the resources of that locality. I will explore each of the four processes in Breakwell's (1992) model: place identification, place continuity, place-related self-esteem, and place-related self-efficacy, and the fifth element, climate, added by Knez (2005).

People's desire to distinctively identify themselves by location. Participants expressed a high level of place identity in this study. Place identity was manifest as both the strong sense of themselves as Tuvaluans as well as the strong sense of themselves as people from their individual islands. Tuvaluans who were raised predominantly on another island due to school or work migration (such as Kina and Ken) still identified themselves according to their home island rather as Tuvaluans from Funafuti where they had been raised. An extreme case was Teba, whose grandfather was lost at sea. For two generations, she and her family were removed from their Nukulaelae home and yet their identities remained connected to that place. Teba's father maintained a lifelong dream to return to his father's homeland, which he was able to fulfill as an old man. Teba first came to Tuvalu as an adult, and moved to the country seeking to learn "what it means to be a Tuvaluan." She learned the language and found a job uniquely suited to allowing her travel between the islands to learn extensively about Tuvaluan cultures in their place.

217

Lanieta and Alamai both spoke about a new Tuvaluan culture that was developing in Funafuti as a result of the gathering of migrants from all of the outer islands into this new location. Alamai said that in Funafuti a new Tuvaluan identity is being formulated that is a composite of the outer island identities. The home island was the place in which people could entirely practice their culture and where place identity could be manifest appropriately. Lanieta said the "only place" where culture can be practiced well is in one's home island community.

They both indicated that a new Tuvaluan language was being created that was not exactly the same as any of the islands' dialects. The language most associated with their home island identity could best be practiced only on their home islands.

Sueina, Ken, Kou, and Kina all discussed that weaving and other handicrafts are best practiced on one's home island. Kina was clear in her belief that she was unable to learn the style of weaving and handicrafts of her island because she was not raised there. Her limited physical interaction in the locality of her identity actually hindered her ability to actively express her identity through certain culturally prescribed actions. Kou explained that not only do outer island migrants to Funafuti have limited access to resources to conduct these activities, but the resources are actually different. The species of pandanus that are available on Funafuti are not the same as those on Niutao. Again, full participation in one's identity is hindered by lack of access to her identity's central place. These and other distinctively identified cultural actions are based within unique localities. The localities and the locality-based actions contribute heavily to personal identity.

Desire to maintain residency in a familiar or otherwise psychologically compatible location. The desire to maintain residency in their location is evident throughout Tuvalu's history in which Tuvaluans have increasingly migrated for school and employment to Funafuti and abroad. These migrants are gaining opportunities to live permanently away from Tuvalu, but they don't. They return home to their island for extended stays between stints at work or school, and they retire home to Tuvalu at the end of their lives. Lanieta said that even given Tuvalu's social problems, it continues to be a good place for Tuvaluans to live. Regardless of the changes occurring with recent development, and even regardless of recent social ills such as overcrowding, Lanieta is indicating a clear preference for life in Tuvalu above life elsewhere.

Tuvaluans are addressing this aspect of sense of place directly with the threat that climate change will literally take their location from them. This desire to maintain residence in their country is expressed in very powerful ways (see 7.2 Tuvalu's Future). Many Tuvaluans state that they will not migrate no matter what the future holds with climate change. Even Tuvaluans who would consider permanent migration from climate change express that they are only willing to consider this migration as a last resort. Every other possible option must be exhausted, including trying to raise the islands higher than the rising sea, before agreeing to move. Tafue said that losing the Tuvaluan homeland would mean losing a sense of belonging. Tuvalu is place that is psychologically compatible to Tuvaluans. It is where they experience a sense of home. When speaking of the possibility of permanent migration, Vete clearly stated that this was the worst possible option for Tuvaluans, though one that may eventually and unfortunately come to pass. ***Feeling good or proud of their location.*** Highly connected with Tuvaluans' desire to stay in Tuvalu and to protect their homeland from the rising sea is their strong sense of love for Tuvalu. Participants are particularly proud of the lifestyle that is afforded by the land in Tuvalu, which is a place of bounty. Vete said the Tuvaluan life was a life of no stress. However, Tuvaluans also refer to the subsistence lifestyle as one that requires a lot of hard work. It is not easy to work the *pulaka* pits, to cook traditional foods, etc. However, this work is rewarded with the knowledge that all of your living needs will be provided by land. Kou compared the bounty of Tuvalu to the scarcity found in other regions of the world. Tuvaluan life that is integrated with the land is compared favorably to modern life that involves job-related stresses, and is compared favorably to live in other developing areas of the world where survival is perceived by Tuvaluans to be tenuous.

Even the recent changes in terms of political and economic development are looked upon with pride. Education and employment opportunities have become standard and ubiquitous goals for Tuvaluan parents. Tuvaluans work wage employment jobs to pay school fees and provide educational opportunities for their children and the other youth in their families so that those youth will have more opportunities for gainful employment in Tuvalu and abroad. Support for this new cultural mandate provided part of the motivation for Tuvaluans to Separate from Kiribati. As part of the Gilbert and Ellice Islands Colony, Tuvaluans were denied access to scholarships that were distributed evenly throughout the island groups. There were simply more Gilbertese people and despite being members of the same colony, Tuvaluans were treated as a distinct and separate people. Tuvaluans believed that students from their island group deserved more. The decision to separate from Kiribati and then to become independent from England was similarly looked on with extreme pride by Tuvaluans, who strongly desired self-determination for the people in their island group. Despite being grouped with Kiribati for almost a century, Tuvaluan sense of place (and sense of community) remained most loyal to the Tuvaluan/Ellice Islands.

Ability to care for their needs within their location. Tuvaluans' pride for their country and desire to stay on their homeland is highly connected with their ability to meet subsistence needs by working the land, whether they are actively working the land or are working wage employment jobs. Even participants who have lived away from their home islands for much of their lives and who rely on wage employment discussed the bounty provided by working the lands. Participants spoke about the wide variety of foods that were available locally. The local foods are not only sufficient for feeding one's nuclear family, but also for feeding the extended family and even neighbors, as Lanieta explained. More modern cultural needs can also be fulfilled in Tuvalu. Jobs are available in Funafuti, as are the hospital and university campus. Secondary school students may travel to Vaitupu or Funafuti for education, and post-secondary students can earn degrees on Funafuti. The education-employment loop can be fulfilled entirely in Tuvalu, although many Tuvaluans now choose to complete at least part of their education overseas. Wage employment positions and individual sales of handicrafts and copra are also available in Tuvalu, especially in Funafuti. Money can be earned domestically to pay for electricity, imported goods, or school fees. Even as Tuvalu becomes a more globalized country, the increasing development allows for this globalization to be achieved without necessarily traveling abroad.

Climate identity (urban- versus country-person attitude). In Knez's study, the focus was on urban- versus country-person attitude, which is applicable in Tuvalu for people who prefer to live in the outer islands versus people who prefer to live in Funafuti. Although the outer islands are diverse in terms of cultural and linguistic traditions, they are more similar to each other in terms of rural island lifestyle compared to Funafuti, Tuvalu's urban center. Noa, for example, said that life in Funafuti was full of excitement and opportunity. On the outer islands, life is less connected to the outside world because the trade ships come through Funafuti and there is no international air travel. Although imported goods, internet, Western-style housing, and other aspects of Tuvalu's increasingly globalized lifestyle are present, a greater proportion of the population on the outer islands continue to maintain a subsistence lifestyle. The outer islands are recognized as the place to maintain cultural traditions and language.

The urban- versus country-person climate identity issues also come into play for Tuvaluans who travel abroad. Tuvaluans are able to maintain a certain style and quality of life in Tuvalu that is not possible in foreign countries. During my first trip to Tuvalu, one woman told me of her time abroad she and her family "suffered" because of the disconnect from extended family, neighbors, and the close-knit community. The communities in Tuvalu are physically close to each other. Houses are close. The traditional thatch structures have open walls. The layout and spacing of homes fosters close-knit community norms. In the United States, as a counter point, neighborhood housing is closed-walled and physically divided by yards, fences, and property lines. People may or may not know their neighbors. The way that many neighborhood spaces are designed, people may not even know what their neighbors look like. Foreign spaces therefore may not be conducive to maintaining Tuvaluan way of life.

In terms of climate, Tuvalu is located in an equatorial tropical region of the South Pacific. It is hot year-round, with a wet and a dry season, both of which more or less approximate summer conditions in temerate countries. Tuvalu is not mountainous, which means that the physical makeup of other islands in the region, such as in Fiji and Samoa, are vastly different to Tuvalu. Cold winters that occur further from the Equator are entirely foreign to Tuvaluans. When a delegation went to England to negotiate for independence, Tomu told me the experience was "awkward" because it was winter in the UK. Many Tuvaluans have little to no personal experience with such cold weather.

Research question 2: Sense of community in Tuvalu. What is the relationship between community connections and the wellbeing of the Tuvalu people? As presented in Chapter 1, McMillan and Chavis (1986) outlined four

220

components within the psychological sense of community, including feeling of belongingness, mutual influence, sense of needs fulfillment, and emotional connection to the community. When discussing the cultural norms (traditional and modern) and the threat of climate change, participants expressed each of these elements as well as a normalized strong sense of community. The Tuvalu culture holds with it an expectation of community involvement and mutual care. I will explore these cultural norms in relation to the four components of sense of community identified by McMillan and Chavis.

A feeling of belongingness, or the extent to which people perceive themselves to be members of the community. Tuvalu is a small country both in terms of population and available land. People on each island live near to one another. Their lives are highly integrated both in terms of physical proximity and therefore continuous interaction, and in terms of structured activities and an expectation of community involvement. Social norms require participation in community activities and events. The expectation of involvement is strong enough that someone who refuses to participate is considered aberrant. There is also a semi-formalized penalty or punishment system that perpetuates cultural and community involvement for those who do not appropriately participate in community and culture.

Participants identified highly with their home island community, regardless of whether they currently live on that island or if they were raised there. On Funafuti, each island maintains separate and active island-specific community groups. The Niutao community, for example, meets as a whole community once a month. Youth, women's, and sports groups may meet more regularly. Through meetings, activities, and events with each group, Tuvaluans maintain a continuous connection to their home island community even when they are away from it. Kou explained that the connection to the home island community is not only a matter of cultural support on Funafuti, but that the Funafuti and Niutao portions of that island community actively support each other. Funafuti is the place for work and for money, and Niutaoans who live there are responsible to send monetary support back to Niutao. Niutaoans who live on their homeland, in turn, are responsible to send local foods and other resources to their community members living in Funafuti. In such ways, community connection and belongingness is active and ongoing.

Influence of the community on the individual and vice versa, or mutual degree of impact of a person on the community and of the community on a person. Because of the highly collectivist nature of Tuvaluan cultures, members of each island community as well as church groups perceive a high level of responsibility toward the care of others. The reverse is also true. Participants expressed a sense of security that their communities could and would come to their aid in a time of need. These cultural manifestations of mutual influence between individual and community are particularly apparent in the guest and gift cultural norms of Tuvalu. The dual perception of community involvement as both a responsibility and a resource during times of need is supported in previous literature (Nowell & Boyd, 2010). The mutual influence of person and community in Tuvalu is exemplified by the requirements to give

221

of oneself and to give of one's belongings. This expectation of giving and receiving is what Kina called, "a cycle of support." Tuvaluans are secure that their community will care for them because they are just as active in caring for others. This is manifest in sharing of resources and food, and also in large community activities such as giving time and effort for manual labor to build community structures, such as the Talafai building the church and preschool.

However, even this activity of community support required support. The Nanumaga women's group organized themselves to provide food for the Talafai while they were working, realizing that the Lofeagai community would not be able to feed the youth workers any more than they were able to complete the work themselves. Mutual influence of this type is also recognized during and after times of disaster. During the most recent tsunami warning, Noa explained that the Funafuti youth group organized themselves to alert everyone of the wave threat in the middle of the night. After Hurricane Ofa, Alamai said that the community groups organized themselves to help rebuild the houses that were destroyed on Vaitupu. These examples show a high degree of mutual influence in community participation. Coming together, people are able to support others and in turn know that they will be supported when they are in need.

A sense of needs fulfillment though community involvement, or the satisfaction one gains from active community membership. Lanieta told the story of the Talafai building the Lofeagai church with great pride. Similarly, Noa spoke with pride about the role played by the Funafuti youth during the tsunami warning. Tomu said that "the most important thing" in his life the extent to which he contributed in the community. Community involvement in Tuvalu is expected, is hard work, and can achieve remarkable things. Kou talked about the 2014 General Assembly that will be happening in Niutao and how the community has already been active in their preparations for more than a year. This high level of activity is necessary of every Niutaoan living on the home island or in Funafuti in order to achieve the goals set by the island leadership to make this enormous event successful. Every community member has their own role for participation and contribution to make large events happen. For feasts and *fateles*, the island leadership decides on an event, the men gather the food, the women prepare the food, and the island leadership conducts the event. These interconnected roles assure that everyone is involved in the proper functioning of the community. Tomu explained that the *maneapa* is a place to "prove" Tuvaluan cultural traditions because this is the space in which everyone comes together to fulfill their roles in the community.

An emotional connection to the community and community functions. The participants of this study were not shy in talking about how much they love Tuvalu, their home island, and their cultural community. They also talked a great deal about their pride for activities and achievements of their island groups. But some of the most visceral reactions of emotional connection to the Tuvaluan community and culture were exhibited when participants expressed their displeasure with future possibilities of migration. These emotional expressions included flat refusal among some Tuvaluans to leave even if it means they will die by staying. There was also denial that the world could be so unfair as to require Tuvaluans to go. For others, there was acceptance of permanent migration as a possibility but only after every other possible option, no matter how costly, had been fully pursued.

Research question 3: Sense of place and sense of community in Tuvalu. What is the relationship between land and community connections in Tuvalu culture(s)? The psychological theories driving the exploration of sense of place and sense of community are based on research that has been in large part conducted in Western societies. Some previous research on the psychological sense of community among indigenous peoples (e.g., Bishop, Colquhoun, & Johnson, 2006; Foster-Fishman, et al., 2005; Fried, 2000; Oneha, 2001) has indicated that community and place are greatly interrelated. In many Western populations and other cultural communities around the world, people no longer directly interact with land to sustain their lives and may not live in the same place (home, city, or even country) as their forebears. Communities that are indigenous to their location are more likely to lead lives that are intricately connected with their space because cultural norms and community activities were developed in that space over a period of multiple generations (Oneha, 2001).[55] In these cases, sense of place and sense of community overlap highly and may in fact be extensions of each other. Many examples of this overlap arose during this study into the cultural norms and expectations in Tuvalu. I will discuss some of these examples within the context of Tuvaluan activities settings that blend community activities with land and natural resources, and the context of cultural communities that are defined by land divisions (islands).

Activity settings blending place and community. Activity settings are spaces in which people gather for the purpose of accomplishing a particular goal or activity. When using an activity setting as a unit of analysis, a researcher will consider the people who are involved, the process of decision-making and other power structures, the goal outcome, the time spent, the behavioral expectations, and other functions and processes inherent to the setting (O'Donnell, Tharp, & Wilson, 1993).[56] Examples of the activity settings used here to are the *pulaka* pits, weaving and other handicrafts settings, and the community *maneapa*. These three examples cover the range of creating traditional and local foods, traditional and local materials, and traditional and local gatherings.

Pulaka is the staple crop of Tuvalu. Prior to the availability of imports including rice, *pulaka* was the foundation of Tuvaluans' diets. Here I am using *pulaka* pits as the example activity settings, but this could be substituted with fishing boats, breadfruit or banana trees, coconut palms, etc. In a *pulaka* pit the people that are present for the growing activities are men. Knowledge is passed between them, predominantly from father to son. Traditionally, there would be a family that has a particularly strong knowledge base and skillset regarding

---

[55] Tuvaluans are also increasingly living non-subsistence lives. See below for further discussion.

[56] For further discussion on theory, please refer to 8.2 Activity Settings Theory.

pulaka growing. Every day, men are expected to go to work in the *pulaka* pits. The immediate goal of this work is to tend to the crops and/or to harvest for immediate or upcoming consumption. In addition, longer-term goals include providing for the future sustenance needs of the family or the community. For example, in preparation for the 2014 General Assembly in Niutao, men on that island are already planting and tending to species of *pulaka* that require years to grow. The efforts put forth by the men in *pulaka* pits reveal the cultural expectation of hard work as well as the role of men in the wider community to provide food for family members and the community. Without the land, this activity setting does not exist. Without the cultural community roles and expectations of this activity, the setting would be entirely different.

Women in Tuvaluan culture are responsible for weaving the mats and for creating other woven articles and handicrafts. The related activity settings include settings for gathering the natural resources, preparing the resources (e.g., the two-week process of preparing pandanus leaves for weaving), and the actual weaving or crafting. Men may also participate in some of these settings, although the primary cultural responsibility is on the women, who are the focus here. The knowledge and skills of these activities are passed from mother to daughter (or son). All of these activity settings require land directly or indirectly. The gathering settings require direct access to land from which to harvest the necessary resources. The preparation and weaving/crafting settings require a previous access to land for harvesting. Women from the outer islands who live on Funafuti are able to participate in crafts such as sewing pillowcases, but they have no ability to weave due to their lack of access to pandanus on the island. Women prepare mats and handicrafts as part of their responsibility to their family, to the women's groups they belong to, and in fulfillment of their cultural role within the community. Once again, both the land and the community are necessary. Without the land, certain settings are impossible. Without the community roles and norms guiding the activities, the land becomes a different activity setting entirely.

A community's *maneapa* is the gathering space in which community leaders meet, in which community-wide meetings are held, and in which functions such as feasts and *fateles* are held. In each of these cases, a *maneapa* is a community-oriented location for activities. Each of these activities utilizes the food and materials created in the previously mentioned activity settings. The activities held in the *maneapa* include protocols for community behavior. All participants have their culturally assigned roles. Mats are laid on the floor. Food is served. Adornments are worn. The activities held in the *maneapa* are in some ways a perfect culmination of other activity settings in terms of the cultural connection to place and the cultural connection to community. Each island's *maneapa* is cherished as the location of these many community gatherings, and its importance is recognized in the power structures and hierarchies on the island. The space is important specifically because of its communal function. The activities that happen in the space, when conducted in complete compliance with the culture, will use natural resources from the island as community members carry out their cultural obligations and roles.

224

Community norms defined by land divisions. The connection to one's home island community is of the utmost importance to most Tuvaluans. They are involved in the island-wide community as well as smaller island-specific groups such as youth groups and women's groups. Even after a person or family migrates away from their home island for work or school, they maintain this community connection according to their island. In essence, the place dictates who is "community." On Funafuti, each island has its own gathering spaces, including a *maneapa*, sports courts, and other structures. These structures may be used by other island communities, but only in specific cases such as inter-island sports competitions. People living on Funafuti are not prohibited from interacting with people from other islands. In fact, the high level of interaction in the workplace, in shops, with neighbors, etc., has given rise to a new Tuvaluan dialect and identity that is an amalgam of multiple island dialects and identities. However, this new Tuvaluan identity does not supersede or discount the strong identification of people with their home island. Island-specific gatherings are frequent, and a person's home island is considered to be part and parcel of their identity.

Research question 4: Sense of place, sense of community, and climate change. How might global climate change affect the Tuvalu community as well as the land? Climate change is affecting natural systems around the world. In Tuvalu, participants discussed coastal erosion, tidal flooding, unpredictable/unseasonable weather, drought, and sea level rise as current and ongoing changes they are witnessing. The thesis of this study is that impacts to land, weather, and sea *necessarily* impact the lives of humans in small to devastating ways. Participants gave examples of these human impacts of climate change. Homes have been swept away during storms. People have had to move their homes inland or build houses on stilts to protect against such risks. Land is incrementally eroding as the sea rises. Shorelines and interior lands are becoming saline as the sea level rises and therefore raises the height of the King tides. Now, monthly tidal flooding seeps through the rock and soil, causing *pulaka* to yellow and wilt. Trees and brush along the shoreline die from saltwater inundation, leaving behind rocky shores that are even more susceptible to erosion. Unseasonable weather makes growing more difficult based on past weather patterns, upsetting planting and harvesting schedules. Changing weather patterns can also make sea faring more unpredictable and, thus, dangerous when the water becomes unexpectedly rough.

During the 2011 drought, Tuvalu nearly ran out of water. A state of emergency was declared and foreign aid poured in with desalination units and bottled water to mitigate the disaster. With the large number of catchment tanks that have been added to the country's households over the past decades, Tuvalu is currently at its least vulnerable to drought in terms of water storage capacity. And yet this was not enough when the drought dragged on. Tuvaluans' lives were affected directly by their strictly limited access to freshwater. Freshwater had to be reserved for cooking and drinking only, leaving bathing, washing, and other activities to be carried out with sea water or brackish well water.

Tuvaluans had to travel to checkpoints to collect a daily ration of two-buckets per household.

The most extreme potential impact of climate change to Tuvalu is the devastation of the land and therefore of the community that will occur if the sea rises one meter or more as is projected. If massive adaptation efforts are not implemented with the full support of foreign nations and organizations for funding and infrastructure, Tuvaluans could lose their entire country. This extreme impact to the land will have obvious and far-reaching impacts to the lives of the people who live on this land. Participants expressed clearly their connection to place and the fact that their cultural community norms are best practiced only on their homeland. Culture is dynamic by nature, but some Tuvaluans fear that if this impact comes to pass, their culture will change quickly and drastically in ways beyond their control, as Tuvaluans lose the space in which their culture was developed over a period of centuries. Tuvaluan lives are highly interconnected with both the land and the communities in which they live. Climate change is currently affecting both of these things, and will continue to do so into the future. This is the cultural impact of climate change.

Tuvaluans have recent experiences with cultural changes, and can look to these examples of change to purposefully develop models and programs to preserve their culture despite future changes relating to climate change. For example, with the increasing urbanization of the Tuvaluan population, many Tuvaluans are leading non-subsistence lives away from their home islands. In some ways, Tuvaluans on Funafuti are living in increasingly "Western" ways as Tuvalu becomes a more globalized country. However, despite barriers to practicing their home island culture in an urban setting, Tuvaluans on Funafuti maintain their home island connections and adapt new Tuvaluan traditions. These experiences can aid future cultural adaptations.

8.2 Activity Settings Theory

Tuvalu is home to dynamic cultures that are in an extended period of development and change. As previously discussed, there is no one time in Tuvalu's past that can be considered "real" Tuvaluan culture, free from outside influence. The first Tuvaluans came from other places. Tuvaluans have a long history of periodic trade and interaction with other Pacific Island peoples. Since the 1500s, Tuvaluans have been periodically visited by European explorers.[57] Christianity was adopted into Tuvaluan culture in the 1800s, around which time the Tuvalu islands came under the purview of the British. Tuvalu was grouped with Kiribati and formally colonized in 1915.[58] The Americans came in World War II, physically changing the shape of three of the islands. Tuvaluans increased foreign trade and migration for wage employment through the phosphate and mariners industries. Education came to be a primary goal of Tuvaluan parents for their children. Between the .tv funds and foreign aid,

---

[57] http://tuvaluislands.com/history.htm
[58] http://tuvaluislands.com/history2.htm

Tuvalu has experienced a boom in development over the past two decades, from roads to internet connection. Through all of this, Tuvaluan cultures have adapted because Tuvaluans are adaptable as their contexts change. As Feue said, "On average I think that the Tuvaluans are renowned as being adaptable."

In this state of cultural dynamism and adaptability, climate change has been introduced. Climate change has caused changes in Tuvaluan cultures and daily lives in large and small ways. Homes are moved and/or constructed differently, temporary but extraordinary water restrictions were enacted during the drought, and concerns for the future have created a pervasive ambient stress. Because the full extent of climate change and the timeline on which it will occur cannot be accurately forecast (due to scientific uncertainty and uncertainty regarding whether future human actions will exacerbate or mitigate these impacts), it is impossible for anyone to know what exactly will happen to Tuvalu's future communities and when. Fears that climate change poses an overwhelming threat to culture are *understandable*. However, given the adaptability of the Tuvaluan people, there is hope that these fears are not *justified*. To explore the precedence of ability of Tuvalu cultures to absorb change from outside influence without losing culture, I turn to Activity Settings theory.

Although there is no point in time in which Tuvalu's cultures were "pure" and "free" from outside influence, I will discuss traditional activity settings and modern activity settings in the general terms that have been used throughout this paper. Traditional settings are meant to include subsistence and cultural gatherings and activities that were a part of life prior to colonization, such as settings related to fishing and agriculture, weaving and handicrafts, and community gatherings. The modern settings in this explanation will include those related to paid employment, education, and modernity that are relatively recent additions to Tuvaluan life, such as schools, shops for imported goods, wage employment workplaces, restaurants, and other settings related to the market economy.

As presented, when people participate in multiple shared and interconnected activity settings with each other over an extended period of time, they begin to develop intersubjectivity, or shared interpretive meanings of events in their lives. These shared meanings and shared interpretations of events by a group create a 'culture' of thought and experience. When communities have a strong intersubjectivity, they share expectations for roles, behaviors, and attitudes of others. They interpret events similarly. The culture of this intersubjectivity is only as static as the people who participate in these shared activity settings, which is to say, not at all. People change over time. The activity settings change over time. New activity settings are created, and these settings interact with each other, changing the quality and outcome of the community's intersubjectivity. Two hundred years ago there was no cultural expectation that parents would send their children to USP because the settings leading to this expectation did not yet exist. Activity Settings theory is therefore a useful tool in understanding cultural changes over time by exploring the changes to settings and introduction of new settings over time. I will now apply this theory as a model for understanding recent cultural changes in Tuvalu.

Traditional Tuvaluan cultures are enacted in a vast array of settings – in the home, at the shore, in the sea, in *pulaka* pits, in the bush, at the *maneapa*, etc. Each of these settings has norms, expectations, and perhaps explicit rules that guide the behaviors and outcomes of the people and the activities. There are certain people allowed to be present, each with their own roles in the setting. There are different power structures, including how decisions are made, who can speak when, and what supportive roles are necessary for the activity to succeed. There are related settings that must occur before or after to ensure all settings are able to continue to function. There are different natural resources, tools, and materials that are necessary, and more. Together, these elements determine the process and outcomes of each setting. When people participate in multiple shared activity settings, they develop intersubjectivity, which over time leads to a shared culture (See Image 67). Traditional activity settings lead to and perpetuate traditional culture.

As extensively discussed in this paper, Tuvaluan cultures are not only made up of traditional activity settings. Many outside influences over many generations have led to the creation of new activity settings, each with their own participants, rules, expectations, resources, outcomes, power structures, and related settings. Tuvaluan community members participate in these new activity settings *and* in the traditional activity settings. The intersubjectivity developed by these many shared-settings makes up modern Tuvaluan cultures (see Image 68). The three example groups of activity settings in this model are school-related, employment-related, and modernity-related settings. These activity settings are highly interrelated in the sense that they support and perpetuate each other. Employment-related settings bring in money that allows for parents to afford school fees and modern appliances, imported goods, etc. Modernity settings increase the expense of living in Tuvalu and therefore require participation in work-related settings. School-related settings increase Tuvaluans' competitiveness for jobs, which better allow them to participate in work-related settings. In addition, both work- and school- related settings may

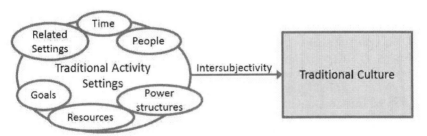

Image 67. Participation in multiple traditional activity settings with associated elements (related settings, time, people, goals, resources, and power structures) leads to the development of intersubjectivity and then to shared traditional culture.

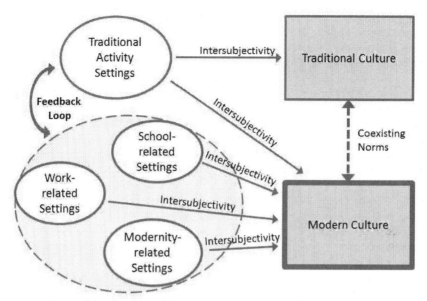

Image 68. Participation in multiple traditional and modern activity settings leads to the development of intersubjectivity and thus to shared modern culture. The school, work, and modernity-related settings are highly interrelated and perpetuate each other. The modern settings and traditional settings also have a feedback loop in which they affect each other. There is a perception among participants that modern Tuvalu maintains both modern cultures and traditional cultures.

include foreign migration, which increases the influence of outside cultures including the increase of Tuvaluan modernity.

Although not as closely related as the interconnected modern activity settings, traditional activity settings do affect and are affected by these new settings, as noted in the model as a feedback loop. For example, fishing is now conducted predominantly with the use of outboard engine motorboats rather than canoes. *Pulaka* may be cooked on gas stoves. The Boxing Day feast and *fatele* for the Niutao community is in honor of the students of the community. Concurrently, the new focus of Tuvaluans on education and work to support education means that many youth and adults are spending more of their daily lives in modern activity settings and less time in traditional activity settings. Modern activity settings are influenced by traditional settings by shared participants, spaces, expectations, knowledge, values, etc. Schools are full of youth whose parents and grandparents maintain traditional activity settings. These youth bring that knowledge with them to school.[59] Work settings are full

---

[59] Youth will also bring school-derived knowledge with them to traditional activity settings. However, as was noted in Chapter 4, youth who participate

of Tuvaluans who are seeking to balance their desire to live on the land with their desire to provide education and modern amenities to their children. None of these activity settings exist in a vacuum. They interact with each other in dynamic ways.

Participants in the study implicitly and explicitly expressed a belief that Tuvaluan cultures are not only made up of these modern settings or the values they espouse. There are plenty of Tuvaluans who are keeping traditional activities, knowledge, and values alive and active today, although the traditional activity settings are influenced by modern settings.[60] Tuvaluans remain committed to their island communities and community groups. They participate in community functions, feasts, and *fateles*, and come together to support other Tuvaluans through building structures, sharing food and resources, and giving of themselves by being present and active in cultural events. Although in this model I show that traditional activity settings contribute to the intersubjectivity that makes up modern Tuvaluan cultures, I would like to stipulate that there is a strong sense among the Tuvaluan participants in this study that traditional culture is alive and well. Tradition and modernity coexist in modern Tuvalu. The outside influences and new activity settings have not displaced traditional culture or activities. Tuvaluan cultures change, but they have not been lost.

The evidence of Tuvalu's dynamic and adaptable cultural past provides hope for the future. Tuvaluans have shown beyond a doubt over the last century that they can absorb extensive amounts of change from outside influence and new cultural directions and maintain their culture. Climate change is affecting the lives of Tuvaluans and will continue to do so into the future. Some of these changes will be dramatic and unprecedented. However, colonization was dramatic and unprecedented. The development associated with the .tv boom and recent donor aid was dramatic and unprecedented. In the decades and centuries to come, Tuvaluans may need to actively envision ways to maintain their cultural values and traditions under the press of extraordinary outside forces. But climate change is only one player in the cultural change that Tuvalu is navigating. And "Tuvaluans are renowned as being adaptable."

---

predominantly in school settings away from their home islands are increasingly feeling less equipped to conduct some traditional activities such as weaving. During our interview, Kina wondered aloud if primary schools should begin teaching this traditional knowledge to students. Should this occur systematically, youth would increase their knowledge of both traditional and modern activity settings, and the feedback loop between traditional and modern settings would likely increase as more actors spend more time in both activity setting categories.

[60] It should be noted that traditional culture will therefore also be affected by the intersubjectivity created by participation in modern settings. However, this model focuses on the creation of modern culture, as influenced by traditional and modern activity settings, to focus on the ways in which Tuvaluan culture persists even as it adapts.

The younger generations in Tuvalu are being raised in the midst of these cultural changes and with the reality of a changing climate and island environment. Participants discussed the changing reality of their ability to practice cultural activities to the expert degree of their forebears as they spend more and more time being educated and working away from their home island. Additionally, I spoke with parents who discussed the changing values with which they raise their children. For example, eating order during meals is beginning to change so that children may eat before elders. Parents are also expending increasing effort and resources to provide their children with advanced educational opportunities. These changes result in generational differences between younger and older generations. It is possible, although it was not explored deeply in this study, that in addition to a different practical ability to engage with the culture, the younger generations experience a different connection to the culture. The younger adults who were interviewed who discussed a declining cultural expertise (in terms of cultural activities like weaving) expressed regret at this change and a concurrent love for and strong emotional connection to their culture regardless. Interviewed participants and other Tuvaluans I spoke with during the study commonly expressed that many Tuvaluans, especially elders, would be unwilling to leave the country even if it meant they would die. Among the participants, there was no increase in hypothetical willingness to leave Tuvalu among younger generations. The only apparent relation between participants' potential willingness to migrate (after every other possible mitigation and adaptation effort had been exhausted) were those who had spent a great amount of time overseas for work and/or school in their lives regardless of their age. As new generations spend more and more time overseas for education, it is possible they may become more willing to migrate.

Because minors are not a part of this study, the experiences of the youngest Tuvaluans are not represented. This is promising area for future studies because today's teenagers were born in a country that was already aware of climate change and its potential impacts. This alone could cause great changes in the ways in which teens experience climate change versus adults. Similarly, the adults raising the next generation may teach their children differently (encouraging different values or life goals) according to the reality of climate change. This topic was not explored in this study, although adaptations in parenting styles and directives according to other cultural changes were apparent and would suggest the need to explore this topic in future research.

8.3 International Discourse on Climate Change in Tuvalu

Tuvalu has multiple media outlets, none of which have a strong international presence. As such, most of the media representation of Tuvalu and Tuvaluans that are played out on the world stage are produced by foreigners, as is the case in the current study. Because these representations are foreign-made, it becomes necessary to view them from a critical perspective and to ask what exactly these representations are saying to their global audiences (Hall, 1997; Mithlo, 2008; Said, 1978). Critical psychology explores power, including the assumptions that are made about a population and how that can lead to false claims based on the ideology of another culture (Davidson, et al., 2006; Fox, Prilleltensky, & Austin, 2009). This section critically explores several examples of international media representations of Tuvalu and Tuvaluans within the context of climate change. This critical analysis should not diminish the positive role of awareness and education that these representations achieve on a global scale, nor should it suggest that all representations of Tuvalu in climate change media and research are negative. Rather the analysis aims to provide a guide to improving the cultural responsiveness of future representations by avoiding common pitfalls. This dissertation is also a foreign representation of climate change issues in Tuvalu. Much consideration has been given to the quality of this representation and its contribution to the international discourse on this topic. However, this paper remains a product of an international researcher and as such should be subjected to the same critical lens that I am now applying to peer literature.

The representation of indigenous peoples by others is an important topic to consider, especially by non-indigenous people. Historically, stories of native peoples have been appropriated by colonizing nations, who then tell the stories from a colonial perspective, reflecting colonial values, meanings, and storytelling techniques (Gunn Allen, 2003). It therefore is easy to misrepresent indigenous people through the storytelling translation. Kilpatrick (1999) has shown that critiquing representation should include an exploration of the sociocultural reality of the representer and the representee. For example, colonial stories of indigenous peoples (especially those who have been colonized) often focus on the "inevitable" destruction of indigenous society and the "inevitable" loss of indigenous cultures. All cultures and societies are dynamic. They shift and change as they move through time and interact with others, but there is nothing "inevitable" about their future end. "It is tempting to get caught up in questions of 'correctness' says Kilpatrick, but it is equally important to understand what exactly the representations are saying to the audience" (Kilpatrick, 1999, p. xv). For example, the question of the "inevitability" story should not merely be, 'Is it really inevitable?' but should also include the question, 'Why are you claiming it is inevitable?'

International journalists and researchers take on a storytelling mantle when relating the experiences of indigenous populations to a global audience who may be unfamiliar with the subject matter. These stories, journalistic or academic though they may be, are still external stories reflecting external preconceptions and oftentimes misrepresenting indigenous peoples. In the case of Tuvalu and climate change, a critical exploration of academic and popular media reveals a pattern of language and representation that harkens back to the colonial era. The discourse surrounding climate change is simply the most recent conversation in which these patterns can be seen. In light of the important role Tuvaluan leaders play on the world stage in political, legal, and moral arguments over current actions and future impacts of climate change, it becomes increasingly important to critique the representations of Tuvalu and Tuvaluans by foreign media and academic literature to understand why certain stories are told. Representations by media and academic literature have the power to legitimize and to dismiss the statements and mission of Tuvaluans in the audience's minds.

The Guardian has published several articles on the topic of climate change in Tuvalu. The Guardian is one of the most prolific international news outlets worldwide in terms of climate change in Tuvalu and is likely responsible for a large proportion of global awareness of the threats Tuvalu is facing. The critical analysis I apply here should not diminish this very important role that this news source and indeed these articles undoubtedly play, but should instead offer a guide for future discourse. One article addressed the political concerns of Tuvalu regarding the rising sea (Adam, 2009). The article, titled *Increase in Sea Levels due to Global Warming Could Lead to 'Ghost States'*, briefly addresses these international political concerns. This stated purpose is at odds with the image that accompanies the article, a stock photo by Chad Ehlers/Getty Images of 'paradise' – a lagoon scene in which white sand slopes down into clear blue water. A palm tree bows over the sea and a topless brown-skinned woman walks away from the camera, thigh deep in the water with her long hair cascading down her back. The article discusses two countries facing the possibility of displacement from the rising sea – the Republic of Maldives and Tuvalu. Physically, the space represented in this image could be either. Culturally, it is neither. Maldives is a Muslim country in which women dress and behave conservatively (Fulu, 2007). Tuvalu's population is predominantly Christian, and the women dress very conservatively. Moreover, women do not leave their hair down, but typically pull it up into high buns or braids. They do not go topless at the beach. This image does not represent the people of the Maldives or Tuvalu as people who are facing the uncertain legal future as 'ghost states.' Rather, this image represents a (male) tourist ideal of a tropical paradise, in which the scenery is beautiful and the women are sexually available. As part of a tourist piece about either country, such an image would be questionable at best. In a piece dealing with the potential of "catastrophic consequences" from climate change to these islands, this image is alarming. This image does not frame Tuvalu or Maldives by their culture, their people, or their government. Instead, this image frames these countries as a tourist paradise, implying that that is their value to the world.

Some of the language within the article also poorly represents Tuvaluans and climate change issues. The article reviews recent comments by Francois Gemenne of the Institute for Sustainable Development regarding the international legal questions of the changing climate. Adam reports Gemenne's words at one point without a direct quotation, "Gemenne said there was more at stake than cultural and sentimental attachments to swamped countries." Referring to a thousands-year-old connection to one's homeland as a "sentimental attachment" downplays the value and importance for a people to maintain their homeland. The statement actively dismisses this attachment by claiming it is at most a minor concern compared to what is at stake. Adam also states that:

> Experts say it is a matter of time before global warming drives up sea levels the one or two metres it would take to force permanent

evacuation of islands such as Tuvalu, the highest point of which is four metres above water.

These anonymous experts have crafted a ticking clock for Tuvalu in which it is only "a matter of time" before their worst fears are realized. In reality, though scientists agree that climate change is certain, there is great uncertainty in the predictions of how much the sea will rise and when (IPCC, 2007; Niepold, Herring, & McConville, 2007). Much of this uncertainty is due to social uncertainty – how will the human race respond to this slow crisis? If far-reaching climate change mitigation efforts are put into effect soon, adaptation efforts to preserve Tuvalu's shores could succeed. Predictions of two meters of sea level rise are typically accompanied by the worst-case-scenario version of climate models in which the assumption is that humans do nothing to prevent this catastrophe. Furthermore, this statement can be seen as an example of foreigners discussing the inevitability of this country's end. There is no consideration of the drastic measures Tuvaluans are willing to enact in order to save their country (see, e.g., 7.2 Tuvalu's Future). There is only an indication that foreign experts have already decided the fate of Tuvaluans.

Statements such as these take away the agency of Tuvaluans by deciding for them what will and will not happen, what actions will and cannot be taken, and perhaps most importantly what *should* happen. In the colonial era, there was a common discourse in European cultures about the "White man's burden," a concept that indicates only White people are capable of making responsible decisions in this world (Said, 1978). Colonization was justified because non-White civilizations were perceived as having no ability to care for themselves. Colonizing nations refused to recognize the agency of indigenous people around the world. They used infantilizing language to justify taking control of land, resources, and people. The colonizers perceived themselves to be adult-like, always knowing what was the best course of action, while the needs and judgments of the colonized populations were childlike at best. Remnants of these sentiments remain active in modern society and can be seen with the use of patronizing or infantilizing language that dismisses the agency of indigenous peoples.

Another article from the Guardian discusses the dichotomy of Tuvalu's internet domain assignation of .tv and the concurrent threat of climate change (Baram, 2005b). This article entitled *That Sinking Feeling* was republished in the Guardian's Weekly Review three weeks later under the new title *Drowning in Money* (Baram, 2005a). The titles alone are worthy of critique. Hilia Vavae, Director of the Meteorologial Office in Tuvalu, was very clear in explaining to me the problem with media characterizations of the islands as "sinking." She noted that many publications will talk about the "sinking islands" when in fact the problem is not that the islands are sinking. The sea is rising. The difference in phrasing shifts the onus of responsibility from those who are causing the sea to rise (polluting industrialized countries) to the islands themselves – as though they, sinking, are the cause of their problems. The second title, *Drowning in Money,* is a reference to the article's secondary thesis that the income generated from .tv has been spent irresponsibly on paradise-ruining infrastructure rather

234

than on climate change adaptation and mitigation efforts, which I address below. The subheading of the article reveals the tone of the story:

> Tuvalu, population 11,000, was the world's third-poorest state until an internet deal made it rich overnight. Then came dire warnings that global warming would soon flood the islands. So what did the natives do with their windfall? Lay new roads and start building discos.

The source for Baram's article is Paul Lindsay's documentary *Before the Flood* (2004) rather than Tuvaluans themselves. Thus, Baram is representing Tuvaluans based on a representation of Tuvaluans. Baram states that Tuvalu became "rich overnight" with the receipt of $40 million. Baram does not mention that this is $40 million over ten years (Lerner, 2001) or that Tuvaluan private citizens did not receive this money. Instead, Baram explains that "For the Tuvalans [sic], with an average annual income of about $1,000, this was a life-changing sum. The islanders became, or at least reacted as if they had become, very rich." Statements such as these make it sound as though every Tuvaluan had access to this money, and they went on a collective spending spree. This article indicates that Tuvaluans behaved very irresponsibly, and uses language which backs up this assertion, e.g. with the patronizing question "So what did the natives do with their windfall?" Baram speaks as though a collective choice were made to develop infrastructure irresponsibly rather than responsibly stop the destruction of climate change:

> Defiant in the face of the rising water, the Tuvalans [sic] are using the windfall to develop the land that is soon to disappear. Buildings are being raised, nightclubs, restaurants and hotels are being planned and built, newly bought cars are cruising on newly laid roads. Modernisation is hitting the islands at the 11th hour.

Baram is quick to point out the negative impacts that have accompanied the development of infrastructure, which is deemed a "luxury." These include dietary issues such as obesity, high blood pressure, and diabetes, as well as increases in trash. These negative impacts of development in Tuvalu are supported in this study. Baram then goes on to say, "But still, the Tuvalans [sic] had their newly-acquired money. With that they could buy themselves a new future. Or at least borrow more time." This victim-blaming argument presupposes that $40 million over ten years is enough to adapt to the impacts of climate change, and further ignores the fact that many adaptation efforts require infrastructure to be already in place. Baram creates a false dichotomy of 'development versus preventing climate change,' which indicates that Tuvaluans themselves have chosen for their country to be at risk. Baram later contradicts this framing by arguing that Tuvaluans did try to stop climate change, but gave up too quickly:

> For a while, vast amounts of money were spent in an attempt to raise international awareness of Tuvalu's predicament. Tuvalu joined the UN, at a cost of $1.5m a year. In diplomatic terms, membership is not that expensive, but renting an office and secretarial services in New York is.

The imprecise phrase "for a while" insinuates that for a short time only, Tuvalu was politically involved in the international discussion about climate change, and that that time is firmly in the past. Again, Tuvaluan agency is in question. In reality, Tuvalu continues to be highly active in the global conversation, advocating for the Kyoto treaty, and more recently for agreements in Copenhagen, Mexico, and Durban. Tuvalu is a member of the Alliance of Small Island States (AOSIS), a global conglomeration of island nations who have combined their political power on issues of island wellbeing, such as climate change.[61]

Baram does actually report that Lindsay addresses the issue of development in the film. Lindsay speaks to the inclination of outsiders to blame Tuvaluans for the danger to their country. Lindsay says, "Many self-righteous people in the West would judge them for giving up the fight. But all the Tuvalans [sic] wanted is what we all want: comfortable houses, cars, good lives" (Lindsay, 2004 as quoted in Baram, 2005a,b). This quote nearly frames development as the basic human right that it is. Unfortunately, Baram answers this quote in the article with a statement about government instability in Tuvalu. This juxtaposition makes it sound as though Tuvaluans are purposefully holding up climate action by electing new governments. This same paragraph ends with the comment, "But while the political system wrangles over the best way to face the rising tides, the sea keeps going up, and the dollars keep drifting away." This statement frames the issue as though Tuvaluans are to blame for the climate change risk to their country by purposefully refusing to address it and by taking irresponsible actions with their money. Baram's article ends with a comment that Tuvalu's paradise does not exist any longer after their recent increase in development. Similar to the photograph in Adam's 2009 article, such comments say to the world that Tuvalu is only worth saving because of its value as 'paradise.' According to Baram, that value is gone.

Representation in academic articles and in news media can be dissimilar in many ways. News media tend to be more prosaic, as reporters are attempting to relay aspects of the human story in only a few short paragraphs or pages to people who may be entirely unfamiliar with the subject matter. News media may be more inclined to rely on the shortcuts of cultural narratives (such as the hero's journey or rags-to-riches tales) to draw the audience into quick understanding and verisimilitude. It would therefore stand to reason that the narrative related by a foreign reporter may not wholly align with the experiences of the local population. Academic research, on the other hand, delves deeply into specific theories, events, meanings, and other phenomena through either an objective lens or an openly reflexive subjective lens. Either way, biases are to be stated and/or controlled for, and the cultural narratives of the researcher ought not dominate the representation of the subject matter. However, we know this is not the case. Cross-cultural research has shown that our cultural biases are at

---

[61] http://www.sidsnet.org/aosis

times so implicit to our worldview that we simply do not recognize them (Greenfield, 1997). Said (1978) revealed the powerful cultural biases that shaped Western academic study of "the Orient" and how inaccurately these studies represented the people they purported to understand. Similarly, Pacific Island cultures are misrepresented in some academic literature in a way that reveals their history of colonization and marginalization.

The APA report on the psychology of climate change gave a comprehensive overview of this burgeoning subfield of psychology (Swim et al., 2010). The report compiles psychological and other social science research about climate change and identifies six areas in which psychologists can positively contribute to climate change research. This very thorough and well-documented 108-page report mentioned island communities in only one paragraph. In a section addressing the psychological barriers that may prevent people from acting in relation to climate change, Swim et al. state:

> For example, interviews with Pacific Islanders who live on very low-lying atolls found that one group is already purchasing higher ground in Australia, while another trusts that god will not break the Biblical promise never to flood the Earth again after the flood that Noah and his entourage endured (p. 68).

The article cited for this information is Morteux & Barnett (2009), see below, which does actually discuss the meaning of climate change to Tuvaluans. In a report which spans global literature in an enormous, though young, field, it is perhaps acceptable that a country with as small a population as Tuvalu is mentioned only once. However, that Pacific Islanders (or islanders in general, for that matter) are referenced only once reveals a bias within the reporting: marginalization of these communities. In fact, the APA report did note that one limitation to the literature review is that it holds a developed-nations bias:

> Although climate change is global, much of the relevant psychological research has been done in North America, Europe, and Australia... Perhaps more importantly, though, are possible differences among these and other countries in extent of economic development and associated wealth.

However, the report fails to make the leap that a tendency for research to come from North America, Europe, and Australia also constitutes a continental bias. Islanders are underrepresented in this report, and even the underrepresentation goes unnoticed. The Mortreux & Barnett citation, as reported by the APA task force, divides Pacific Islanders into two neat groups—those who realize that climate change is going to destroy their island and have made plans to migrate to Australia, and those who base their climate change denial on Biblical belief. As discussed in this current study, aspects of this representation are accurate; however this is hardly an exhaustive portrayal of Pacific Islanders and does little to capture the true extent of cultural and psychological questions that are faced because of the changing climate in island communities. This representation reveals the need in academia to conduct further research on the experiences of non-mainstream communities. In the global context of climate change, this need is to address developing nations, island communities, and indigenous peoples.

237

The APA report's representation also fails to address the critical nature of the Mortreux & Barnett article, which delves into the underrepresented or poorly represented experiences of Tuvaluans regarding climate change.

There is a widespread assumption around the world that climate change will or should result in population migration from Tuvalu. However, that assumption is not held by many Tuvaluans and should not be considered a foregone conclusion by the rest of the world (Mortreux & Barnett, 2009). Mortreux & Barnett explored Tuvaluans' expectations, beliefs, and intentions regarding climate change in Funafuti. While it is true that they uncover a belief among some that God will protect Tuvalu from flood, this is only one finding among many. As in any country, Tuvaluans are diverse in their interpretations of scientific evidence and opinions on how best to respond to these interpretations. Mortreux & Barnett argued that if the rest of the world has determined that migration is the only course of action for Tuvaluans, they have made this decision without consulting the Tuvaluans themselves. These findings are supported in this current study, in which participants are clear that migration is not up for consideration currently, and may never be so, even if it means "to stay here and die here for my country," in Kou's words. Tuvaluan cultures are highly integrated with the space that is occupied by the community. To Tuvaluans, migration is not a hypothetical or theoretical argument and it is not a foregone conclusion. Tuvaluans deserve the right to draw their own conclusions rather than have foreign researchers decide for them that migration is necessary, and then refuse to entertain other possibilities.

An academic publication that poorly represented the Tuvaluans who were included was a Nature article titled *That Sinking Feeling* (Patel, 2006). The opening paragraph introduces the reader to Tuvalu and to Tuvaluans with a short vignette, "Hilia Vavae, the director of the Meteorological Office, sounds excited in her modest, laid-back way. 'There is a…' she struggles for the right word '…flooding!'" (p. 734). Patel cites two other Tuvaluans in his piece, then-Prime Minister Maatia Toafa and Pepetua Latasi, the climate change coordinator of the Environmental Department. Prime Minister Toafa is described as "a casual and jovial fellow who kicks off his sandals and props his feet on the table as we speak" (p. 736). These descriptions are likely meant to give the audience a quick insight into the island lifestyle that typifies Tuvalu. However, in an academic article, these descriptions place unprofessional appearances on powerful and intelligent Tuvaluan leaders. That Ms. Vavae should excitedly struggle for the word "flooding" or that Prime Minister Toafa should be "casual and jovial" while speaking about his country's future gives the false impression that Tuvaluans are not serious, or perhaps cannot be serious, about the consequences of climate change. Their statements regarding climate change are therefore placed under scrutiny of their legitimacy and accuracy. Such descriptions feed into the patronizing colonial mindset which holds that indigenous people are not capable of caring for their country and that someone else must therefore do it for them (Deloria, 1998; Hall, 1997). These patronizing and at times infantilizing descriptions minimize the credence that readers will give to the statements of those thus described. Mithlo (2008) for example describes her decision not to describe the lives and personalities of the indigenous artists in her book:

> Given the decades of analysis by mainly non-Native writers who treat Native American artists as specimens, a personalized appraisal (what the artist looks like, where she was born) is, at this time, inappropriate. Just as I will not describe, for example, how a scholarly theorist looks, his age, or his residence, I refuse to dissect Native women's lives for personal examination. Their words, their narratives will be assessed as intellectual data in a manner similar to the published works of academics (pp. 21-22).

Indeed, while Patel's article cites only three Tuvaluans, more than twice as many foreign researchers are cited. The foreign researchers are not described or characterized to give insight into their looks or personality. Patel does not reflect the foreigners or their words in the playful light that the Tuvaluan scientists and leaders receive. The statements of these foreigners are therefore not placed under the same scrutiny as the playfully described Tuvaluan leaders and scientists. The foreigners are given a name and a title or organization only. In addition, the foreigners' words, opinions, and knowledge are cited with the credence of fact, although Patel does not always cite their scholarly publications. In this way, a foreigner discussing published research is cited with as much authority as a foreigner whose research or opinions may or may not be supported by fact. Without the appropriate citations, it is impossible to know. The name and title description of the foreigner, however, gives the allusion of credibility to their words in the same way that Director Vavae's excitement and Prime Minister Toafa's bare feet diminish their credibility to the audience. Patel describes Arthur Webb as "a coastal ecologist in the Fiji offices of the South Pacific Applied Geoscience Commission" (p. 736) without any further characterization. Webb shows Patel images of WWII air and seacraft and:

> He explains how, in 1943, US troops built a makeshift seawall and land-reclamation project along the length of the lagoon foreshore. After the troops left, locals built homes and roads on this 25- to 30 metre-wide stretch of rubble, which then began to erode (p. 736).

Webb's anecdote may be based in fact and extensive research or it may be something he heard from a friend of a friend of a friend. The audience does not know, because Patel's citations hold no reference to shore erosion of this type. In the article, however, the erosion described by Webb is treated as fact supported by Webb's title and office. Also, as previously discussed, language like this contains strong themes of victim-blaming because it shifts the onus of responsibility for Tuvalu's erosion from foreign-caused sea-level rise to domestic land use practices. This anecdote insinuates that the threat to Tuvalu is perhaps Tuvalu's fault, and is perhaps only a fantasy brought on by the erosion of land that was not stable to begin with.

Having met with Ms. Vavae, I can confirm Patel's experience of her willingness to contact foreigners to tell us when and where we can find examples of the flooding brought on by sea-level rise. During my two week stay in August 2010 (six months before and after the occurrence of King tides),

Tuvalu experienced high tidal flooding in the center of the island. Ms. Vavae explained to me that while King tides flooding has always been common in Tuvalu, flooding at other times of the year is only a recent occurrence with the rising sea level. After I first met her, Ms. Vavae emailed me to let me know when the seawater began bubbling up from the center of the island. Contrary to Patel' experience, I found Ms. Vavae, others in the Meteorological Office, and many Tuvaluan leaders in government agencies and NGOs to be full of information addressing the uncertainties he raises in the article but does not answer with the words of Tuvaluans. Patel cites (or does not cite) multiple foreigners who suggest that sea-level rise is not the big concern to Tuvaluans that journalists and researchers sometimes make it out to be. Without citing her work (see below), Patel quotes the words and opinions of Carol Farbotko, "a cultural geographer from the University of Tasmania":

> In her interviews with officials and community leaders, she has found that climate is a vague, long-term concern. People get much more worked up about problems such as waste disposal, a fetid and ubiquitous problem; over-population; and the accelerating erosion of traditional culture in the age of the Internet and DVDs ... 'Oh, it's a very important concern,' is the standard and slightly mechanical response to questions on climate change, Farbotko says. In her experience, and in mine, some Tuvaluans refuse even to talk about climate, or dismiss it with a weary wave of the hand (p. 735).

As discussed earlier, quotes such as these, which describe the "fetid and ubiquitous problem" of waste, create a sense that the Tuvaluan paradise is already gone. Furthermore, Patel speaks of Tuvaluans' refusal to talk of climate change as though they do not find it to be an important concern. This quote is followed by a description of Tuvaluans' Christianity and God's promise to Noah that there would be no further flooding. As discussed in this current research, Tuvaluans employ a wide variety of coping mechanism to address the uncertainty and ambient stress of climate change. Tuvalu has only one airstrip and one plane with two flights a week between Tuvalu and Fiji. If a flood comes and Tuvaluans must leave, how will 11,000 people on nine islands and atolls evacuate? Where will they go? Who has the money to migrate? Will they be together as a family, as a community, as a country, or will they be spread out in the world? What will happen to the culture? What will happen to their daily lives, in which they must work in foreign lands? In the face of such uncertainty, of course people must rely on faith. It is psychologically healthy for people to seek ways to cope with this vast uncertainty, and faith is a common strength used by people to navigate uncertain lives (Bishop, Colquhoun, & Johnson, 2006; Hobfoll, 1988, 1998; Nowell & Boyd, 2010). Faith allows Tuvaluans to maintain their daily roles, responsibilities, and relationships, which continue despite future threats of climate change.

Furthermore, in the above quote Patel cites Carol Farbotko (though does not cite her work) in a way that insinuates she agrees that Tuvaluans are unconcerned with climate change. This insinuation is a disservice to Tuvaluans and to Farbotko herself. By suggesting that not even Tuvaluans care about climate change, Patel is diminishing the risks and realities of climate change. Throughout the article, Tuvaluans who express concerns are patronized and foreigners who diminish these concerns are regarded as experts. By stating that Tuvaluans are less concerned by climate change than they are by garbage, Patel is implicitly arguing that the climate change threat is invalid. If not even Tuvaluans are in a constant state of panic and despair regarding climate change, why should the rest of the world be concerned? As discussed in this current study, Tuvaluans like all people cannot and will not cease all other life activities for the next century while the issues of climate change are resolved or come to a head. Tuvalu as a country is active in addressing climate change, and is simultaneously active in all other aspects of life.

Farbotko's work in Tuvalu is highly critical of researchers who place the onus of responsibility on Tuvaluans while simultaneously taking away their power of self-determination (Farbotko, 2010a, 2010b, 2012). In her article *Wishful Sinking: Disappearing Islands, Climate Refugees and Cosmopolitan Experimentation*, Farbotko (2010b) criticizes articles that portray the islands as "laboratories" in which the world can first glimpse the impacts of climate change from a safe distance. Farbotko criticizes foreign researchers who adopt a wait-and-see policy with regards to climate change, which in essence claims that the only value Tuvalu has to the rest of the world is if the country does, in fact, disappear. Should this happen, other countries will then have proof of what might happen with climate change, and they can then respond appropriately and more knowledgably. In this way, Tuvalu and other small island countries become 'canaries in a coal mine' – except of course for the fact that they are not canaries and should not be viewed as disposable indicators of the risk to the rest of the world. They are countries who have a right to maintain their homeland. Indeed ongoing international debates are considering the most just, ethical, and effective ways to support vulnerable populations with climate adaptation, including international carbon taxes, development aid, and the United Nations Framework Convention on Climate Change (see, e.g., Adger, 2001; Cooper, 2000; Grubb, 1995; Kelly & Adger, 2000; Paavola & Adger, 2005)

Farbotko (2010a) explores research and media which presents Tuvalu as a dying country heading toward its 'inevitable' end. Many Western outlets adopt a stance of waiting for Tuvalu's inevitable destruction, typified by non-action or even active counter-movements to block the political process (McCright & Dunlap, 2003). . Farbotko (2012) explores the diverse reactions Tuvaluans have to climate change (as discussed in the current research) as well as the value international media places on Tuvaluans as climate refugees. Farbotko notes, "Such representations can fail to reflect complex engagements with the climate change issue (and with journalists) among Tuvaluans" (p. 126). By addressing climate change in Tuvalu with a sensationalistic or narrow focus, foreign journalists and researchers fail to capture the extraordinarily complex ways that Tuvaluans (as all populations) interact with climate change.

Such representations of indigenous peoples are harmful to their right of self-determination. As shown in the current study, Tuvaluans themselves are discussing options in which their homeland can be maintained. The dynamic nature of their culture, which shifts as all cultures do, is not heading toward an 'inevitable' conclusion. Tuvalu has a long history of cultural change and adaptation, throughout which they have maintained or adapted traditional cultural values and activity settings. Tuvaluans are active in the global conversation about climate change. They are people of agency who concerned about their lives and the future of their country. Tuvaluans from diverse backgrounds have much to say on the topic of preserving their culture as well as on the topic of climate change. In this current research I have sought to represent Tuvaluan words, meanings, opinions, and experiences as accurately as possible through my lens as a foreign researcher. Future research by foreigners would benefit from a critical analysis of relevant research to understand the stories we are portraying.

8.4 Limitations, Implications, and Conclusion

Limitations. There are several limitations that should be noted as they could greatly affect the data, resulting themes, and conclusions of the research. First, I am not Tuvaluan and I do not speak Tuvaluan. As a foreigner, I bring an American worldview, perception, and interpretation of words and events. It is possible that on multiple occasions I understood what was said differently than the intended meaning of the Tuvaluan participants. Furthermore, my understanding of conversations and community events that were conducted in Tuvaluan was limited to what was translated to me. These limitations were tempered by the welcoming support of my host family, nearly all of whom were fluent in English and some of whom were comfortable conversing with me in limited English and my few sentences of broken Tuvaluan. My host family was very conscientious of my desire to learn about the Tuvaluan culture and the communities in Funafuti. They brought me to family and community events and patiently explained to me what was happening, what I should do, and what was being said. A great portion of the ethnographic field data was thickened through Tuvaluan explanations so that I was not only describing what I saw through my American perspective, but was also able to capture my family's descriptions of what was happening and why. Many times, people I had just met took on this mantle of translation and explanation when I was alone or sitting away from family members. Just as Tuvalu's powerful guest culture made it possible for me to conduct cold visits with many people during my first field visit, these same cultural norms meant that many Tuvaluans went out of their way to help me understand their culture despite my language limitation.

The small interview sample size should be noted as well. Only 18 Tuvaluans from a population of around 11,000 participated in the interview portion of the second study, which was the analytical focus of this research. These participants represented each of the islands, but there is a question as to the comprehensiveness of this representation since many of the islands were represented by only one person who may not be indigenous to that island (e.g., Tafue served as pastor on Vaitupu but is from Nukulaelae). Themes that arose within this sample may not be universal to all Tuvaluans and additional interview participants may have raised additional themes. Similarly, there were no interview participants under the age of 18. It is possible that themes that arose from the adult interview sample do not comprehensively address issues, beliefs, or potential future courses of action common among younger people in Tuvalu. These limitations to the interview sample are tempered by the ethnographic and participant observation components of the study, which contextualized and thickened the resultant themes from the interviews with shared conversations and activities with dozens of Tuvaluans during the study period. This limitation was further tempered by the diversity of interview participants, who included elders and young adults, men and women, government veterans, students, workers, and homemakers, bringing a wide range of viewpoints to the analysis.

The interviews were conducted in English, which limited the participant pool to those who were comfortable speaking my language. It is possible that this restriction means that certain views common in Tuvalu among non-English speakers simply did not emerge. Furthermore, even among fluent speakers, there were moments in which key words, phrases, or concepts stumbled over translation. One simple example is searching for the right word, such as during the interview with Kina about Nui's history:

KINA: They said that our ancestors, or whatever we called that they'd been intruded – what is that?

MICHAEL: Invaded.

LAURA: Invaded.

KINA: Invaded, invaded by the Kiribati canoes.

The meaning was not lost. In fact, it is obvious that we understood immediately what she intended to say. It is my experience in speaking with people for whom English is a second language, as well is when I am speaking in a foreign language, that the intention of meaning often overrides the exact choice of words. Even when conversing with other native English speakers, I have often had the experience of a word being on the tip of my tongue and the other person knowing what word is eluding me. However, some translation difficulties posed a greater challenge because there is not an appropriate translation into English. When Sueina was telling the story of Setema on Niutao, we came across an example of this:

SUEINA: So they use their, uh, their island words. We call it like, uh, I don't know how to explain it in English. It's, they have a name, I think Grandpa knows.

LAURA: It's like a, ah, a chant? Or like a, kind of like a prayer or something like that?

SUEINA: No, it's like a, it's like magic that when you say it, it will happen, eh?

LAURA: Like a spell?

SUEINA: Yeah, kind of like a spell. So they – but it's a bit different. Like spell, like if you said to the – 'Go and do that one,' like you're doing magic to that one.

LAURA: Oh, like if I say something to you then you have to go do it?

243

SUEINA: Yeah but, but no. You know those words, it's island
                 words. But it's from before, for they used to use that
                 one, like those words they are going to say them.

There is no suitable translation for what we were discussing. If I had been able to conduct this interview in Tuvaluan, I may still struggle with reporting this conversation in English, but within the conversation there would have been a more proficient understanding of the concept. Additionally, because the language of the study was English, conversations of climate change relied upon English language scientific language and other jargon common to educational systems and international news media surrounding climate change. It is possible that Tuvaluans speaking Tuvaluan discuss climate change in very different terms, which are not represented in this study. My lack of Tuvaluan language skills remains a barrier. I intend for this research to be the first in a series of longitudinal studies throughout my career. In future studies, it is my intention to become fluent in Tuvaluan so that I can eventually work toward closing this translation gap.

Another limitation is the relatively short period of time that I was able to spend in Tuvalu. My first stay was two weeks and my second was three weeks. Again, my interaction with the community was greatly enhanced during these short periods of travel by the generosity of my host family. I was able to participate in daily family life – the everyday workings of culture – such as meals, prayers, games, etc. These are events I would have missed if I were solely reliant on interviews with people in their offices or short stops by people's homes. In addition, I was invited to community functions, parties, and even political meetings because of the generosity of my host family. It is my firm belief that my short time in Tuvalu was maximized thanks to them. I have also been able to converse periodically with my Tuvalu adviser Ms. Lanieta Faleasiu, as well as with host family members and friends, through email and Facebook. I have been able to follow events in Tuvalu through these media and check in with my friends even when I am away.

I was not present during the 2011 drought in Tuvalu. During my field research in December 2011 and January 2012, multiple people mentioned that I should have been present to see what it was like when the drought was happening. The photos used in this study from Stephen Boland were originally shared on Facebook in October during the drought emergency, and were the most comprehensive visual images I was able to find at the time. The use of these images and participants' stories are the best record of this important event that I am able to record.

A final limitation that should be noted is that the entirety of this study took place on Funafuti. I was not able to travel to the outer islands. I sought to mitigate the gaps that might arise from staying only on Funafuti by speaking with Tuvaluans who were from or who had experience with each of the outer islands. Regardless, as one of the major cultural themes states, Funafuti is for money and for working. The people from the outer islands who live on Funafuti are there for school or for work, or have accompanied those who are there for school or for work. Their descriptions of the outer islands and the dynamic of

244

support between family members on Funafuti and the outer islands were told through that lens. I have no reason to believe that these support systems would have been described differently by people on the outer islands. However, there remains a strong possibility that certain themes did and did not emerge due to the participant pool. In future studies in Tuvalu, I hope to close this research gap by traveling to the outer islands. Specifically, I hope to travel to Niutao in 2014 during the EKT General Assembly meeting to experience this significant event with my host family.

Implications of research. As an exploratory qualitative study, this research can be applied in a variety of practical ways in Tuvalu and abroad, as well as for future climate change research. The Tuvaluan government and religious leadership are already extremely active in the global communities dealing with climate change. These leaders are advocating for extensive and comprehensive global mitigation and adaptation efforts, spearheaded by wealthy nations like the United States, Australia, and Japan. Climate change must be addressed first and foremost by the nations that are most responsible for its occurrence (Soderbergh, 2011). Industrialized nations must reduce their carbon emissions drastically and immediately for there to be hope of preventing the worst impacts of climate change. This requires agreeing upon and implementing a plan to that addresses vastly diverse risk analyses and political considerations (Hultman, Hassenzahl, & Rayner, 2010). Climate change impacts are a complex interplay between regional vulnerability and the rate of change based on emission levels and other climate change drivers (Hallegatte, Przyluski, & Vogt-Schilb, 2011). Global models for climate change projection must be "downscaled" to improve forecasting ability for local areas (Oreskes, Stainforth, & Smith, 2010). This is especially important for island nations, in which the difference of even a few kilometers can be the difference between ocean, atoll, or mountain (Hamilton, 2012).

Although these events are happening with unprecedented swiftness on a geological time scale, a matter of centuries is extremely slow in terms of the lifespan of humans. Regardless, to prevent ecological devastation that will greatly threaten the survival and welfare of people in the coming centuries, extensive actions must be taken in the coming years. Industrialized nations, and especially the wealthy nations among them who are the worst polluters, must mitigate climate change by overhauling energy systems to reduce emissions and retrofitting industries to be more sustainable. Concurrently, wealthy nations and donor organizations must support the sustainable development of poorer nations. Development is a human right and should not be prevented by developed (and highly polluting) nations under the guise of limiting climate change. Rather, development should continue to be supported and where appropriate, this development should be supported with technologies and economic systems that provide long term political, economic, and environmental independence and sustainability for these developing nations.

The results of this qualitative cultural study can be used to assist in this ongoing global advocacy effort. This study addresses the ongoing cultural changes in Tuvalu as the context in which climate change has been introduced.

As discussed in 8.3 International Discourse on Climate Change in Tuvalu, some seek to use these cultural changes to minimize or dismiss the impacts of climate change in Tuvalu. This study clearly shows that cultural change is necessarily a part of Tuvaluan culture (as it is with all cultures). The threats of climate change include population upheaval, which could cause an unprecedentedly quick rate of change that would be difficult for even the most adaptable populations to absorb. Although climate change is occurring within the context of other cultural changes, it is unique because of its potential enormity and because it is an external force over which Tuvaluans have no direct control. Tuvaluans have in the past generations embraced Christianity, education, paid employment, and development into their cultural norms and activity settings. They have chosen separation from Kiribati and independence from England. Tuvaluans have been able to exert a limited measure of control over the impacts of modernity to their culture, land, and community. Climate change, on the other hand, is occurring in a way that Tuvaluans cannot reject. The addition of roads and motorbikes or the problems of waste management cannot justifiably be compared with the threat of losing an entire nation.

Similarly, this study offers a record of land, cultural, and community impacts of climate change that are already occurring and that are feared to occur in the future. Participants have discussed the practical ways in which their lives have already been affected by climate change, including adaptations they have had to make due to sea level rise, erosion, and tidal flooding; their experiences with the 2011 drought; property loss and damage during extreme weather events; damage to crops and other natural resources during flooding and extreme weather events; and the ambient stress from fears for Tuvalu's future when participants think forward to the ways climate change may affect their lives and the lives of future generations. This record of the human impacts of climate change may be useful in some advocacy settings to communicate the climate change threat above and beyond changes to natural systems. The people who live within these natural systems are affected as well, and they deserve consideration.

As Tuvalu moves forward, the government and private citizens will continue to enact various adaptations to protect their land and wellbeing from climate change. Tuvalu has a number of cultural strengths explored in this study that will aid in these adaptation measures. For example, Tuvalu's guest and gift cultures have proven invaluable in the response during and after short-lived disaster events. Community groups mobilize themselves to spread the word about upcoming risks, as was experienced during the recent tsunami warnings. Community groups mobilize themselves to aid in the reconstruction of damaged homes and property, as was experienced after Hurricane Ofa in Vaitupu. Community groups mobilize themselves to support families and other community groups who are rebuilding by providing food and resources. People who are displaced by housing loss find family and neighbors willing to provide shelter and care. Tuvaluans' ability to give of themselves in daily life and in times of great need is an invaluable support network that will be utilized into the future as Tuvaluans help each other cope physically with climate change. Future adaptation strategies can tap into these community support systems in both official and unofficial ways. The government and outside donor organizations can support the functioning of cultural community systems when implementing preparation, adaptation, and recovery efforts.

Similarly, these community supports are invaluable to the implementation of spiritual, emotional, and psychological coping interventions in various incarnations. The ongoing workshops provided by the EKT are a great example of the use of strong cultural networks to aid in the education and understanding of the population about climate change. By using Biblical interpretations of the climate change phenomenon, these workshops enable Tuvaluans to discuss and address climate change in a culturally-relevant, psychologically healthy, and proactive way. Similar interventions may become necessary in the future to deal with change, loss, and threat associated with climate change. Through religion, island community groups, extended family networks, and other already active support networks, Tuvaluans have multiple culturally relevant avenues through which to address current and future psychological coping needs of community members. Tuvalu's culture is strong with examples of individuals' obligations to support and care for the wellbeing of the community. These cultural systems can be utilized and supported by the government and donor agencies.

Finally, many participants expressed concern for the future of Tuvalu's cultures if climate change forces population upheaval or other quick and far-reaching changes. The fear is that the culture will be lost or irreparably damaged if Tuvaluans are no longer able to live as Tuvaluans in Tuvalu. This fear is real and reasonable. However, I believe that recent cultural shifts in Tuvalu provide a template for preserving traditional culture despite contextual changes in the community. Activity Settings theory offers a way to understand the blending of traditional and modern life so as to maintain Tuvaluan culture with adaptations. As the land and community change, whether due to climate change or other influences, Tuvaluans can maintain traditional activity settings as a major part of their community life. Shared experiences in these settings means that Tuvaluan culture is preserved through the intersubjectivity created by ongoing expectation and execution of traditional culture in these new contexts. These are the ways that Tuvaluans have shown an aptitude for adaptation and cultural preservation. Even if the context changes dramatically in the future, Tuvaluans can create new iterations of cultural activities that will preserve the intentions and traditions. For example, women on Funafuti may sew pillowcases instead of weaving, but their women's groups remain active and dedicated to their island community and the handicraft traditions of their island. Imported foods are now available and common in Tuvalu, but Tuvaluans still gather for feasts and *fateles* even as rice is increasingly substituted for *pulaka*. Tuvaluans have naturally and instinctively maintained those values and traditions that are most important to their culture. If climate change increases the rate of change, Tuvaluans may find themselves needing to consciously and purposefully adapt these activity settings quickly to maintain their traditions. History has shown this is possible. Tuvaluan culture survives.

Future research in climate change and related topics in other cultural settings can benefit from this research. Using exploratory qualitative research methods, including ethnography, participant observation, qualitative interviewing, and photographic imagery, a short durational field excursion can yield extensive results about cultural and community needs and strengths regarding climate change adaptation. In a short-term data collection period, the support of community collaborators, host families, and other key informants can greatly increase cultural understanding. Similarly, participants should come from a range of diverse population indicators to ensure maximum usefulness and applicability of study results. Exploratory qualitative studies can assist in the design and implementation of climate change adaptations and coping interventions according to cultural strengths, norms, values, and decision hierarchies. Population outreach should be based on cultural norms as well as on the regional needs of the community. Qualitative research provides a detailed look into these local needs and strengths to heighten the relevance of climate change research and interventions.

Future research built from this study will include a more detailed exploration of the role of religion in climate change in Tuvalu, particularly the role of the Church of Tuvalu. This will include a more in-depth analysis of the role of Christianity in Tuvaluan culture. In addition, my future research in Tuvalu will address the cultural norms, strengths, and community needs in outer island communities regarding climate. I would also like to explore potential generational differences in Tuvaluan cultural connectedness and climate change experiences, including a sample of high school students who are growing up within the context of a Tuvalu dealing with climate change, as well as an exploration of parenting as it relates to climate change. In addition, I would like to explore shifting perceptions of climate change, particularly after events like the 2011 drought. Future research could further explore the extent to which the population supports the government's directions in climate change advocacy, and will explore ways that the lay Tuvaluan community is involved and can be involved in these efforts domestically and internationally. Finally, future research could include studies conducted in Tuvaluan by myself or a translator to explore potential language effects of discussing climate change issues in English versus Tuvaluan.

Conclusion. Tuvalu is a low-lying nation in the South Pacific that will experience an extreme threat from climate change over the next century. This exploratory qualitative research studied the human impacts of climate change in Tuvalu by exploring the culture through the psychological theories surrounding sense of place and sense of community and their interconnection with each other and with climate change. Resulting themes from the study revealed that climate change is considered within the context of ongoing cultural changes in the country. Tuvalu's culture is strong with norms and obligations of community involvement and support, including guest and gift cultural values. Tuvalu's nine islands and atolls are unique in their cultural and linguistic history but are interconnected in terms of identity and support, mutually influencing each other throughout the country's history. Funafuti is the urban center of Tuvalu and the

248

place that has seen the most dramatic cultural changes over the past few decades.

The impacts of climate change are already being seen in Funafuti and the outer islands as changes to the land, sea, and weather. Tuvaluans lives are already being affected in small and sometimes large ways during extreme events. Tuvaluan cultural norms provide many strengths through which Tuvalu can and will adapt to the changing climate just as they have successfully adapted to many cultural and contextual changes throughout the country's history. Tuvaluans have a justifiable desire to maintain their homeland but lack the physical resources to bring this about without outside assistance. The government is active in the international community advocating for mitigation and adaptation efforts to be enacted to save the Tuvaluan homeland.

This study provides records of the cultural impacts of climate change in Tuvalu as well as the cultural strengths that Tuvaluans are utilizing and will continue to utilize in the future. Activity Settings theory offers a potential guide to Tuvaluans to aid in translating their natural adeptness in cultural adaptability to conscious and purposeful adaptation for cultural preservation should climate change force a dramatic upheaval of the cultural context. Future research will explore the role of Christianity in climate change in Tuvalu, the needs and strengths of outer island communities, and the actions of lay Tuvaluans in addressing climate change at home and abroad.

Appendix A: Reflexivity

Who I Am

Talofa.

My name is Laura Kate Corlew. Many people call me Kati, though others call me Laura. In Tuvalu, I go by Laura. I am a White American woman who was raised in Memphis, Tennessee. I went to university in Murfreesboro, TN, where I met my husband Michael. Michael and I moved to Chicago, Illinois, where we served as fulltime volunteers with the Claretian Volunteer Program. I worked predominantly with gangs and gang-affiliated youth, and with homeless and impoverished populations. Michael worked with a peace and social justice agency called 8th Day Center for Justice. We loved Chicago.

Five years ago we moved to Honolulu, Hawai'i where I joined the Community and Cultural Psychology graduate program. My interests in social justice were melded with my interests in environmental justice, and from there I became interested in the human impacts of climate change. Michael studies history, and is particularly interested in human rights within the context of workers' history and the political economy. These interests eventually took us both to Tuvalu.

My mother is Sally Hermsdorfer, a teacher by profession who is currently a principal at a Catholic high school in Memphis. My father is Arthur Hermsdorfer, a pharmacist who retired a few years ago and has since found himself busier than ever with his church and community service, and with working his land. My older sister is Anna Hermsdorfer, a radiographer with a major medical center in Memphis. My older brother is Joel Hermsdorfer, an engineer and retired Army captain and war veteran who will be graduating from law school one week before I attain my PhD. His wife is Lieutenant Commander Kate Hermsdorfer, a Naval Oceanography Officer with the U. S. Navy. My younger sister is Mary Delgado, a Spanish teacher who is currently pursuing her Master's degree. Her husband is David Delgado, a lawyer and a friend from childhood. His family has more or less already been our family for two generations. Their marriage only made it official.

I have adopted family as well. My husband was adopted as a baby, and so his side of the family spans blood relatives and adopted relatives alike. It's a very extensive family, and I still have not met everyone. Also, Michael and I placed our son Ian for adoption at birth with Molly and Eric Alspaugh who are, along with my parents, some of the best parents in the universe. By placing our son for adoption, we gained another arm of our extended family. All of these families are integrated into who we are. This is where I come from.

My Tuvaluan Family

I met my Tuvalu family in the summer of 2010. My grandfather is Sir Tomu Malaefone Sione, GCMB, OBE, a knight of Queen Elizabeth II and a retired Tuvalu government minister of 40 years. He is the head of his clan, a highly respected elder from his island of Niutao. I call him Grandpa Tomu or just Tomu. His wife Segali (whom I call Grandma) speaks very little English,

250

and I speak very little Tuvaluan. We have become extremely close anyway and I love her dearly. I have two generations of Tuvalu siblings: Grandpa Tomu's children and their spouses, and his grandchildren. I'm not sure why they all came to be my siblings. His oldest granddaughter (university student Lilly) was introduced to me as my sister, and it seemed strange to me to consider the next older generation, who are my age, to be my aunts and uncles. But I guess family doesn't always have to be so well-defined.

My Tuvalu siblings that I have met in person are Tomu's daughter Enna, who works with the Taiwanese Embassy in Tuvalu, and her husband Isala, a People's Lawyer; Tomu's son Ken, who is a police officer who works with the prison on Funafuti, and his wife Kou; his son Hindu's wife Sueina; and an adopted son from Fiji, Joe. Hindu, and Tomu's other sons Salaifenua and David (Limoni), and his other daughter Salaifina, have been away during both of my trips to Tuvalu, though we have met through Skype and through stories. Everyone in this family has welcomed me warmly and without hesitation. I am touched by their generosity and welcome.

To be clear, I have done nothing to deserve this. When I first began to study cultural research methods in the fields of Cultural and Community Psychology, and with Cultural Anthropology, I quickly learned that there is a, shall we say, rite of passage that is common if not ubiquitous in the fields. A researcher travels to a foreign country and integrates into the community and is at some point "adopted" into the culture. As a reader, I have often recognized that these stories are meant to signal legitimacy – the researcher has come to know the culture so well that community adopts the person into a family, gives them a new name, or otherwise indicates to the rest of the world that *this person knows what they're talking about because they are basically one of us now.*

When I was with the Claretian Volunteers, I traveled to Q'eqchi' Mayan villages in Guatemala with Father Tom Moran. Father Tom was celebrating his 50th year as a Catholic priest that year. He had spent decades in Guatemala working for justice, education, land rights, and other issues with these communities. He had been chased out of the country on threat of death, twice, by the government during the political upheavals in the 1970s and 1980s. I was fortunate enough that year to witness one of these villages conduct a very elaborate and extensive ritual to recognize Father Tom as a Mayan priest. He was 'one of them.' Father Tom had spent his life working for the welfare of this community. This is a true story of recognition and legitimacy.

That is not the case for me.

I was welcomed into my Tuvalu family months before I met any of them in person, before I ever stepped foot into Tuvalu, before I ever had a spoken conversation with a person from Tuvalu. That I was accepted into this family says absolutely nothing about *me.* Rather, the welcome I have received speaks volumes to the amazing generosity of spirit of my Tuvalu family and of the Niutaoan and Tuvaluan cultures. Like other Pacific Island countries, Tuvalu is known for its welcoming guest culture. I have been told that in Tuvalu the island of Niutao is especially known for their love and their welcome. I can

251

certainly attest from personal experience that my family is very strong in this cultural practice. My adoption story is a story about Tuvalu.

I began to prepare for my dissertation research on 'the cultural impacts of climate change' in early 2009. By the end of the year, I had decided that Tuvalu was the place I would go to explore this broad topic. I didn't know anyone from Tuvalu, but the Pacific is a connected place. Living in Hawai'i, I learned that I knew people who knew people in Tuvalu, and it seemed to be a good place to bring focus to this study.

In early 2010, I was fortunate enough to receive a small grant which funded a preliminary research trip to Tuvalu. I would get to travel to the country, meet with people, begin to develop a baseline understanding of the culture, and most importantly, *ask people* what kind of research would be useful to Tuvaluans within this broad topic. I could develop my research proposal in collaboration with Tuvaluans. I was especially excited about this opportunity because of my lack of personal experience with the culture. I knew that if I designed a study on my own in Hawai'i, there was no telling how incredibly wrong I might get it. Beginning the research process in Tuvalu greatly increased my potential of telling the story right.

I made some plans, bought my tickets, and hit the internet. I searched for contact information to organizations working with community, culture, or climate change. I started sending emails asking if it would be possible for me to stop in to say hello and ask a few questions when I arrived. One of these emails went to the Luaseuta Foundation, which worked with community, culture, *and* climate change. It read:

> Aloha,
>
> My name is Kati Corlew and I am a student of Cultural Community Psychology at the University of Hawaii in the United States. I was reading about the Luaseuta Foundation online, and I am very impressed with the work you do to improve the wellbeing of the people of Tuvalu. Next year, I will be conducting a small study about the psychology of climate change-- the meaning of climate change to communities. Past research has mostly been done in the USA and Europe, which means that developing nations and island nations are not well represented. When I do my study, I would like very much to be able to portray the meaning of climate change to communities in Tuvalu.
>
> Next month (from July 29 to August 12), I will be visiting Tuvalu for the first time. Tuvalu has really captured my heart, and I want to do all that I can to learn about Tuvalu people and culture so that when I do my research, I am able to show Tuvalu's perspective and not just my own. When I am visiting, would it be okay if I come by to talk with someone at the Luaseuta Foundation about Tuvalu's people and about climate change? I would be very honored if you would be willing to share your thoughts with me.
>
> Thank you,
>
> Kati Corlew

Geoff Ludbrook wrote back within hours:

Talofa,

Welcome to Tuvalu.

I'm in Australia at present but I suggest you contact Sir Tomu below. He can introduce to whom you need to meet.

Also he can provide you with accommodation ... which will save you a lot as the main island hotels are very expensive. Also this moves you straight in to the community and provides a cross section of people to talk to, etc.

There are no credit card facilities on the island so having enough Australian dollars helps (country's currency)... otherwise most things are available.

kind regards

Geoff Ludbrook

I looked up "Sir Tomu" on Wikipedia and found out he was Sir Tomu Sione, the former Governor General. I wrote back to both Geoff and Sir Tomu:

Aloha,

Thank you, Geoff, for your kind advice and for directing me to Sir Tomu. I am greatly looking forward to my visit to Tuvalu and hope to learn a lot from the community. Sir Tomu, if you are able to meet with me while I am in Funafuti, I will be greatly honored. As I mentioned in my original email, during this trip I am seeking to learn as much about the Tuvalu community, culture, and history as I can from the people of Tuvalu. I would also like to get advice from community members about how best to learn about the community's experience of climate change so that next year I can do this in a Tuvaluan way (not every method that works in a laboratory will work all over the world-- that's been a big problem with international studies in the past, in my opinion). I hope I will have a chance to meet with you soon.

Mahalo,

Kati Corlew

Sir Tomu wrote back almost immediately:

Laura K Corlew

Greeting and talofa

Thank for your information to me that you intend to visit Tuvalu in the near future and learn about the ways our community lived.

We fully appreciated it and are also looking forward to meeting you here in Tuvalu.

Please let us know your arrival time for us to meet you at the airport.

Best regards.

Sir Tomu M Sione

Over the next few weeks, I received a series of very helpful emails from Geoff giving me all manner of unsolicited advice about traveling in Tuvalu, what to expect with food and culture, and how to interact with people. I couldn't believe my luck. A week before I departed, I received one final message from Geoff:

Oh,

Need to check Man or woman?

sorry

G

I laughed out loud. Some years ago I had emailed for six months with a man in a volunteer house I was going to visit in Ireland, and only realized he was not a woman two days before my trip. His name had been unfamiliar to me, and I had guessed the gender wrong. Laura and Kati are both common enough names in America, but for those Western readers who may be skeptical of the need for this question, take a moment to guess the genders of my Tuvaluan friends Feue, Kina, Vete, Kokea, and Jopeto. I came to learn that Kati is actually a male's name in Tuvalu, or near enough to one that there was some question as so whose room I should share at the house. This is why I go by Laura in Tuvalu.

These emails show the welcome I received as a traveler to Tuvalu. However, it was my arrival in the country that made me realize the depth of Tuvalu's guest culture. When I stopped at the customs desk at the airport, I was asked the local address where I would be staying. "I don't know," I said. She looked up, surprised. "But you're staying with Tomu, aren't you?" Now I was surprised. "Um, yes. How did you know?" She told me he had come to the airport the day before to tell them that his granddaughter was coming and to help me if there were any issues at customs.

Tomu's son Ken was waiting for me outside. In his friend's taxi, we drove several blocks to the house I would be staying in, which turned out to be in the row of houses for government ministers, next door to the Prime Minister. I was surprised to find out that Sir Tomu was the Minister of Health at the time. Tomu welcomed me, introduced me to the family members who were present, and said, "You are part of the family now. You are my granddaughter now."

My Place in This Study

Throughout both of my research trips and during my time in Hawai'i throughout this study, I have had continual personal contact with many Tuvaluans. Tomu's family has treated me like family. I have come to consider many people I have met as good friends. In Hawai'i, I keep in touch through email and Facebook. While in Tuvalu conducting the study, a number of my interview participants were family members or friends. During many of these interviews, participants reference other conversations we had had. The interviews were a chance for them to expand upon topics we had discussed and to explore others that might not have come up otherwise. Tomu and Lanieta have been incredible "key informants" for me because of their continual willingness to patiently explain everything until they are sure that not only do I understand what they are saying, but that I understand what *they* mean when they say it.

Given these interactions, it is clear and without doubt that I have a role in this study. In qualitative research, interviews and conversations are conducted within a relationship, even if the relationship only lasts as long as the conversation. In Cultural and Community Psychology, there is not necessarily a desire to create a division between researcher and participant. There can be great value in developing collaborations and relationships in which participants feel just as welcome to ask questions as to answer them, and to periodically check in with the researcher to make sure she understands what is being said. Kou asked me, "You get it?" after telling me the story of Setema. Lanieta asked, "Does it make sense to you people?" after explaining the various rules guiding public speaking and women. Conversations like this reveal the power of participants in research to direct conversations and ensure the researcher understands. I have learned a lot from these relationships. It is my desire to pass on this knowledge to others as accurately as possible.

Appendix B: The Outer Islands

In this section, I will give a brief introduction of each of the outer islands as they have been described to me. My Tuvalu family is from the island of Niutao. Having heard a great deal more about Niutao than the other islands, I am able to say more in its unique description. It is my hope that these pages will provide some insight into the diversity of experience and identity that spans the Tuvaluan islands.

Nanumea. Nanumea is the northernmost island in Tuvalu, and the second largest at 3.87 km². Nanumea is shaped like a Y with another islet to the north, Lakena. The lagoon is not as large as Funafuti's lagoon, but it is open and beautiful. Kokea said:

> You can swim, it's all right. Nothing, no sharks. But people are mindful because the American passage is quite big, quite big and very deep. But the sea level is, I think it's coming up a little bit there. I mean, sharks can certainly go there but I don't, if sharks roam there they go back again. [Laughter] ... There's what we call the easterly side there, where the wind blows. There's a very good beach there. Really quite sandy beach.

The "American passage" is the ship passage that was blasted into the reef during World War II when the Americans came to Nanumea and two other islands in Tuvalu. The Americans blasted a passage in the reef for their large ships, and built a landing strip on the island, which has since become overgrown. Kokea told me, "They have a map where to put up the airstrip, and also to blast the passage. So their passage is still in there. It's quite an asset to Nanumea for fishing." The passage and the airstrip both remain, although only the passage is still in use. Kokea said:

> Yeah, the airstrip is definitely still there but all the coconut trees are growing. So, you still have the landowners with the lands [that became] the airstrip. They have these coconuts growing there but they don't bear as much fruits as the other ones that are not in the airstrip. [Laughter]

While the Americans were present, Nanumeans were evacuated to live on Lakena. Although it is a smaller islet than where Nanumeans live, it is large enough to support settlement if need be. Kokea told me:

> This other island is Lakena. They called it Lakena, which is quite a big island if we compare. It is almost like Niutao... So Nanumea is quite a big island – the main island, and Lakena is an islet to the north of the main settlement.

Nanumeans do not grow *pulaka* on the main island. They travel by boat to Lakena and maintain *pulaka* pits there. Nobody lives on Lakena, and nobody has except for during WWII. In the olden days, Nanumeans traveled to Lakena by canoe, but these days everyone uses an outboard engine. Kokea told me that although motorboats might save human energy, the time saved is not very much because the canoes were quite fast.

Nanumea is notable as one of the focal points of the Chambers' anthropological studies in Tuvalu beginning in the 1970s and continuing on to the present:

KOKEA: I remember I had a book, but this is a couple of Americans – a couple of Americans, a married couple, they said to me in Nanumea, they came here and they went to Nanumea. And they wrote about Nanumea, very good book. I can't remember what.

LAURA: Is it the Chambers?

KOKEA: That's right, the Chambers. Yeah, the couple, the Chambers, yeah… That's a nice guy there, with the wife.

LAURA: Yeah. I saw their book in the library.

KOKEA: Oh, that's good. Chambers here, Anne and

LAURA: Anne and Keith.

KOKEA: Keith Chambers. Ah, they really wrote a very good article about Nanumea. The houses and all that. That book there.

Feue also spoke fondly of the Chambers' visit as a notable event in Nanumea's history. Kokea spoke of the feasts that were prepared for the Chambers with pride. Nanumea feasts were also praised by Jopeto who said, "Nanumea, they celebrate the wedding from Saturday until like one week."

Nanumaga. Nanumaga[62] is another island in the northern group in Tuvalu. It is about the same size as Funafuti by landmass, but while Funafuti is spread out over dozens of kilometers as scattered islets stretching around a large lagoon, Nanumea is a compact oval-shaped island. Regarding the island's basic social structure, Lanieta said:

We have one primary school and we have a health clinic, all these services. Like, we have policemen from the police force looking after the safety of the island, and we have a pastor who is looking after the whole island. Yeah, I think the setting up is just the same all through all the other outer islands.

Nanumaga is also known for local stories about a "large house under the sea."[63] Deep underwater along the walls of the coral cliff that raises the island, evidence of ancient human habitation were found, going as far back as 8,000 years ago – the oldest evidence of settlement in the Pacific Islands.[64]

Lanieta recalled growing up on the island before the modern push of development came in full swing. There were no jobs to be had on the island, only a subsistence lifestyle, growing food, fishing, weaving, and building

---

[62] Sometimes spelled "Nanumanga." The "g" in Tuvaluan is pronounced "ng."

[63] tuvaluislands.com/history.htm

[64] http://tuvaluislands.com/history-caves.htm

structures from island resources. Her father made a little income in the only way available to the island. Lanieta said:

> My dad is really good in making handicrafts, so in addition to copra cutting he earned money from handicrafts, my dad used to make. That's life. And we don't buy good clothes. We don't buy shoes, we don't have shoes at the time. That was in early 80s.

Each island has a special feast day that celebrates something of importance in the island's history. Nanumaga Day is in April, and is called Aso te Fakavae.[65] Lanieta explained its origins:

> This was from a long time ago. It's like a contribution put in together by the community members for money... and then they call it the Fakavae. Fakavae literally means foundation. And then, I don't really know why they put in the money together. Maybe they have the plan for it, but then things went wrong and all the money is gone. I don't know where it has gone to. [Laughter] But that's how it started.

Every year, Aso te Fakavae is celebrated with feasts and *fateles*. On Funafuti, everyone receives a day off from work for their home island's feast day. They are major events for celebration. When I asked Lanieta if there was something that Nanumagans were known for, unique among all Tuvaluans, she gave me a smile and a nod and said:

> Yes, there is. People from Nanumaga they are well known for – people refer to it as *kaiuu*. *Kaiuu* means selfish. But they are not. They are not *kaiuu*. They are more like, I don't know the proper words, but ... they spend money wisely. Not even money – everything else. They spend *things* wisely. But other people, other people on the other islands, they refer to Nanumaga people as *kaiuu* [Laughter]. They are not, they are not. We are very thoughtful in everything we do. Food, clothes, water, and whatever, light. Like Nanumaga people in the olden days, we only light the lamp for eating. After that, switch off the lamp, save the kerosene for the next night... So the moonlight, we are very fond of it, the Nanumaga people. Because when the moon is out, we can do all our jobs in the night. We continue weaving in the night. We continue carving the handicraft in the night, using the moonlight. Because we save the kerosene.... [Laughter] Yeah, that is Nanumaga people, that's how they do things.

Nui. Each of the Tuvaluan islands has a different dialect of Tuvaluan. They are all mutually intelligible, with the possible exception of Nui's language. Teba told me that in Nui, "They are almost similar to Kiribati. The Gilbertese people... the language is similar, very similar." Although Tuvalu and Kiribati were grouped together as the Ellice and Gilbert Islands while they were colonized by the British Empire, the two groups actually have little historical and cultural ties between them prior to colonization. Tuvaluans are Polynesian

---

[65] "Day of Foundation"

258

and the i-Kiribati are Micronesian. Kina tells me that Nui alone has a linguistic connection to Kiribati, because their language is:

A pidgin Kiribati. It is a mixture of Kiribati and Tuvaluan language. You know? People of Kiribati can understand us, some of the words. And the other island in Fiji which is Rabi, we have the same words. And then the dialect, what you call the dialect, is quite different. We have our own and I always think that that was a blessing... But out of the eight islands in Tuvalu, we have a very different language. We understand the Kiribati people and the Rabi people when they talk, and if we talk, they said that they really find it hard to understand. Because some of the words are truly no doubt it's a Tuvaluan word and they just changed it.

When asked about why there is this difference, Kina shook her head and said she did not know, nor did she really want to know:

No, I just heard a legend from, that our people in the past, they were attacked by the boats. That was the legend that I heard. But I am not interested in finding out why, because either the legend is true or just a makeup story that was made by other people. They said that our ancestors ... [were] invaded by the Kiribati canoes, you know, and they killed the men and they married to the women. And that's when they started to have this kind of mixed [Laughter] language.

As she explains it, I begin to understand why she would find this violent story so distasteful, especially considering that the outcome was the "blessing" of this unique language. And so she shrugs it off as part of the island's legend: perhaps true, but then again, perhaps not.

Vaitupu. Vaitupu is one of the central islands in Tuvalu, and also the largest island by landmass, with 5.63 km². The land is densely connected as opposed to the wide dispersion of small islets in the Funafuti atoll. It is shaped similar to a very fat checkmark. Motufoua high school is located in Vaitupu. It is one of Tuvalu's two secondary schools (along with Fetuvalu high school in Funafuti). Motufoua is a boarding school. Jopeto, now a student at the University of the South Pacific, Tuvalu campus, described the differences between the schools:

JOPETO:	They said that Fetuvalu is more high standard than Motufoua, but the discipline is more better in Motufoua than in Fetuvalu.
LAURA:	How do you decide which high school to go to, here or on Vaitupu?
JOPETO:	Our parents decide where to go to. Because most of the parents know that Motufoua is more well-behaved than this kind of school. Students here, they can just, it's up to them if they want to go to school or go out. It's more.
LAURA:	And Vaitupu is more strict?
JOPETO:	Yeah, it's strict, but it's good.
LAURA:	Which one did you go to?

259

JOPETO: Motufoua.

Many students board at Motufoua. Dormitories are set up for the students, who swell the island's population to about 1,600, the second largest population after Funafuti. Motufoua high school experienced a great tragedy in 2000, when a fire broke out in the girl's dormitory. Tafue was serving as pastor on Vaitupu at the time, and spoke of the tragedy with visible emotion:

> When the girls' dormitory got burnt, and 18 of them got burnt in the dormitory including their matron. I think that was the biggest thing that ever happened here in Tuvalu in modern days... that was the darkest day I believe in the whole of the country. The whole of the country. Vaitupu mourned for weeks.

Nukufetau. Nukufetau has the second-largest lagoon in the Tuvalu group, after Funafuti. It has the third largest landmass, spread out in a thin strip of islets around a rectangular lagoon. Metia said that Nukufetau is "just the same" as Funafuti, except that Funafuti's lagoon is bigger and Nukufetau has "many more islets than here." Jopeto described Nukufetau:

> Nukufetau is a nice island, and it's 3.6 kilometers big. It is the third largest island in Tuvalu, of the eight islands of Tuvalu. And Nukufetau, too, it's a sandy island. It's not as long as Funafuti. And people, they fish and they gather. And every function that they have in Nukufetau, they always go there. Because it's like the culture, too, of the Nukufetau people. You should attend.

Nukufetau is one of the three islands that the Americans inhabited during World War II. An airstrip was also erected on this island, but as on Nanumea, it is no longer in use.

People from Nukufetau are known for speaking very rapidly. Metia also made note of this and the importance of Nukufetau's functions in understanding what is unique about the island, "I think the language and especially in dancing, you can see the differences... you can act that because you are from that island." Nukufetau's island holiday celebrates the school that was built there—the first school in Tuvalu. Jopeto explains:

> In Nukufetau, the only important building is the school, where the school is. Because it's interesting, an important building, it is the first school in Tuvalu...
>
> The Nukufetau day, we have it on February 11th. It's about the first school that was first raised in Nukufetau. The first school to reach Tuvalu, it was in Nukufetau. So they celebrate it on that day. It's an important day.

The school is not, of course, the only important building, although it may be the most notable. The Nukufetau *maneapa* is also important for community gatherings, *Kaupule* meetings, and other important functions. Jopeto took a picture of the Nukufetau *maneapa* on Funafuti (see Image 69), but said, "Nukufetau *maneapa* on the main island is more bigger than this *maneapa*. And it's more full of decorations, you know? It's like, local inside. Made of local mats, and it's decorated with local mats." Jopeto also spoke briefly about functions on Nukufetau by comparing Nukufetau weddings to those on

Image 69. Nukufetau *maneapa* on Funafuti (Major, 2011).

Nanumea. Where Nanumea weddings may last a week, "In Nukufetau it's just, getting married and finishing that time. They have a Sunday lunch, if you are married on Sunday, then Sunday lunch and then finished."

Nukufetau is also known for its unique fishing styles, materials, and skills. Jopeto said:

How they catch a fish... *maiava*. That's the only thing that Nukufetau can catch more than the other islands. Like, they used a special fishing material to catch those kinds of fish. It's only the Nukufetau people. They're smart in doing that. It's like, 'Oh, no wonder he is from Nukufetau because he's good.'

Metia explained that when Nukufetau men go fishing, they go two at a time to work together scooping the fish out of the water in a large net in a practice that is unique to their island. He said:

METIA: When people get a fish, you hold that thing and the fish comes into the net. But the net is, each side has a big stick. Not a net like this, but a big stick. People just hold up the stick at each end, they just bring it up. So the fish is inside.

MICHAEL: So almost like a hammock for a fish?

METIA: Yeah.

Nukulaelae. Nukulaelae is the second-most southern island after Niulakita. It is also the second smallest according to landmass and population after Niulakita. These two tiny islands are the only Tuvaluan islands south of Funafuti. With fewer than four hundred people, and only 1.82 km² of land, Nukulaelae maintains a friendly community. Reverend Alefaio Honolulu, who served as pastor on Nukulaelae for several years, told me that, "On Nukulaelae, there are no videos on Sunday. That is the custom. No alcohol. It is a good place, very friendly. They give birds to the pastor, and fish" (Corlew field notes, 2012). Tafue, who is from Nukulaelae, told me that people from Nukulaelae were competitive in nature, which reminded me of a bit of information Jopeto had told me in passing:

261

TAFUE:	They love competing. These people love competing in anything they do. Simple as fishing. If we decided to go fishing, even if we are on one canoe, you in the front and me at the back, we compete starting from there. Everything is a competition.
LAURA:	I heard Nukulaelae was the first winners of the Tuvalu games.
TAFUE:	Yes.
LAURA:	Yes. [Laughter]
TAFUE:	Yes, hmm, and well it's the smallest island, population wise, it's the smallest in the whole of Tuvalu, but because of that competitive spirit, you know, they managed to do things which raises a lot of questions. But that's the way they do it.

Tafue, who is a minister with the Church of Tuvalu, told me that Nukulaelae had also traditionally worshipped an entity they called the Unknown God prior to the coming of Christianity. This Unknown God had many of the aspects of the Christian God they now know in Tuvalu. To Tafue, this is evidence that Tuvaluans were not a people of complete evil and darkness before their conversion. They did not know the true, Christian God yet, but were already trying to worship Him, even in their isolation. He told me the story of Christianity's arrival in Nukulaelae:

Every full moon there was a, they called him half-human half-god but in reality, he's half-human and half-demon. He is a cannibal. The islanders were not cannibals. So he demanded from them a sacrifice every full moon. So every full moon people, take one of the eldest of the families in rotation up to him. They give it to him and that's his meal. And then they continued on to this rock and worshipped it. Just before the arrival of Christianity, people have managed to kill this half-demon. Two brothers killed him. So, they lived in peace worshipping [the Unknown God] because they don't know. But all the attributes of this god that they worshipped were more or less very similar to the attributes we attribute to God now. The most powerful and loving god who sustained us.

Niulakita. Niulakita is the smallest island in Tuvalu with a landmass of only 0.42 km ² and a population of 35 people (8 families).[66] Alefaio was the pastor on Niulakita as well, and said that:

Niulakita is like the Garden of Eden, as far as he is concerned. People eat banana, crab, prawn, fish, birds, all local foods. Birds are sold here on Funafuti $2/each as one way for to the island to make money (but very little money, and there is very little reliance on money, imports, electricity, etc.) Guano is there. Everything grows very green, very

---

[66] www.tuvaluislands.com/islands/islands.html, 2002 Census.

large *pulaka*. There is no alcohol, very strict. If someone drinks, they are taken to the *maneapa* and receive speeches about respect (Corlew field notes, 2012).

Niulakita is not traditionally part of Tuvalu's 'group of eight.' Niutao, which is a very small island in the north of the country, had become overpopulated. Niulakita, which is traditionally uninhabited, was given to Niutao to move some of their population and ease the strain on the island's resources.

Niutao. Niutao is my host family's island. Niutao is a laid back place, I have been told. Sueina said,

SUEINA: Also our language, the way that we talk, the Niutaoans, we talk slowly and you can understand properly. Not like others, like the Nukufetau, they speak fast. We have different dialects for language.
LAURA: Does Niutao speak the most slowly?
SUEINA: Yeah, yeah, the most slowly of the eight groups. [Laughs].

When I asked Teba what dialect of Tuvaluan she spoke since she first moved to Tuvalu and learned the language, she laughed and said, "I don't know – Niutao." The joke, of course, is that she speaks slowly even though she is fluent now. She also says, "The Niutaoan people have this way of speaking that is sort of like singsong." The language is very beautiful when spoken. Niutao is a very friendly place. Sueina tells me that Niutao is known for being the most welcoming of all the islands, and that Niutaoans are very welcoming to outsiders:

If you sit at a house and you see some people walking around on the road, even though they are Tuvaluans or no matter what, if they are Tuvaluans or *palagis* like you people, we just call out to them, "Come and drink, come and eat!" That's our culture. But not for most of the Tuvalus. But us, the Niutao people, we are different because we have love. They always call that the Niutao people, that they have much love than other Tuvaluans.

Ken also explains how very welcoming the people from Niutao are:

In Niutao... There is another culture, but I love that culture... The people are friendly, you know, you walk around and the families, they just call you come and eat or something to drink. Yeah, it's different from other islands. Mostly you'll see each other, you make some local food and then you can share it with your neighbors, and others.

In Niutao, there are two large *pulaka* pits in which every family goes to grow. Kou tells me that in Niutao, even if a family does not have anyone working, they can still live because there is so much food from the land and from the sea. She tells me, "That time I stay in Niutao, I think Niutao is a beautiful island." Sueina explains that even though Niutao has access to many modern amenities, they are not as prevalent as in urban Funafuti:

Like here [in Funafuti] we have twenty four hours for electricity. And back at home we only have, from the morning we start the generator at six and then we have to off it at four. And then after that, from six in the evening until ten, then we off it again.

I was told that in Niutao there are three very important structures in the community. The first is the sea wall. Niutao is a small island by size, only 2.53 km², but it has a large lagoon-like pool in the center. The Niutao people erected a seawall that divides this water, connecting one side of the island to the other, spanning it like a bridge that can be crossed on foot or motorbike. Ken told me:

> I think the Niutao sea wall reflects sort of, Niutao building our sea wall. That's important for us. That's like our main island, our lands where the sea will come and take all the sand. That's another one too, the Niutao sea wall... that's because when you go to Niutao we have no lagoon there. Only ocean side, same side, both sides. So you can see waves all the way.

The second important structure is the new *maneapa*. It is the larger of the two *maneapas* in Niutao, and also houses a museum-like array of traditional island tools, weaponry, and materials on the walls. Most of these are replicas, with small cards explaining how they are used as a means to honor and preserve Niutao's cultural history. In the center of the *maneapa* is a hole in the floor where stones can be filled in. Throughout the rest of the country, Tuvaluans use large, hollow wooden boxes as drums during the traditional songs. But in Niutao, they fold mats and use them as drums. They place them on top of gravel to soften the blow. The *maneapa* also houses a large, painted stone at one end where the chief will sit during functions (see Image 70). Ken described it, saying it is "like a chair, but it's just to put his back to rest. And also put the hand back. And all the guards will sit around." Niutao regards the chief with a number of honors to recognize his place in the community. Feue explained:

> You know, in Britain they have the crown. Now, the traditional chiefs in Niutao have got their own head gear that symbolizes that he is the chief. Now, there is a special place for him to sit in the community hall, which is the *Falekaupule*, as Niutao refers to that. And that's a secret sort of spot. Nobody sits at that place unless you are the appointed chief.

The third place of importance in Niutao is the church. The events surrounding the building of the church are what Niutao commemorates during their island feast day, called Setema. While Ken was showing me videos of the island, he pointed out the church in the community:

KEN:	But this one is a church, this side's church. The bell, so they can ring the bell and everybody comes in, comes for church.
LAURA:	Is there just one church on the island?
KEN:	Right now, we have two churches on the island. This church, and the other one is Seventh Day Adventist.
LAURA:	So this is the one that was built by the Australians, and the Setema?
KEN:	You heard about that, eh?

Image 70. Stone in Niutao *maneapa*. Screengrab from home video (Sione family, 2012).

Ken cut me a sideways glance as he asked that question. What do I know of this story? And what do I think of it? The story of Setema is a long and complicated one that highlights the complexities and sometimes the confusion the occurred during Tuvaluans' early contact with *palagis*. Sueina explained:

> During the Setema, that's our Niutao day... That's a time when they build the chapel... because before there's no, they never, they don't understand properly, eh? People are like, darkness was still there. So they asked those Europeans to come and build a chapel, and then after that thing was finished, the owner of the company asked them to pay their debts. But they don't have any money, but they just told those people to come and build for them [Laughs].

The church was completed, but the Tuvaluans had no way to pay for the labor and materials that the foreigners had put into the construction. Now accidentally and badly in debt, the Niutao people were in danger of being caught under the thumb of this *palagi* who was demanding that if they did not pay the money, they would be beholden to him for labor and resources. In essence, in exchange for this church, he would own the people of Niutao. Sueina continued:

> That *palagi*, that boss of that company asked them... that if they don't settle their bill, I don't know what he's going to do with the Niutao people, eh? But the Niutao people in the olden days, they have like

265

what do you call that? It's like, from their ancestors, like they do with magical words... it's island words. But it's from before, they used to use that one. Those words, they are going to say them. So they used those kind of words and then they came up with thinkings to collect, there's a shell, there's a seashell in the sea, it's round. We call it the *alili*.

The Niutao people hatched a plan to trick the *palagis* into thinking they had paid their debt. They collected a box full of *alili* shells as "payment" for the construction of the church. But the shells were not meant to be received by the *palagi*. Nalu explained:

The Niutao people collected all these things, put in the box. So the ship arrived in my island. So these people, there were six of them taking the box out. So they tied the box with, because no lock. They tied the box with coconut leaves... took it down, the box ...my great grandfather went in the same canoe taking down the box.

They tied it with coconut leaves and string made from coconut rather than tying the box with a rope that would be more secure. The coconut leaves were fragile. The men, including Nalu's great grandfather, took the box to the ship to be hoisted aboard. But as the ship's crew lifted it, the bindings broke and the box opened. It fell into the ocean, spilling the entire "payment" along with it. The plan was a success. The foreigners were shocked by their folly when bringing the money on board the ship. Sueina told me, "So that the boss said 'Oh, it's okay. Forget about the credit. It's all done.' Because it's their own fault. They didn't take care of that bag of money." Only there was no money inside, she explained with a laugh. This is the story of Setema, a reminder to the people of Niutao how their church was built, and how they escaped their debt. As Kou said:

If that box goes up to where the English guys are, and they check it out, then they would find out that it's not our money. And that's why they make the thing fall down. So the English guys, they say the box is money... that's why we are free from those English guys. Because the thing is fallen down. You get it?

266

References

Adam, D. (2009). Increase in sea levels due to global warming could lead to 'ghost states', The Guardian (Environment ed.). London. Retrieved from http://www.guardian.co.uk/environment/2009/sep/29/sea-levels-ghost-states on 3/20/11.

Adger, W. N. (2001). Scales of governance and environmental justice for adaptation and mitigation of climate change. Journal of International Development, 13(7), 921-931.

Allice, I. A. (2009). Negotiating the flood: The encounter with climate change in Tuvalu. (Unpublished master's thesis). York University, Toronto, Ontario.

Altman, I., & Low, S. M. (Eds.). (1992). Place attachment. NewYork: Plenum.

Anglin, A. E. (2012). Exploratory study of youth perceptions of tourism in selected schools in Liberia, Costa Rica. (Unpublished master's thesis). University of Hawai'i, Mānoa, Honolulu, HI.

Anthony, S., Izuka, S. K., & Keener, V. W. (2012). Fresh water and drought on Pacific islands. In J. J. Marra, V. W. Keener, M. L. Finucane, D. Spooner, M.H. Smith, M.H. (Eds.). Climate Change and Pacific Islands: Indicators and Impacts. Report for The 2012 Pacific Islands Regional Climate Assessment (PIRCA). Honolulu, Hawai'i, USA.

Barem, D. (2005a). That sinking feeling. The Guardian. Retrieved from http://www.guardian.co.uk/theguardian/2005/mar/04/features11.g21 on 11/13/10.

Barem, D. (2005b). Drowning in money. The Guardian. Retrieved from http://www.guardian.co.uk/theguardian/2005/mar/25/guardianweekly.guardianweekly1 on 11/13/10.

Barnett, J. & Campbell, J. (2010). Climate change and small island states. Washington, DC: Earthscan.

Baum, A. (1987). Cataclysms, Crises, and Catastrophes: Psychology in Action. Washington, DC: American Psychological Association.

Bayer, J, & Salzman, J. (Producers and Directors). (May 2007). Time and tide. Wavecrest films.

Beckford, G. (2011). Drought-stricken Pacific islands down to last few days of water. Reuters, October 7, 2011. Accessed on 3/24/12 from http://www.reuters.com/article/2011/10/07/us-pacific-drought-idUSTRE7960F120111007.

Benns, M. (2011). Tuvalu 'to run out of water by Tuesday'. The Telegraph, October 3, 2011. Accessed on 3/24/12 from http://www.telegraph.co.uk/news/worldnews/australiaandthepacific/tuvalu/8804093/Tuvalu-to-run-out-of-water-by-Tuesday.html .

Berzon, A. (2006). Tuvalu is drowning. Salon, March 21, 2006. Accessed on 3/26/12 from http://www.salon.com/2006/03/31/tuvalu_2/.

Bhattarai, B. (2011). Assessment of mangrove forests in the Pacific using Landsat imagery. (Unpublished master's thesis). University of Nebraska, Omaha, Nebraska.

Bishop, B., Colquhoun, S., & Johnson, G. (2006). Psychological sense of community: An Australian Aboriginal experience. *Journal of Community Psychology, 34*(1), 1-7.

Breakwell, G. M. (1992). Processes of self-evaluation: Efficacy and estrangement. In G. M. Breakwell (Ed.), Social psychology of identity and self-concept. Surrey: Surrey University Press.

Brokopp Binder, S. (2012). Resilience and disaster recovery in American Samoa: A case study of the 2009 Pacific tsunami. (Unpublished master's thesis). University of Hawai'i, Mānoa, Honolulu, HI.

Brodsky, A. E. (2009). Multiple psychological senses of community in Afghan context: Exploring commitment and sacrifice in an underground resistance community. *American Journal of Community Psychology, 44*, 176-187.

Budescu, D. V., Broomell, S., & Por, H. (2009). Improving communication of uncertainty in the reports of the intergovernmental panel on climate change. *Psychological Science, 20*, 299-308.

Burns, W. C. G. (2003) Pacific island developing country water resources and climate change. In *The World's Water: The Biennial Report on Freshwater Resources 2002-2003*, (113-131) Washington, DC: Island Press.

Canberra, D. W. (2006). Call for action on 'drowning' islands. *The Age, January 5, 2006.* Accessed on 3/26/12 from http://www.theage.com.au/news/national/labor-calls-for-action-on-drowning-islands/2006/01/04/1136050495632.html.

Cardazone, G. M. (2010). Exploring the meaning of community service to adolescents in Hawai'i: A photovoice study. (Unpublished Master's thesis). University of Hawai'i at Mānoa, Honolulu.

Carlson E. D., Engebretson, J., & Chamberlain, R. M. (2006). Photovoice as a social process of critical consciousness. *Qualitative Health Research, 16*(6), 836-852.

Carter, R. (1986). Wind and sea analysis: Funafuti lagoon, Tuvalu. *Technical Report No. 58 of PE/TU.3.* Committee for Co-ordination of Joint Prospecting for Mineral Resources in South Pacific Offshore Areas (CCOP/SOPAC) work Programme and South Pacific Regional Environmental Programme and UNDP Project RAS/81/102 Investigations of Mineral Potential of the South Pacific.

CCSP, 2008.*The effects of Climate Change on agriculture, land resources, water resources, and biodiversity in the United States*: Synthesis and assessment product 4.3 report by the U.S. Climate Change Science Program and the Subcommittee on Global Change Research. P. Backlund, A. Janetos, D. Schimel, J. Hatfield, K. Boote, P. Fay, L. Hahn, C. Izaurralde, B.A. Kimball, T. Mader, J. Morgan, D. Ort, W. Polley, A. Thompson, D. Wolfe, M.G. Ryan, S. R. Archer, R. Birdsey, C. Dahm, L. Heath, J. Hicke, D. Hollinger, T. Huxman, G. Okin, R. Oren, J. Randerson, W. Schlesinger, D. Lettenmaier, D. Major, L. Poff, S. Running, L. Hansen, D. Inouye, B.P. Kelly, L. Meyerson, B.

Perterson, R. Shaw. U.S. Department of Agriculture, Washington, DC., USA 362 pp.

Central Statistics Division (2010a). Demographic Indicators. Retrieved from http://www.spc.int/prism/country/tv/stats/Social/Demog_Popn/demogra phic_.htm on 11/02/10.

Central Statistics Division (2010b). Tourism and Migration Statistics. Retrieved from http://www.spc.int/prism/country/tv/stats/Tourism_migration/Tour_su mmary.htm on 11/02/10.

Chambers, A. F., & Chambers, K. S. (2007). Five takes on climate and cultural change in Tuvalu. *The Contemporary Pacific, 19*(1), 294-306.

Chambers, K. S. (1984). Heirs of Tefolaha: Tradition and social organization in Nanumea, a Polynesian atoll community. (Unpublished doctoral dissertation). University of California, Berkeley, California.

Chambers, K., & Chambers, A. (2001). *Unity of Hearts.* Prospect Heights, IL: Wavel and Press, Inc.

Chapman, P. (2012). Entire nation of Kiribati to be relocated over rising sea level threat. *The Telegraph, March 7, 2012.* Accessed on 3/26/12 from http://www.telegraph.co.uk/news/worldnews/australiaandthepacific/kiri bati/9127576/Entire-nation-of-Kiribati-to-be-relocated-over-rising-sea-level-threat.html.

Chowdhury, M. R., Barnston, A. G., Guard, C., Duncan, S., Schroeder, T. A., & Chu, P. S. (2010). Sea-level variability and change in the US-affiliated Pacific Islands: Understanding the high sea levels during 2006-2008. *Weather, 65*(10), 263-268.

Cline, R. J. W., Orom, H., Berry-Bobovski, L., Hernandez, T., Black, C. B., Schwartz, A. G., & Ruckdeschel, J. C. (2010). Community-level social support responses in a slow-motion technological disaster: The case of Libby, Montana. *American Journal of Community Psychology, 46*(1-2), 1-18.

Coelho, C. A. S., & Goddard, L. (2009). El Nino-induced tropical droughts in climate change projections. *Journal of Climate, 22*, 6456-6476.

Cohen, D., & Nisbett, R. E. (1997). Field experiments examining the culture of honor: The role of institutions in perpetuating norms about violence. *Personality and Social Psychology Bulletin, 23*(11), 1188-1199.

Cohen, D., Nisbett, R. E., Bowdle, B. F., & Schwarz, N. (1996). Insult, aggression, and the southern culture of honor: An "experimental ethnography." *Journal of Personality and Social Psychology, 70*(5), 945-960.

Commonwealth update. (1999). Tuvalu.

Connell, J. (2003). Losing ground? Tuvalu, the greenhouse effect and the garbage can. *Asia Pacific Viewpoint, 44*(2), 89-107.

Cooper, C. M., & Yarbrough, S. P. (2010). Tell me--show me: Using combined focus group and Photovoice methods to gain understanding of health issues in rural Guatemala. *Qualitative Health Research, 20*(5), 644-653.

269

Cooper, R. N. (2000). International approaches to global climate change. *World Bank Research Observer, 15*(2), 145-172.

Corlew, L. K. (2011). Creating a collaborative proposal for climate change research in Tuvalu. *The Community Psychologist, 44*(2), 29-32.

Corlew, M. R. (2012). Nothing is timeless: Exploring economic change in Tuvalu through oral histories. *University of Hawai'i at Mānoa Spring Symposium, April 28, 2012.* Honolulu, HI.

CNN Tech. (2009). Drowning island pins hopes on clean energy. *CNN Tech, July 21, 2009.* Accessed on 3/26/12 from http://articles.cnn.com/2009-07-21/tech/tuvalu.cleanenergy_1_tuvalu-solar-power-clean-energy?_s=PM:TECH.

Creswell, J. W. (2007). Qualitative inquiry & research design: Choosing among five approaches, Second edition. Thousand Oaks: SAGE Publications.

CRISP (2007). Funafuti atoll coral reef restoration project (Republic of Tuvalu). Baseline Report, June 2007. Coral Reef InitiativeS for the Pacific.

Davidson, H., Evans, S., Ganote, C., Henrickson, J., Jacobs-Priebe, L., Jones, D. L., Prilleltensky, I., & Riemer, M. (2006). Power and action in critical theory across disciplines: Implications for Critical Community Psychology. *American Journal of Community Psychology, 38*(1-2), 35-49.

Deloria, P. J. (1998). Playing Indian. New Haven, Connecticut Yale University.

Dix, C. V. (2011). Tuvalu: Balancing climate change and development initiatives in Small Island Developing States. (Unpublished master's thesis). Saint Mary's University, Halifax Nova Scotia.

Doherty, T. J., & Clayton, S. (2011). The psychological impacts of global climate change. *American Psychologist, 66*(4), 265-276.

Ede, P. M. (2003). Come hell or high water. *Alternatives Journal, 29*(3), 8-9.

Ells, P. (2000). *Where the hell is Tuvalu? How I became the law man of the world's fourth-smallest country.* Great Britain: Virgin Publishers.

Encyclopedia of the Nations (2003). World leaders, Tuvalu, Saufatu Sopoanga, Prime Minister. Retrieved 10/31/10 from http://www.nationsencyclopedia.com/World-Leaders-2003/Tuvalu.html.

Faaniu, S., & Laracy, H., (Eds.). (1983). *Tuvalu, a History.* Tuvalu: Institute of Pacific Studies and Extension Services, University of the South Pacific, and the Ministry of Social Services, Government of Tuvalu.

Farbotko, C. (2005). Tuvalu and climate change: Constructions of environmental displacement in the *Sydney Morning Herald. Geografiska Annaler, 87*B(4), 279-293.

Farbotko, C. (2008). Representing climate change spaces: Islographs of Tuvalu. (Unpublished doctoral dissertation). University of Tasmania, Tasmania, Australia.

Farbotko, C. (2010a). 'The global warming clock is ticking so see these places while you can': Voyeuristic tourism and model environmental citizens on Tuvalu's disappearing islands. Singapore Journal of Tropical Geography, 31, 224-238.

Farbotko, C. (2010b). Wishful sinking: Disappearing islands, climate refugees and cosmopolitan experimentation. Asia Pacific Viewpoint, 51(1), 47-60.

Farbotko, C. (2012). Skillful seafarers, oceanic drifters or climate refugees? Pacific people, news value and the climate refugee crisis. In K. Moore, B. Gross, and T. Threadgold (Eds.) *Migration and the Media.* New York: Peter Lang Publishing.

Farbotko, C., & McGregor, H. V. (2010). Copenhagen, climate science and the emotional geographies of climate change. *Australian Geographer, 41*(2), 159-166.

Finucane, M.L. (2009). Why science alone won't solve the climate crisis: Managing climate risks in the Pacific. *Asia Pacific Issues*, 89, 1-8.

Finucane, M. L. (2010). Human dimensions of drought in Hawai'i: An exploratory study of perceptions of and responses to drought risk by farmers, ranchers, and service providers in Hawai'i. *East-West Center Research Program.* Honolulu, HI.

Fitchett, K. (1987). Physical effects of Hurricane Bebe upon Funafuti Atoll, Tuvalu. *Australian Geographer, 18*(1), 1-7.

Flegal, K. M., Carroll, M. D., Ogden, C. L., & Curtin, L. R. (2010). Prevalence and trends in obesity among US adults, 1999-2008. *Journal of the American Medical Association,303*(3), 235-241.

Fletcher, C. H., & Richmond, B. M. (2010). Climate change in the Federated States of Micronesia (Sea Grant Report). University of Hawaii.

Foster-Fishman, P., Nowell, B., Deacon, Z., Nievar, M. A., & McCann, P. (2005). Using methods that matter: The impact of reflection, dialogue, and voice. *American Journal of Community Psychology, 36*(3/4), 275-291.

Fox, D., Prilleltensky, I., & Austin, S. (2009). Critical psychology for social justice: Concerns and dilemmas. In D. Fox, I. Prilleltensky, & S. Austin (Eds.). *Critical psychology: An introduction, 2nd edition.* Thousand Oaks, CA: Sage Publications, Ltd. 3-19.

Fried, M. (2000) Continuities and discontinuities of place. *Journal of Environmental Psychology, 20*, 193-205.

Friedman, L. (2010). If a country sinks beneath the sea, is it still a country? *Nations,* 08/23/2010.

Fritze, J. G., Blashki, G. A., Burke, S. & Wiseman, J. (2008). Hope, despair and transformation: Climate change and the promotion of mental health and wellbeing. *International Journal of Mental Health Systems, 2*(13). Retrieved October 9, 2010, from http://ijmhs.com/content/2/1/13

Fulu, E. (2007). Gender, vulnerability, and the experts: Responding to the Maldives tsunami. *Development and Change, 38*(5), 843-864.

Funk, M. (2009). Come hell or high water. *World Policy Journal, Summer,*93-100.

General Environment Briefing. (2010). Government of Tuvalu.

271

Gifford, R. (2011). The dragons of inaction: Psychological barriers that limit climate change mitigation and adaptation. *American Psychologist, 66*(4), 290-302.

Goldsmith, M. R. (1989). Church and society in Tuvalu. (Unpublished doctoral dissertation). University of Illinois, Urbana-Champaign, Illinois.

Goldsmith, M. R. (2005). Theories of governance and Pacific microstates: The cautionary tale of Tuvalu. *Asia Pacific Viewpoint, 46*(2), 105-114.

Greenfield, P. M. (1997). You can't take it with you: Why ability assessments don't cross cultures. American Psychologist, 52(10), 1115-1124.

Grubb, M. (1995). Seeking fair weather: Ethics and international debate on climate change. *International Affairs, 71*(3), 43-496.

Gunn Allen, P. (2003). Pocahontas: Medicine woman, spy, entrepreneur, diplomat. New York: HarperCollins.

Hall, S. (1997). *Representation: Cultural Representations and Signifying Practices.* London: Sage Publications.

Hallegatte, S., Przyluski, V., & Vogt-Schilb, A. (2011). Building world narratives for climate change impact, adaptation and vulnerability analysis. *Nature Climate Change, 1135*(1), 151-155.

Hamilton, K. (2012). Appendix B: Future regional climate – models and projections. In J. J. Marra, V. W. Keener, M. L. Finucane, D. Spooner, M.H. Smith, M.H. (Eds.). Climate Change and Pacific Islands: Indicators and Impacts. Report for The 2012 Pacific Islands Regional Climate Assessment (PIRCA). Honolulu, Hawai'i, USA.

Harrison, B. (2002). Photographic visions and narrative inquiry. *Narrative Inquiry, 12*(1), 87-111.

Hidalgo, M. C. & Hernandez, B. (2001) Place attachment: Conceptual and empirical questions. *Journal of Environmental Psychology, 21*, 273-281.

Homer, S. (2000). Online world covets Tuvalu's domain: Information technology developing nations. *Financial Times London, 3*, 20.

Hughes, H., & Gosarevski, S. (2004). Does size matter? Tuvalu and Nauru compared. *Policy, 20*(2), 16-20.

Hultman, N. E., Hassenzahl, D. M., & Rayner, S. (2010). Climate risk. *Annual Review of Environment and Resources, 35*, 7.1-7.21.

Hunter, J. R. (2002). A note on relative sea level change at Funafuti, Tuvalu. *Antarctic Cooperative Research Centre. Retrieved 10/09/10 from* http://staff.acecrc.org.au/~johunter/tuvalu.pdf.

Intergovernmental Panel on Climate Change (IPCC). (2007). *Climate Change 2007: Synthesis Report. Contribution of Working Groups I, II and III to the Fourth Assessment Report of the Intergovernmental Panel on Climate Change* . Geneva Switzerland: IPCC. 104 pp.

Jorgensen, B. S., & Stedman, R. C. (2001). Sense of place as an attitude: Lakeshore owners attitudes toward their properties. Journal of Environmental Psychology, 21, 233—248.

272

Jurkowski, J. & Paul-Ward, A. (2007). Photovoice with vulnerable populations: Addressing disparities in health promotion among people with intellectual disabilities. *Health Promotion Practice, 8*(4) 358-365.

Karl, T. R., Melillo, J. M., & Peterson, T. C. (eds). (2007). Global Climate Change Impacts in the United States. Cambridge University Press, 2009.

Kelly, P. M., & Adger, W. N. (2000). Theory and practice in assessing vulnerability to climate change and facilitating adaptation. *Climatic Change, 47*(4), 325-352.

Kempton, W. (1991). Public understanding of global warming. *Society and Natural Resources, 4,* 331-345.

Kidner, D. (2007). Depression and the natural world: Towards a critical ecology of psychological distress. *The International Journal of Critical Psychology, 19,* 123-146.

Kilpatrick, J. (1999). *Celluloid Indians: Native Americans and film.* Lincoln, Nebraska: University of Nebraska Press.

Knez, I. (2005). Attachment and identity as related to a place and its perceived climate. *Journal of Environmental Psychology, 25,* 207-218.

Lazrus, H. (2009a). Weathering the waves: Climate change, politics, and vulnerability in Tuvalu. (Unpublished doctoral dissertation). University of Washington, Seattle, Washington.

Lazrus, H. (2009b). Perspectives on vulnerability to climate change and questions of migration in Tuvalu. In: A. Oliver-Smith and X. Shen, eds. *Linking environmental change, migration, and social vulnerability.* Seattle: United Nations University, Institute for Environment and Human Security, 32–41.

Leiserowitz, A. (2005). American risk perceptions: Is climate change dangerous? *Risk Analysis, 25,* 1433-1442.

Lerner, M. (2001). What's in a domain? The CBS Interactive Business Network. New York: News World Communications, Inc. Retrieved from http://findarticles.com/p/articles/mi_m1571/is_33_17/ai_78127733/ on 3/20/11.

Levine, A. (1982). *Love Canal: Science, Politics, and People.* Lexington, MA: Lexington Books.

Locke, J. T. (2009). Climate change-induced migration in the Pacific Region: Sudden crisis and long-term development. *The Geographical Journal, 175*(3), 171-180.

Lindsay, P. (2004). *Before the Flood.* UK: Mediarights.

Lusama, T. M. (2004). Punishment of the innocent: The problem of global warming with special reference to Tuvalu. (Unpublished master's thesis). Presbyterian Church of Taiwan.

Lykes, M. B., Blanche, M. T., & Hamber, B. (2003). Narrating survival and change in Guatemala and South Africa: The politics of representation and a liberatory Community Psychology. *American Journal of Community Psychology, 31*(1/2), 79-90.

273

Mann, C. C. (2005). *1491: New Revelations of the Americas Before Columbus.* New York: Alfred A. Knopf.

Manzo, L. C. (2003). Beyond house and haven: toward a revisioning of emotional relationships with places. Journal of Environmental Psychology, 23, 47-61.

Marra, J.J., Keener, V.W., Finucane, M.L., Spooner, D., Smith, M.H. [Editors] (2012). Climate Change and Pacific Islands: Indicators and Impacts. Report for The 2012 Pacific Islands Regional Climate Assessment (PIRCA). Honolulu, Hawai'i, USA.

Marra, J. J., Merrifield, M. A., & Sweet, W. V. (2012). Sea level and coastal inundation on Pacific islands. In J. J. Marra, V. W. Keener, M. L. Finucane, D. Spooner, M.H. Smith, M.H. (Eds.). Climate Change and Pacific Islands: Indicators and Impacts. Report for The 2012 Pacific Islands Regional Climate Assessment (PIRCA). Honolulu, Hawai'i, USA.

McCrae, R. R. (1984). Situational determinants of coping responses: Loss, threat, and challenge. *Journal of Personality and Social Psychology, 46*(4), 919-928.

McCright, A. M., & Dunlap, R. E. (2003). Defeating Kyoto: The conservative movement's impact on U.S. climate change policy. *Social Problems, 50*(3), 348-373.

McCright, A. M., & Dunlap, R. E. (2011). The politicization of climate change and polarization in the American public's views of global warming, 2001-2010. *The Sociological Quarterly, 52*, 155-194.

McGeehan, K. M. (2012). Cultural and religious belief systems, tsunami recovery and disaster risk reduction in American Samoa in the aftermath of the September 29, 2009 tsunami. (Unpublished master's thesis). University of Hawai'i, Mānoa, Honolulu, HI.

McMillan, D. W., & Chavis, D. M. (1986). Sense of community: A definition and theory. Journal of Community Psychology, 14, 6-23.

Mimura, N., Nurse, L., McLean, R.F., Agard, J., Briguglio, L., Lefale, P., Payet, R., & Sem, G., (2007). Small islands. Climate Change 2007: Impacts, Adaptation and Vulnerability. Contribution of Working Group II to the Fourth Assessment Report of the Intergovernmental Panel on Climate Change, M.L. Parry, O.F. Canziani, J.P. Palutikof, P.J. van der Linden and C.E. Hanson, Eds., Cambridge University Press: Cambridge, UK, 687-716.

Mithlo, N. M. (2008). "Our Indian Princess": Subverting the Stereotype. Santa Fe, New Mexico: School for Advanced Research.

Mortreux, C., & Barnett, J. (2009). Climate change, migration and adaptation in Funafuti, Tuvalu. Global Environmental Change, 19(1), 105-112.

Munroe, D. (1982). The lagoon islands: A history of Tuvalu 1820-1908. Dissertation in Philosophy. School of History, Philosophy and Politics. Macquarie University.

Nicholls, R. J., Wong, P. P., Burkett, V. R., Codignotto, J. O., Hay, J. E., McLean, R. F., Ragoonaden, S., & Woodroffe, C. D. (2007). Coastal

274

systems and low-lying areas. Climate Change 2007: Impacts, Adaptations and Vulnerability. Contribution of Working Group II to the Fourth Assessment Report of the Intergovernmental Panel on Climate Change, M.L. Parry, O.F. Canziani, J.P. Palutikof, P.J. van der Linden and C.E. Hanson, Eds., Cambridge University Press, Cambridge, UK, 315-356.

Niepold, F., Herring, D., & McConville, D. (2007). The case for climate literacy in the 21st Century. Submitted for publication to the Fifth International Symposium on Digital Earth http://www.isde5.org.

Nine, C. (2010). Ecological refugees, state borders, and the Lockean proviso. *Journal of Applied Philosophy, 27*(4), 359-375.

NOAA (2010). National Oceanic and Atmospheric Administration website, Education page. Retrieved from http://www.climate.noaa.gov/index.jsp?pg=/education/edu_index.jsp& edu=literacy on 10/28/10.

Norris, F. H., Baker, C. K., Murphy, A. D., & Kaniasty, K. (2005). Social support mobilization and deterioration after Mexico's 1999 flood: Effects of context, gender, and time. *American Journal of Community Psychology, 36*(1-2), 15-28.

Normille, D. (2010). Hard summer for corals kindles fears for survival of reefs. *Science, 329*, 1001.

Nowell, B. L., Berkowitz, S. L., Deacon, Z., & Foster-Fishman, P. (2006). Revealing the cues within community places: Stories of identity, history, and possibility. *American Journal of Community Psychology, 37*(1/2), 29-46.

Nowell, B. L., & Boyd, N. (2010). Viewing community as a responsibility as well as resource: Deconstructing the theoretical roots of psychological sense of community. Journal of Community Psychology, 38(7), 828-841.

O'Donnell, C. R. (2006). Beyond diversity: Toward a cultural community psychology. *American Journal of Community Psychology, 37*(1-2), 1-7.

O'Donnell, C. R., & Tharp, R. G. (2012). Integrating cultural community psychology: Activity settings and the shared meanings of intersubjectivity. *American Journal of Community Psychology, 49*(1-2), 22-30.

O'Donnell, C. R., Tharp, R. G., & Wilson, K. (1993). Activity settings as the unit of analysis: A theoretical basis for community intervention and development. American Journal of Community Psychology 21(4), 501-520.

Oneha, M. F. M. (2001). Ka mauli oka 'o-ina a he mauli ka-naka: An ethnographic study from an Hawaiian sense of place. *Pacific Health Dialog, 8*(2), 299-311.

Oresekes, N., Stainforth, D. A., & Smith, L. A. (2010). Adaptation to global warming: Do climate models tell us what we need to know? *Philosophy of Science, 77*(5), 1012-1028.

275

Ornelas, I. J., Amell, J., Tran, A. N., Royster, M., Armstrong-Brown, J., & Eng, E. (2009). Understanding African American men's perceptions of racism, male gender, socialization, and social capital through Photovoice. *Qualitative Health Research, 19*(4), 552-565.

Paavola, J., & Adger, W. N. (2005). Fair adaptation to climate change. *Ecological Economics, 56*(1), 594-609.

Pacific Country Report. (2006). Sea level & climate: Their present state. Tuvalu. *Australian Agency for International Development (AusAID).*

Parks, B. C., & Roberts, J. T. (2006). Globalization, vulnerability to climate change, and perceived injustice. *Society and Natural Resources, 19*, 337-355.

Patel, S. S. (2006). That sinking feeling. *Nature, 440*, 734-736.

Paton, K. L. (2008). At home or abroad: Tuvaluans shaping a Tuvaluan future. (Unpublished master's thesis). Victoria University of Wellington, Wellington, New Zealand.

Paton, K. L. & Fairbairn-Dunlop, P. (2010). Listening to local voices: Tuvaluans respond to climate change. *Local Environment, 15*(7), 687-698.

Perry, M. (2009a). UPDATE 6 – Samoa tsunami toll may exceed 100, hundreds injured. *Reuters UK, September 30, 2009.* Accessed on 3/24/12 from http://uk.reuters.com/article/2009/09/30/quake-pacific-idUKSYD51634720090930.

Perry, M. (2009b). Pacific quakes stir panic but tsunamis tiny. *Reuters UK, October 8, 2009.* Accessed on 3/24/12 from http://uk.reuters.com/article/2009/10/08/us-quake-pacific-idUSSYD42800820091008.

Perry, N. (2011). Tuvalu water crisis may point to global problems. *Boston Globe, October 14, 2011.* Accessed on 3/12/12 from http://www.boston.com/news/world/asia/articles/2011/10/14/tuvalu_water_crisis_may_point_to_global_problems/

Proshansky, H. M., Fabian, A. K., & Kaminoff, R. (1983). Place identity: Physical world socialization of the self. Journal of Environmental Psychology, 3, 57-83.

Resture, A., & Resture, S. (2005). Seashells on the seashore: Women's participation in the shell trade on Funafuti and Nukufetau, Tuvalu. In I. Novaczek, J. Mitchell, & J. Vietayaski (Eds.) *Pacific Voices: Equity and Sustainability in Pacific Island Fisheries*. Suva, Fiji: Institute of Pacific Studies, University of the South Pacific.

Rhodes, S. D., Hergenrather, K. C., Wilkin, A. M., & Jolly, C. (2008). Visions and voices: Indigent persons living with HIV in the southern United States use Photovoice to create knowledge, develop partnerships, and take action. *Health Promotion Practice, 9*(2), 159-169.

Richmond, B. M. & Morton, R. A. (2007). Coral-grave storm ridges: Examples from the tropical Pacific and Caribbean. In N. C. Kraus & J. D. Rosati (Eds.). *Coastal Sediments '07: Proceedings of the sixth International Symposium on Coastal Engineering and Science of Coastal Sediment*

Processes, May 13-17, 2007. Reston, VA: American Society of Civil Engineers. 572-583.

Rogan, R., O'Connor, M., & Horwitz, P. (2005). Nowhere to hide: Awareness and perceptions of environmental change, and their influence on relationships with place. *Journal of Environmental Psychology, 25,* 147-158.

Rudiak-Gould, P. (2011). Climate change and anthropology: The importance of reception studies. *Anthropology Today, 27*(2), 9-12.

Said, E. W. (1978). Orientalism. New York: Random House, Inc.

Sarason, S.B. (1974). The psychological sense of community: Prospects for a community psychology. San Francisco: Jossey-Bass.

Schoen, A. A. (2005). Culturally sensitive counseling for Asian Americans/Pacific Islanders. *Journal of Instructional Psychology, 32*(3), 253-258.

Secretariat of the Pacific Regional Environment Programme (SPREP). (2011). Pacific Regional Environment Programme Strategic Plan 2011-2015. Apia, Samoa: SPREP.

Sharma, K. D. & Gosain, A. K. (2009). Application of climate information and predictions in water sector: Capabilities. Draft White Paper, Geneva International Conference Center, Geneva Switzerland, 31 August -- 4 September.

Shea, E. L. (2004). Final report: ENSO forecasting and applications in the Pacific: Supporting the transition from research to operations.

Sheehan, G. (2002). Tuvalu little, Tuvalu late: A country goes under. *Harvard International Review, 24*(1), 11-12.

Simons, C. (2007). Global drowning: Ocean may soon swallow a nation. *Rome News-Tribune, December 16, 2007.* Accessed on 3/26/12 from http://news.google.com/newspapers?id=yq81AAAAIBAJ&sjid=1iQM AAAAIBAJ&pg=2482,935373&dq=drowning+tuvalu&hl=en.

Soderbergh, C. (2011). Human rights in a warmer world: The case of climate change displacement. Working paper available at: http://lup.lub.lu.se/record/1774900.

Soeriaatmadja, W., & Ghosh, A. (2005). Indonesian Tsunami toll is at 172,161, Ministry says (Update 3). *Bloomberg News, January 20, 2005.* Accessed on 3/24/12 from http://www.bloomberg.com/apps/news?pid=newsarchive&sid=asqOuy 49USgM&refer=asia.

Sogivalu, P. A. (1992). *A Brief History of Niutao.* Suva, Fiji: Institute of Pacific Studies, University of the South Pacific.

Song, J. (2011). Hawai'i: Waves as high as two metres hit islands. *The Star, March 11, 2011.* Accessed on 3/24/12 from http://www.thestar.com/article/952325--hawaii-waves-as-high-as-two-metres-hit-islands.

Sonn, C. C., & Fisher, A. T. (1998). Sense of community: Community resilient responses to oppression and change. *Journal of Community Psychology, 26*(5), 457-472.

Spenneman, D. H. R. (2006). Freshwater lens, settlement patterns, resources use and connectivity in the Marshal Islands. *Transforming Cultures eJournal, 1*(2).

Stedman, R. C. (2002). Toward a social psychology of place: Predicting behavior from place-based cognitions, attitude, and identity. *Environment and Behavior, 34*(5), 561-581.

Strauss, A., & Corbin, J. (1998). Basics of qualitative research: Techniques and procedures for developing grounded theory, Second edition. Thousand Oakes: SAGE Publications.

Swim, J., Clayton, S., Doherty, T., Gifford, R., Howard, G., Reser, J., Stern, P., & Weber, E. (2010). Psychology and global climate change: Addressing a multi-faceted phenomenon and set of challenges. A Report by the APA's Task Force on the Interface Between Psychology and Global Climate Change.

Taiwan News. (2011). MOFA issues yellow travel alert for Tuvalu. *Taiwan News, October 3, 2011*. Accessed on 3/29/12 from http://www.taiwannews.com.tw/etn/news_content.php?id=1724595.

Taylor, A. J. W. (2000). Tragedy and trauma in Tuvalu. *The Australasian Journal of Disaster and Trauma Studies, 2000-2*, n.p. Accessed from http://www.massey.ac.nz/~trauma/issues/2000-2/taylor.htm.

Taylor, A. (2011). PICTURES: Earthquake in Japan. *National Journal, March 11, 2011*. Accessed on 3/24/12 from http://www.nationaljournal.com/pictures-earthquake-in-japan-20110311.

Telavi, M. (1983) War. In S. Faaniu & H. Laracy's Tuvalu: A History. Institute of Pacific Studies and Extension Services and University of the South Pacific and the Ministry of Social Services

The Holy Bible, New International Version, NIV. (2011). Colorado Springs: Biblica, Inc.

Timmerman, A., McGregor, S., & Jin, F. (2010). Wind effects on past and future regional sea level trends in the Southern Indo-Pacific. *Journal of Climate, 23*, 4429-4437.

Triandis, H. C. & Gelfand, M. J. (1998). Converging measurement of horizontal and vertical individualism and collectivism. *Journal of Personality and Social Psychology, 74*(1), 118-128.

Triandis, H. C., McCuster, C., & Hui, C. H. (1990). Multimethod probes of individualism and collectivism. *Journal of Personality and Social Psychology, 59*(5), 1006-1020.

Tuvalu Millennium Development Goals Report. (2010/2011). Department of Planning and Budget, Ministry of Finance and Economic Development, Government of Tuvalu.

Tuvalu-News.tv. (2006). Eco-tourism team from Japan. *Tuvalu-News.tv, 11/10/06*. Accessed on 3/27/12 from http://www.tuvalu-news.tv/archives/2006/10/ecotourism_team_from_japan_wed.html.

Twigger-Ross, C. L., & Uzzell, D. L. (1996). Place and identity processes. *Journal of Environmental Psychology, 16*, 205-220.

278

Tzeng, E. & Wu, L. (2011). MOFA issues yellow travel alert for Tuvalu. *Taiwan News, October 3, 2011.* Accessed on 3/24/12 from http://www.taiwannews.com.tw/etn/news_content.php?id=1724595.

UNFCCC (1992). United Nations Framework Convention on Climate Change, adopted 9 May 1992 in New York, USA. Retrieved from http://unfccc.int/essential_background/convention/background/items/13 49.php on 10/28/10.

UNFCCC (2005) Climate change, Small Island Developing States. Issued by the Climate Change Secretariat (UNFCCC), Bonn, Germany.

U.S. Agency for International Development (USAID) 2009. Adapting to coastal climate change: A guidebook for development planners. Can be downloaded from http://www.usaid.gov/our_work/cross-cutting_programs/water/news_announcements/coastal_climate_change_report.html or http://www.crc.uri.edu/index.php?actid=366

Wang, C. C., & Burris, M. (1994). Empowerment through photo novella: Portraits of participation. *Health Education Quarterly, 21,* 171–186.

Webb, A. P. & Kench, P. S. (2010). The dynamic response of reef islands to sea-level rise: Evidence from multi-decadal analysis of island change in the Central Pacific. *Global and Planetary Change,* 1-13,

Weber, E. U., & Stern, P. C. (2011). Public understanding of climate change in the United States. *American Psychologist, 66*(4), 315-328.

Weiss, J. L, Overpeck, J. T., & Strauss, B. (2011). Implications of recent sea level rise science for low-elevation areas in coastal cities of the conterminous U. S. A. *Climatic Change,*

Whiteman, H. (2011). South Pacific islands running out of water. *CNN U.S., October 4, 2011.* Accessed on 3/24/12 from http://articles.cnn.com/2011-10-04/asia/world_asia_south-pacific-island-drought_1_tuvaluan-atoll-water-supplies?_s=PM:ASIA.

Wilson, C. (2012). The Pacific's threatened islands. *Asia Sentinel, January 5, 2012.* Accessed on 3/25/12 from http://www.asiasentinel.com/index.php?option=com_content&task=view&id=4099&Itemid=594.

Wilson, N., Minkler, M., Dasho, S., Wallerstein, N., & Martin, A. C. (2008). Getting to social action: The Youth Empowerment Strategies (YES!) project. *Health Promotion Practice, 9*(4), 395-403.

World Climate Programme – Water (2006). Final report: Expert meeting on water manager needs for climate information in water resource planning. Geneva, Switzerland, 18-20 December, 2006.

Wynne, M. S. (2010). Video Feedforward and self-efficacy in adult tribal language users. (Unpublished master's thesis). University of Hawai'i, Mānoa, Honolulu, HI.

Zinn, H. (1980). *A People's History of the United States: 1492-Present.* New York: Harper Collins.

Made in the USA
Coppell, TX
10 March 2021